Why You Were Born

A Choice We Don't Get To Make!

CHARLES POPE

EXPRESSO
Executive Center 777, Dunsmuir Street Vancouver, BC V71K4
1-888-721-0662 ext 101
info@expressopublishing.com

Table Of Contents

PREFACE

*P*reface This book could affect your concept of life, death, and the hereafter. If you take the time to read through these pages of information you will see this life of living, learning, and accumulated experiences is by design. Our lives will end with death. Whether by accident, war, murder, suicide, disease, or old age, we will die! It is an event that was caused soon after the first humans appeared on the planet.

We are near the end of 6,000 years of mankind's records of living and learning from life's experiences after the first humans appear. The records and history of mankind and events accumulated over six millenniums supply a treasure chest of information to create this personal journey of finding answers for why I was born. There is one book of records that helps me make sense of all the others: The Bible.

Our own opinions and our own sense of what God is telling us throughout the bible can deceive us, unless we believe there a higher power that can be present in our discernment of the scriptures. Appearing from the pages of the Bible, the Holy Spirit becomes the guiding knowledge. The propensity of the Holy Spirit reveals intrinsic truths from the Bible as we open our spiritual minds to the information. When individuals allow the Spirit of God to speak to them from the Bible, they are delivered from the confusion created by carnal men and poor translation. The more we humbly believe, the more united we become with our Creator and His purpose for our mortality.

Believing and receiving the world of God creates an undistracted spirit within us for understanding the things of God. When the believing takes place, you will see the Bible does not support many of the mainstream beliefs of churches. Don't get mad at me; get into this book and see what I have discovered to be hidden from people by centuries of false teachings and manipulation of information promoting certain religious behavior. There is a plan in the Bible that is a different gospel from what mainstream churches promote. Bold words for a common man to write in a book, you may think.

I say they are words no less bold than the inspiration of thousands of witnesses down through history who have lived and died, sharing the inner spirit of their life and their encounter with the Invisible Creator God. The lives they lived are expressed through drawings, hieroglyphic paintings, scrolls of parchment, cave walls, stories, mythology, history books, and the Bible. There is a phrase familiar to most people: Those who do not consider history are condemned to repeat it. I have found this to be a profound statement of consistent truth as I have studied and saw the behavior of mankind. I am a human being experiencing the successes and failures of this life. I confused my understanding of this life with rebellion, hypocrisy, lying, cheating, and stealing my way through the daily struggle for happiness. Life's experiences are a progression of accumulated knowledge, coupled with creative instincts endowed upon o4ur brain's potential to advance ourselves as created human beings, occupying the time and chance conditions of the planet we live upon. We must exert as much effort in how we live as we exert in discovery of the intended way of life.

Our lives will someday answer to our learning. It is crucial what we keep as values for living the life that is intended by our Creator. This book is a straightforward presentation of collected facts and information from the many authors of many different books of history, science, and theological commentaries.

Because there is no way I can cover all the many events and encounters of human history for the last 6,000 years, I will only cite the various people and events that have affected me in the autumn of my life after years of mistakes, fear, being deceived, and clinging to my own stubborn pride about religious beliefs and the subject of Life and Death.

I will present the information available to me through books written by people who make it their life's work to compile and process information of ancient history, history, and science. My story reveals the many choices mankind is allowed, through free moral agency of our spirit, soul, and body. It is not my intent to debate the Bible, medical science, and the documented histories of the events of mankind that are available to anyone who can read. I wish to simply create the story that I found through my personal years of research and desire to figure out why I was even born It is the result of reading hundreds of books over a span of 40 years, trying to sort out the confusion mankind created in this life where we had no choice in the fact that we are born and are alive.

The story may appear arrogant and presumptuous at times; this is because it challenges some beliefs held in worldwide acceptance by Christian religions. Challenging the centuries-old, predigested doctrines for religious teaching is not a new thing. The Protestant Reformation is proof of the desire to be free of manmade traditions about God and how to live life. I claim only the organization of a few of the billions, of bits of information from history, medical science, and the use the Bible as a guide to give motive and reason to the things of science and history. I do not try to debate or argue the many differences of opinions that are available to choose from. My life of living through thousands of experiences is not much different from anyone who has wondered why they are born or have thoughts about death.

I share this story because it is information that helped me to start believing in something that is special to the spirit in us that knows we are born into this world for a purpose greater than we limit ourselves to think. I have no letters of abbreviation showing a doctorate, only the name bestowed upon me by my parents. However, I find no show in the Bible requiring such acknowledgments for Biblical interpretation. My only credentials are a belief in a Creator God and a heartfelt desire to understand what the intended purpose for me being born into this world. My journey in search of truth has taught me to respect the Bible above all the books ever written.

This book outlines the core beliefs of Catholic, Protestant, Jewish, and other religions under the X-ray of what the Bible tells us. This book is not an attack on religions and churches. There is valid truth taught in all churches. This book is my researching from history, science, and the Bible as a timeline guide. It is a comparison with what mainstream Christian churches teach about our destiny and what the Bible says about the purpose of mankind and its destiny.

I have attended churches all my life, listening to preachers proclaim the Gospel. Upon personal research I find they do not preach the complete Gospel. Jesus warned us this would happen. The religions and cults of this world offer many choices for a person to believe. Our choices with what we learn and prove to be true about God's Plan for mankind will decide our destiny. There is a reason we are born, and our destiny is not wings, a halo, and a rocking chair. Our destiny is more than the heaven and hell concepts adopted by most religions.

Satan does not want us to understand what our true destiny is! He has gone to extreme efforts down through time to diminish our potential as human beings made in the image of God. We are, of all the things we discover on this planet and in the universe, God's most important and precious creation. Our eternal destiny is set by God, and God chooses why, when, where, how, and which of two destinies we will inherit.

INTRODUCTION

There are three important days in your life. The day you are born, the day you understand why you are born, and the day you die. Choices will decide your destiny. We all get to make choices about our lives, but there is one choice we do not get to make: We can't choose to be born. One day two people told me they were my parents and that they gave me life. It was their choice, not mine. I had now to live, learn, and sustain my life in a world among billions of other lives. This story is about how I tried to understand why I was born into this world.

This is a long story. It is mostly a thumbnail sketch of ancient history, late history, and recent history, helping me to understand where I am headed in a world that doesn't even know or care who I am. I looked for meaning from religions, cults, and life's experiences. I searched the scriptures of the Bible to find salvation from this life. It was like nailing pudding to a wall. But life starts making sense when I begin to compare ancient history and the sciences with the Bible. People have long sought answers to the many questions raised by the events of the daily news, history, and day to day struggles of life.

A continual set of problems are produced by the prejudices, accidents, wars, governments, and health issues generated by mankind. Political power, cults, and religious orders have become a type of opium for people to feel good while living in a world of many choices. Some people find peace in a hobby of some sort. For some people, gangs fill the need for acceptance and belonging; they join to soothe their feelings of inferiority. Many people find peace and happiness by eating food, drinking alcohol, viewing pornography, sexual promiscuity, taking street drugs, prescription drugs, joining country clubs, resorts, religions, cults, and the like. All these choices have created billion-dollar empires of wealth and prosperity for the people who feed those appetites. Empires of wealth sustained by the search for happiness.

I too have tried some of these choices to achieve feelings of happiness, peace, and security. Sadly, some people turn to suicide or homicide to get relief from their stresses, anger issues, unhappiness, poverty, etc. Our soldiers returning home, after traumatic situations of war, commit murder and often murder themselves for reasons that are not fully understood. The result of these choices and behaviors creates a huge part of the daily news.

Today we have the stress of terrorists from without and within our country. Less fortunate nations are confronted daily with starvation and oppression. For over two hundred years, people have been immigrating and sneaking into this country to escape the oppression and starvation in hopes of an opportunity for a better life. They are trying to escape the carnal whims of those in power who are using their power for personal and selfish agendas. Our nation's outstretched, welcoming arms for people to come and embrace LIBERTY and FREEDOM is proof we are a nation built on Godly principles.

For many years, I found history to be confusing, boring—just a record of continual struggles for controlling power, through a series of religious or political wars. Wars that have destroyed billions of human lives down through the centuries. From antiquity to the present day are wars based upon religious and political agendas. Disagreements, conflicts, hurt feelings, hatred, crimes of lawlessness, crimes of passion within families and religious and political institutions. Domination and control are the main diet of people in power.

As I compiled the information and viewed it through the eyes of my common-man simple logic, my desire to believe and understand life became an interesting journey for me. As I read books written by people with educational backgrounds superior to my own, I found that information must be legitimized by facts. I begin to understand that not all facts presented by people of knowledge are necessarily the truth of the events of history.

I found I first needed to understand how information has come down to us through time. The ancient history of mankind is a long path through a jungle of facts, myths, and opinions of people who lived during or near the time of their documented information. Most of these writers and scribes wrote from information passed down to them from their families and friends. It often creates a tangled web of facts that are not always true; much of history is how the writers of that history interpret it.

This can be confusing at times. Stories are not repeated over and over precisely the way they are told and heard. Much of what is written must be sorted, sifted, compared, and confirmed by other information available. The information that is written or told by different people during the same period of time is not always perceived the same. This is the process I use to create a story about people and events that connect us to our ancient forefathers and bring some light to our purpose for existence.

Anthropologists, archeologists, linguists, historians, and theologians dedicate most of their lives to sifting the sands of artifacts, parchments, and stones covered with pictures and writings to reveal the past. From their studies we develop a sense of awareness in the struggle for existence. We then use this information to help understand our beginnings and life as human beings. Before I could get a grip on choosing my information and facts, I started to understand an important fact about historical information:

Down through time, historical records are removed, added to, and manipulated by people who are motivated to write their version of history. I learned that facts and the truth are two different things. The foundation of modern historical research is called the historical method of study. It is the approach to history that is not based on demonstrable facts. It rests on only this fundamental hypothesis: God has never and does not now intervene or decide the course of History.

Most modern educators do not believe the course of nature can be interrupted or perforated by supernatural powers! The modern historical research of history teaches students to reject everything supernatural from historical text, even when there is evidence of the intervention of a supernatural power seen by eyewitnesses from ancient records. This is the universally needed method of modern historical study in institutions of higher learning. I say, if you find it hard to believe in things you can't see, explain the effects of electricity or radio sound waves! These are supernatural powers that mankind can produce. Nuclear science and many things invisible to the normal vision of mankind does exist.

There is a lot of history in the Bible. Most scholars agree that at least one third of the Bible is history. A lot of that history is personal testament of supernatural intervention. Why do you think mainstream educators, professors of history and such, do not allow into their society of educational priesthood the possibility of the supernatural? At least scientists accept the invisible things they can watch with their inventions.

The reconstruction and interpretation of history to suit political, social, economic, and religious prejudices is how historical prejudice is preserved. Many times, educators, ministers, and writers of textbooks are confronted with conflict between the truth and the beliefs of the society surrounding them. If their writings are to be accepted by the people, they must conform by rejecting truth. This is done when the truth does not promote the political agenda by men or women in positions of power.

I am not saying they are flat out lying! They are just using facts in a deceitful context. It is a process of using facts, emphasizing facts, bearing down on facts, sliding off facts, quietly ignoring facts, and interpreting facts. This is to satisfy the social whims of people for survival of the issue in question. Facts can appear as truth, but truth is inherent to the person's complete revelation of facts without biased interpretations. The facts of history do not automatically organize themselves into a scenario of unmistakable truth and answers.

There is a need for a standard or compass to guide the researcher along the right path to organize the revealed information and facts. Only then will you receive understanding and reason for the questions in historical information.

Geology and artifacts do not answer certain questions, such as when and why certain events became a fact of truth. Ancient Historical records often do not supply motive or accuracy in transmission of facts and information, but the Bible does give us some answers if we are seeking them and are willing to believe what it can tell us.

Two choices are available for the researcher. One is hypothesis, the other is facts and logic. I have chosen facts and logic coupled with the Bible—a willingness to believe in a higher power to confirm man's purposeful existence will create the story I am writing. An injustice is done to the truth of historical events when decisions are founded upon the whims, false ideas, theories, political partisanship, and influence of a religious order in a society.

This is why I have chosen to believe the history and writings of the Bible, comparing them with the academic ancient historical writings during the times associated with the Bible. I believe they support each other as to the inherent truth of why mankind was created with the ability to choose values. Historians express no true respect for the history and wisdom found in the Bible. The Bible is discounted because it is a book with information that requires belief and faith to understand.

The Bible itself reveals why this lack of understanding persists in human thinking: And even as they did not like to keep God in their knowledge, God gave them over to a reprobate mind (Romans 1:28).

I am not saying I understand all of the Bible. I will say it takes a lot of mental effort to understand the many strange writings and stories of the Bible. There is a process the Bible itself teaches that can help you begin to understand much of the information in it. I am not convinced the Bible can make sense without what is called spiritual intellect. I am not speaking of anything religious or spooky.

I am speaking of a phenomenon that even our greatest scientists prove exists within every person's brain. They say it is found near the pineal cone in our brain and can produce enough energy to light a twenty-five-watt lightbulb. It is what they call a spirit essence, an energy that only exists while we are alive. The Bible calls it the spirit in man.

Who knows the spirit of man that goes upward, and the spirit of the beast that goes downward to the earth? (Ecclesiastes 3:21)

It is the conscious you when you're thinking and aware of your thoughts. It is the invisible mirror essence that records information from your physical brain cells as they reason, learn, and understand your life's experiences. Medical science says your brain produces Alpha waves that receive information as Beta and Theta waves from other sources.

It is a scientific process I will try to expand upon later in the book. Another fact for logical interpretation is from scientists who study geology. Science proves there is a distinct break in geological strata, proving the existence of the world long before mankind was created.

No fossil evidence of humans has ever been found in the first strata before the break in stabilized strata. The Hebrew word for form is (tôhû pronounced to'-hoo From an unused root meaning to lie waste; a desolation of surface, that is, desert; figuratively a worthless thing; adverbially in vain: - confusion, empty place, without form, nothing, thing of naught, vain, vanity, waste, wilderness.) and void; (bôhû, pronounced bo'- hoo From an unused root (meaning to be empty); a vacuity, that is, superficially an undistinguishable ruin: - emptiness, void.) in Genesis indicate creation week as a re-construction of the earth's strata to support human, animal, and plant life.

All scientific information shows a catastrophe of events occur long before mankind was created and occupied the earth. Who cares if it is in 7 days or 7 million years? It's here, and we live on it.

It is not my purpose to debate the credibility of the authors of the books of the Bible or its content. History reveals people died for its publication, and we are privileged to own a copy. It is not my purpose to defend it as a "pure" textbook of information. I do not wish to debate how these authors carry a theme of mankind's beginnings, successes, failures, and at times deliverance from their own demise by an invisible God.

Millions of Bibles are sold, and many people believe it to be a holy book written by men who were inspired by God to help us understand what our destiny will be as we choose specific values on the journey of this life. For me, the Bible reconciles scientific findings— especially when I consider the geological changes to earth's strata.

The Bible says it had to be prepared for mankind's existence because of a catastrophe. Bible scholars consider the phrase "in the beginning" is not referring to the original creation of the planet earth. They believe the next verse says a "re-creation" of the earth's surface to accommodate human life. Moses simply used the phrase "in the beginning" because he had no knowledge of the pre-existing events later described by Isaiah and what Jesus says four thousand years later about Satan! In the beginning,

God created the heaven and the earth. And the earth was without form, and void; and darkness was upon the face of the deep. And the Spirit of God moved upon the face of the waters. (Genesis 1:1–2) The Hebrew word for the English word WAS, is a mistranslation. It should be translated, BECAME. This is the true meaning from the Hebrew word hâyâh. After years of study, I do believe the Bible is God's spiritual guidebook, written by many different authors, spanning 4,000 years of early history.

The Bible tells us who God is, how and why God created us. The Bible's distinctive here a little, there a little, information supports a consistent theme of information for choices to decide our personal destiny. There are several opinions about God, the Bible, and its revelations. Opinions cannot change the fact of our existence.

A person must believe in some reason and purpose for all we can experience in this physical life. This physical life is not eternal. It is temporary. From its creation, life is dependent on pre-existing life. As I begin to understand about my life, it becomes my personal responsibility to make choices to preserve it. My life is sustained or destroyed based on choices. Life is an opportunity! My life has a purpose and reason for existing.

This story is the thread of information that becomes the cloth woven from the history of mankind's living experiences I expose to my life. The information only helps to create the garment I will wear during my journey. I will create my own garment by the choices I make based on the information I process. My existence becomes real to me as I compare history, science, and the Bible to reveal experiences lived by others. I then use the Bible as a guide to supply reason, motive, and understanding of mankind's experiences from academic history.

What if someday I am told I have an incurable disease and will soon die? What? All this learning, living, and struggle, and now it will soon be over, and I will die! Why did my parents bother to create me? The preacher says if I am good, I can go to heaven. If I'm not good, I will go to an existing hell and burn forever—writhing, screaming, and wishing I could die. Is this concept even true? The Bible certainly does not support these two destinies. I am sharing my story with you as a common man searching for answers to confirm why I was born. It is not my purpose to argue or debate the many opinions about good versus evil, creation versus evolution, politics versus religion, or the many issues causing people to become angry and upset with each other.

A famous news agency has a catchphrase I would like you to remember as you read my story. We report, you decide. This story is my search for answers to my life. It is based on my personal study of history, science, astronomy, and theology from many books I have read.

I am a person of no reputation among the fine scholars, philosophers, professors, and authors of books with all sorts of facts, information, and opinions. This story is how I come to an understanding for why I was born. It reveals the choices available for me—some good, some bad. History books are full of many choices mankind makes during an appointed time on this earth. There are many writings from ancient and modern times describing the actions of mankind for many thousands of years. These writings are not the only information for understanding our purpose in this life.

I use the Bible as a guide to help me; it begins to show a purpose for my life. A combination of academic history and science. The Bible influences my choices giving me confidence for the destiny I look for. The Bible says that mankind's existence is affected by time and chance.

I returned, and saw under the sun, that the race is not to the swift, nor the battle to the strong, neither yet bread to the wise, nor yet riches to men of understanding, nor yet favor to men of skill; but time and chance happens to them all. (Ecclesiastes 9:11)

We are intellectual beings by nature! Our first and spontaneous exercises from our reasoning is the investigation of cause and effect. From these come our first convictions of our mind's investigation: There cannot be an effect without a cause! Because of this natural intellect, unbelief in the effects of a superior power has never prevailed in the world. Pagan or divine, mankind recognizes one superior being, and we are inferior beings that are responsible to Him. This is the last and highest conclusion of human intellect, no matter if a person worships the SUN which lights each day or the SON of the Creator of the Sun.

The Bible is not a textbook, it is a guidebook! The Bible holds the essence of God's spiritual character and power to guide us in choosing a way of life leading to an eternal existence. However, the choices are solely ours to embrace, and those choices can cause different consequences at the end of the values we choose. God watches the progress of mankind allowing us to choose our own way or His way. God will not force us to choose an eternal existence. The life we choose to live during our physical existence is our freedom and responsibility.

My story is a creation from my personal study of science, physics, astronomy, anthropology, history, politics, and theology. I have a basic high school education and a desire to learn the purpose for which I was born. I do not seek fame and fortune, for I understand they are temporary. I do not wish to debate the age-old arguments that go with religion and politics, evolution, and creation, science, and myths. I simply wish to understand the purpose for mankind's struggles and victories of history and during my life. I sought answers for struggles and victories from History and the present-day struggles of my life in the world we live. A life we did not choose to be born into. A world that has existed long before we were aware of it. There is a valid reason for the daily ritual of get up, survive, and go to bed. I found an answer for me, and only wish to share it for your consideration as one of innumerable choices we are responsible to make on this journey of life.

I can only scratch the surface of the many events and characters of the Bible and how they relate to academic history and myths. Many of the details not found in the Bible are picked up from the records and writings of people down through time. I see mankind as free moral agents with only the power of choice to secure their destiny within the confines of a master plan by a Creator who is willing to share His eternal existence with anyone who will believe the stories and events that reveal His plan.

In a sense, we are all victims of a process that started nearly six-thousand years ago. We do not choose to be born. We simply one day begin to understand we are created through a miraculous process, thoughts into a progressing world of chaos and information from which we select our values and struggle to survive. We are surviving in a world of time and chance, living to achieve happiness, and understanding of why we are here.

The process of knowledge and human creativity starts slowing and become a technological snowball of innovations and technology, which through cooperation and time has brought mankind into the end-time scenario of Bible prophecies. We are at the end of approximately 6,000 years of mankind's existence and development of human potential. The ancient forefathers would have thought we were gods because of our knowledge and technology! It is an impossible task to cover thousands of years and millions of mankind's existence. I have chosen the events and characters inspiring me personally to understand my purpose for living.

I am only scratching the surface of the available information in this 21st century of technology. There are thousands of people, events, wars, reasons, and documented experiences for me to choose. God can use and inspire anyone He chooses for His purposes. He can use them to write or act in the affairs of life that promote His purpose for mankind! I am writing this for me and simply sharing it with you. God uses good or evil people, governments, nations, and empires, causing events to become lessons of history for us to learn. God uses the experiences of people before our time and people living now on this planet to help us make choices.

There is too much order and design for this life to have just happened by itself. God is the potter and mankind is the clay; God works through willing people to carry out His plan for mankind's destiny. God allows us to make our own choices. We can even choose not to believe in God! The choice is ours alone. At the end of our physical lives God has plans for two destinies! He is waiting for us to choose which one of paths of applied knowledge leading to those destinies we will choose!

The information is available, often buried by circumstances, but discovery is possible when we choose to believe in the invisible God who reveals Himself through the things of creation surrounding us.

The heavens declare the glory of God; and the firmament shows his handy work. (Psalms 19:1)

By the word of the LORD were the heavens made; and all the host of them by the breath of his mouth. (Psalms 33:6)

The heavens are thine; the earth also is thine: as for the world and the fullness thereof, thou hast founded them. (Psalms 89:11)

The heaven, even the heavens, are the LORD'S: but the earth hath he given to the children of men. (Psalms 115:16)

The LORD by wisdom hath founded the earth; by understanding hath he set up the heavens. (Proverbs 3:19)

The writer of these passages didn't see what we can now see through Hubble and other telescopes! There is a reason mankind must take the things from earth with him when venturing into the far reaches of the heavens. We are not spiritual beings; we are physical and perishable. We are designed to live our physical lives within the boundaries God has set for us. However, God allows us to learn, create, and use our minds and inventions to explore the depths of the earth and as far as we can reach out into the heavens.

By using the Bible as a guide, I can understand the academic history and science of mankind's beginnings and the potential destiny for the purpose for our existence. By studying foundational academic history and information and combining it with the Old Testament information, using the bible as a guide, I discover an interesting story that answers many of my questions about why we are here.

God has a plan for one of two eternal destinies for mankind. He begins to reveal His plan by first working through individuals who are willing to believe what God is telling them about life. During this process, God worked with many individuals one at a time as they responded to His teachings. After the "flood," the number of individuals God works with grew until He chose to call a nation of people to physical salvation and blessings above the other nations; to have them carry a message to all other nations. The message was the Creator's intentions for mankind—its purpose.

During the journey of this chosen nation, various prophets were inspired by their personal encounters with God to foretell a coming Messiah. One prophet was given an exclusive vision of future nations that would influence the world through empires of domination. The influence of these empires reaches all the way to present day.

Eventually the information reveals a prophesied visit from the "Creator" in the form of a human being. God creates Him to live among His created human beings. He ministered to them and presented changes to the added beliefs adopted by well-intentioned religious zealots. He explained the meaning of grace as a spiritual concept that would save mankind from itself, upon a choice made personally by everyone. This spiritually begotten physical individual became the ultimate sacrifice as atonement for mankind's transgressions. This sacrifice resulted in the firstborn spiritual child of God from physical death, Jesus Christ, the Firstborn Son of the Creator God from physical human life.

This firstborn Son promised to send spiritual power from heaven to merge with the spirit in mankind upon that person's request. The result was an agreement between God and mankind to help an individual make specific choices for behavior. This one-time event prepared the opportunity for all human beings to choose their path for destiny.

This power to choose created a trail of many changes, opinions, wars, actions, and history of man's tries to interpret the meaning of this event for mankind. The deception and perverting of the Faith Once Delivered by the Son of God is deceiving the peoples of the nations, teaching them only parts of the Complete Gospel Message of God through Christ and the Apostles.

This is a grassroots man's testament of the awareness, feelings, failures, successes, personal experiences, and situations in my years of living and learning. It is the reality of how time, chance, and circumstance have brought me to an understanding for my purpose of being born into this world. The history, names, and places found in the Old Testament are the expressions of many different people who have passed the information verbally and in written form. The various characters of the bible influence my belief in a purpose greater than we can imagine.

The first five books, called the Pentateuch, were authored by a special and brilliant man, Moses, at least 1,200 years after the flood of Noah's time and 2,600 years after Adam's time. Therefore, the bible account of history, names, and places is not as detailed as Babylonian and Egyptian records are, but that does not mean it is not correct.

Understand that for the first 1,700 years, people lived 600 to 900 years before they died. Information is well proven by stories repeated and shared over long years of time, being remembered, and passed on to the continuing generations. As the first civilizations of Babylon and Egypt become more organized, after the flood, hieroglyphics and the invention of letters preserved the events in consistent detail. We must understand that by the time world dictatorial empires were controlling the masses of people; tampering and adjusting of the information God had sent becomes the theme of dictators to control people and keep them in the dark about the freedom of choice God supports all people.

During the time of Josephus, there was not as much tampering and adjusting of the information as there was after Josephus, Herodotus, Philo, Eusebius, and later historians. I read about a man in 1864, John Mahan, who said that earlier historians had more correct copies of the Pentateuch and the Jew's Talmud's. He said, when compared with the Pentateuch and Talmud that he could view and translate from scrolls found in the Vatican library and at Constantinople, he discovered a different story than records revealed to the public researchers long after those records were kept from the public in these special libraries.

I will cover this tampering of stricture in more detail as we get to that time in the timeline of academic history. There will be many inserts of information during the story timeline as I progress toward the religious confusion in the world today. The inserts will be shocking compared to mainstream religious teachings about God, and I pray they will not offend my readers to the point of anger. Please let me report, and you decide what you will believe about the things God has provided in His word. The Assyrians, Jews, Greeks, and Romans are famous for cutting and rewriting much of their history to satisfy religious and political agendas. The ancient Church of Rome has perverted the scriptures more than any influence I could find. This is why I believe combining all the academic and biblical information with a timeline that matches the people and places gives us a better story of the past. This combining of information becomes the method that gives me a foundation of logic to choose how I want to live life.

I have learned the books of the Old Testament are not in chronological order. I have found this information to be helpful as far as tying the books and various characters to the timeline of secular history. The books are divided into specific groups of writers: Books of Law, Writings of the Prophets, and "The Writings." History reveals Ezra the Scribe as the most responsible character for canonizing the writings of the Old Testament.

When reading the first five books of the Old Testament I think about the author Moses and when he actually compiles these stories and information. Moses grew up in Egypt and was schooled by the Egyptians. He was taught all the known arts and writings of his time in pharaoh's court. It is unclear when Moses started to author his books.

Academic history reveals Jacob and his twelve sons, especially Joseph, were respected by the Egyptian leaders when they arrived in Egypt about 1737 BC. No doubt the Egyptians studied stories and records of some sort. Considering the intelligence of the Chaldeans and Aramean people from Mesopotamia after the flood of Noah's time, information migrated with them to Egypt, along with the records of the Babylonians who gathered there with Cush and Nimrod after the Tower of Babel event. The

Babylonians and Egyptians are certainly noted to be the first to record their governments and actions.

There is truly little detailed information in Genesis from the creation scenario up to the event of the worldwide flood. The Pentateuch or books of Moses were written based on information from the Egyptian records of kings and governments up until Moses was at least 40 years old. Moses is schooled from that written history while growing up in pharaoh's court as the adopted son of one of the pharaoh's sisters.

From the Exodus to the Promised Land, Moses diarized his life. My point here is that we must consider the stories and information as past tense information written and passed down through the ruling tribe of Judah and priestly tribe of Levi, until it was sorted out and canonized by Ezra the priest over 500 years later. Therefore, there is not much detail from the first five books of the Old Testament. This is where the civil academic records of Babylon and Egypt can fill in a lot of information Moses does not include in his writings.

The Bible is a Priestly document! Though the bulk of it is about the Israelite/Jews, it was preserved by God for the education of mankind, past, present, and future as seen through the eyes of specific people from approximately 2264 B. C. – 100 A. D. The stories of those who meet a relationship with their Creator God!

Another consideration is this: Jesus speaks of events before mankind's creation. In fact, Jesus never writes down one word He says while on Earth! His story is told by the witnesses who lived with Him while He walked the Earth. Even His enemies wrote about His message for life. I believe this is by God's design.

Luke16:31 And he said unto him, if they hear not Moses and the prophets, neither will they be persuaded, though one rose from the dead.

The bible speaks of events long before the creation of man in many of the prophecies and especially the revelation Jesus gives to the Apostle John. The half-brother of Jesus, Jude, is privy to pre-flood information from Jesus.

Jude 1:14-15 And Enoch also, the seventh from Adam, prophesied of these, saying, Behold, the Lord comes with ten- thousands of his saints, (15) To execute judgment upon all, and to convince all that are ungodly among them of all their ungodly deeds which they have ungodly committed, and of all their hard speeches which ungodly sinners have spoken against him.

Biblical information and history become more detailed after God appoints Judah and his descendants to be the keepers of the oracles.

Romans 3:1-2 What advantage then hath the Jew? or what profit is there of circumcision? (2) Much every way: chiefly because that unto them were committed the oracles of God.

Deuteronomy 4:5-6 Behold, I have taught you statutes and judgments, even as the LORD my God commanded me, that ye should do so in the land whither ye go to have it. (6) Keep therefore and do them; for this is your wisdom and your understanding in the sight of the nations, which shall hear all these statutes, and say, Surly this great nation is a wise and understanding people.

Academic history certainly is proof of the Jews' dedication to meticulously record and preserve all government and religious activities. The Chronicles and books of Kings for example. Preservation of the books of Law are part of Israel's war chest, the ark of the covenant and Temple vessels.

This will be a long journey from before the beginning of mankind to the future events ahead of us in this 21st Century. It has revealed the purpose for why we as Human Beings are born, and it reveals one of two destinies we will experience based on the choices we make during our time on this planet.

This will not be an easy read for most people. There will be information that is considered heresy in many religious circles. But this information is not an attack on any specific religion or church; it is simply what I discover about the many choice's men have created from their own interpretations of how to live life. Every person ever born has a right to choose what to believe about their destiny.

However, I have found that information has been manipulated and is often quite different than what the bible teaches about God's plan for mankind. I can only say I am sharing this information with you because once I waded through the many choices of carnal men compared to the spirit of the Bible, it changed my understanding of the reason I was born. It gave me the desire to be the person God has designed in each one of us the potential to become.

It is not about me; it is about the Invisible Creator God and the future He has designed for every person who chooses to believe in the hope of our intended destiny. Our lives can be changed by the truth and a spiritual experience from God if we are open for it. The truth will set you free from a lot of baggage the world has loaded us down with; traditions and burdens we could be free from if we understood our true purpose for being born. Remember, I report, you decide what the choices for your belief system will be to decide your ultimate destiny.

THIS PROJECT IS DEDICATED TO THE SAINTS OF THE FAITH ONCE DELIVERED

To the Saints who have withstood the propensities of carnal-minded men who have buried the Truth revealing God's plan for mankind's destiny.

To the Patriarchs, Prophets, Apostles, and Saints; a prodigy of martyrs, the victims of the enmity and rage imposed upon them by the Religious and Political Governments of their day.

To the Patriarchs: Noah—divinely warned concerning the things not yet clear—moved with reverent fear and prepared an ark for the preservation of all his family and the future of mankind, believing and obeying, and by doing so condemned the world of evil and became an heir of the righteousness according to faith. By faith Abraham also obeyed. He was called to go out to the place which he was about to receive as an inheritance, and he went out not knowing where he was going. By belief and faith in God, he lived as a stranger in the land of the promise, as a foreigner, in tents with Isaac and Jacob, joint heirs of the same promise.

To all Prophets, whose blood was shed from the laying of the foundation of the world of mankind. They willingly suffered, knowing the wisdom from God which says, "I will send them prophets and apostles, and some of them they will kill, and some they will persecute from city to city."

To John the Baptist, a voice crying in the wilderness for repentance and Baptism to a better life, preparing hearts and minds to receive the coming Messiah. To the Apostles, of whom only John did not suffer martyrdom during the persecutions of the Jews and the Romans.

To Stephen, the first to suffer death for embracing the Gospel of Jesus Christ and proclaiming it publicly.

The others, because of profession of their faith in Jesus Christ, were beaten, beheaded, slain, and crucified at the behest of Roman Procurators who appeased the desires of the Jewish Sanhedrin. To the Saints who were tortured, not accepting release so they could obtain a better resurrection. Others who suffered public ridicule, whippings, beatings, and chains of imprisonment. They were stoned, sawn asunder, tested, put to death by murder with the sword; they went about in sheepskins and goatskins, being destitute, being afflicted and ill-treated. These Saints remained faithful to the truth, receiving approval from God, though not yet receiving the promise.

This story is a witness to the 21st century <u>Christians who have an ear to hear the plan of God revealed by the Bible</u>—the Complete Gospel of Jesus Christ that includes the establishment of the coming Kingdom of God.

2Thessalonians 2:10-12 (10) And with all deceivableness of unrighteousness in them that perish; because they received not the love of the truth, that they might be saved. (11) And for this reason, God shall send them strong delusion, that they should believe a lie: (12) That they all might be damned who believed not the truth but had pleasure in unrighteousness.

IN THE BEGINNING

Do I believe the earth is millions of years old as scientists tell us it is? Yes! I do believe the earth is millions of years older than us humans. I believe mankind is a very recent addition to the earth as a planet. Mankind showed up a mere 6,000 years ago, per the best estimates of historical information. Have you ever thought about when the dinosaurs were created? There is no mention of them in the Creation Scenario of the bible.

We dig up their bones now and then and say they are millions of years old while their decayed bodies extracted as a source of oil drawn from deep, deep, within the earth's layered surface. There are few clues as to how these huge beasts were suddenly entombed within the earth. They obviously lived millions of years before God decided to clean up the desolation upon the earth. Myths? Evolutionary theories? No!

I believe dinosaurs were created long before mankind. And I believe mankind was created after these monsters were long buried in the earth. I say mankind was created because it appeals to my ego more than an evolution theory about some lovesick amoeba cells merging into something crawling out of swamp water. I do not believe these cells morphed into an apelike creature, then grew a brain and made up the theory called the evolution of mankind.

There is a more logical feeling of order, design, and superior intellect associated with the term created. I think the chances of Evolution theory for mankind is as possible as an explosion from inside a library full of books and words from all those books ending up in the completed copy of Webster's Dictionary. I have more respect for myself than to believe my ancestors are a progression of apes evolving into mankind (although the behavior of some people can often make you wonder about such a theory).

I see the dinosaurs existing during a pre-mankind period. Evidence from the strata and fossil evidence of the millions of years old earth produces some awesome skeletons of these monsters to show us how they looked and behaved.

Ages like the Mesozoic including the Triassic, Jurassic, and Cretaceous eras 230-67 million years before mankind make sense as a time they would have existed. Cenozoic period and the before mentioned ages are possible per geological studies of the earth as a planet. The Quaternary era consisting of Pleistocene and Holocene ages was the end to Dinosaurs. The latter is a time of the Ice Age and that is followed by a period of flooding. Scientists put the rising of deserts as having begun about 4,000 B.C. In Susa, its lowest levels of excavation from earth strata show traces of human occupation around 4,000 B.C. This data parallels with the time for the creation of mankind.

The bible doesn't put it as straightforwardly as people would like, but the bible does give us some hints about some things that happened long before mankind is created. These things are clues to why the earth becomes without form fit for human life. The Bible says Satan fell as lightening from heaven.

Luke 10:18 And he said unto them, I beheld Satan as lightning fall from heaven.

There is another passage of scripture that says there was war in heaven and one/third of the angels rebelled. Visions were given to some men who later wrote of the same event relating to the comment Luke records as what Jesus says.

Revelation 12:7-9 And there was war in heaven: Michael and his angels fought against the dragon; and the dragon fought and his angels, (8) And prevailed not; neither was their place found any more in heaven. (9) And the great dragon was cast out, that old serpent, called the Devil, and Satan, which deceives the whole world: he was cast out into the earth, and his angels were cast out with him.

Isaiah 14:12-15 How art thou fallen from heaven, O Lucifer, son of the morning! You are thou cut down to the ground, which didst weaken the nations! (13) For thou hast said in thine heart, I will ascend into heaven, I will exalt my throne above the stars of God: I will sit also upon the mount of the congregation, in the sides of the north: (14) I will ascend above the heights of the clouds; I will be like the High God. (15) Yet thou shalt be brought down to hell, to the sides of the pit.

This war is indescribable by mankind. It is a conflict between spirit beings with invisible forces of power and energy scientists have discovered only in the 20th century, which they call atoms. If this happened after the creation of mankind, it most certainly would have made the headlines of historical and biblical records. It would be mentioned just as the flood in Noah's time, the parting of the Red Sea, and many other events of ancient and bible history, don't you think?

I believe long ago, for millions of years, the angels and their Creator fought in a great war. A real Star Wars scenario. Lucifer (light bringer) was the leader of a rebellion with at least one-third of the lesser angels. The earth and moon suffered great destruction as meteors and asteroids were hurled back and forth, creating huge craters on the moons and nearby planets. After the rebellion was had, the earth was left in darkness and void of its original condition.

Darkness was upon the earth. Could this have been the Ice Age that destroyed the enormous beasts we call Dinosaurs? Maybe not. What about our concept of TIME itself? No one knows how much time passes! It really doesn't matter. Time is a phenomenon known only to us earth-bound humans. Time is a continuum related to the rotation of the earth in relation to the Sun. Science defines it thus: Time is a non-spatial continuum of events occurring in irreversible succession from the past, through the present, and into the future.

The Creator suddenly restored the earth to a condition that would support His divinely designs for the created human beings.

Genesis 1:2 And the earth was without form, and void; and darkness was upon the face of the deep. And the Spirit of God moved upon the face of the waters.

The Creator prepared an environment capable of supporting the growth of plants and animals, which would in turn sustain human beings. He then scraped up some dust and molded it into a likeness of His image. The Creator breathed into the first human. We call His spiritual breath of life oxygen.

Medical science tells us unless we breathe Oxygen and consume and digest food from the earth, we die. They admit only a pre-existing life form can produce more life. I once thought that making mankind out of dust was a fairy tale. But after seeing what scientists have discovered in the various elements of the earth, I can understand, how this can be carried out by a Master Creator with unseen powers.

Science has seen these powers through manmade instruments and watches to reveal them. The first two humans were pure and beautiful. They were familiar with the voice of their Creator and for the first time were hearing everything He had to teach them about their new life! The conversation was mostly one-sided, for they were new, innocent, with no questions to ask because they had no pre-existing history of their life. Their experiences in life were just beginning!

Each day they looked forward to hearing from their Creator. It was the only voice they knew, and they listened and believe every word spoken to them by their Creator. Lucifer, defeated from the war in heaven, was now renamed Satan or Destroyer. Remember, Spirit beings are invisible, like the wind!

John 3:6-8 That which is born of the flesh is flesh; and that which is born of the Spirit is spirit. (7) Marvel not that I said unto thee, Ye must be born again. (8) The wind blows where it lists, and thou hear the sound thereof, but canst not tell whence it cometh, and whither it goes so is every one that is born of the Spirit.

Satan created a situation to disrupt the education and trust of God's newly created human beings. He started another rebellion against the Creator by deceiving them into disobeying the very thing God told them not to do. Satan knew they would only listen to the voice of their Creator, so he used a serpent to speak to them. Something they could see and hear! I won't belabor the story further because most everyone knows what happens. Mankind now has thoughts of dealing with the knowledge of what is good and what is evil. Suddenly, Adam and Eve know about choices and the consequences for choosing not to obey their Creator.

I think God knew this was certain to happen eventually. Why? Because later in the timeline of information from the Bible, the redemption for disobedience is characterized as part of a plan for mankind from the foundation of the world—especially the world remodeled by the Creator to sustain physical human life, not the pre-historic world or Jurassic world as labeled by scientists.

Please remember, the Bible is a timeline guide parallel to the academic or secular history of mankind by mankind. Jesus spoke of the plan during His time on earth.

Hebrews 1:1-2 God, who at sundry times and in different manners spoke in time past unto the fathers by the prophets, (2) Hath in these last days spoken unto us by his Son, whom he hath appointed heir of all things, by whom also he made the worlds.

John 17:24 Father, I will that they also, whom thou hast given me, be with me where I am; that they may behold my glory, which thou hast given me: for thou loved me before the foundation of the world.

Hebrews 4:1-3 Let us therefore fear, lest a promise being left us of entering into his rest, any of you should seem to come short of it. (2) For unto us was the gospel preached, as well as unto them: but the word preached did not profit them, not being mixed with faith in them that heard it. (3) For we which have believed do enter into rest, as he said, As I have sworn in my wrath, if they shall enter into my rest: although the works were finished from the foundation of the world.

1Peter 1:19-21 But with the precious blood of Christ, as of a lamb without blemish and without spot: (20) Who verily was foreordained before the foundation of the world, but was manifest in these last times for you, (21) Who by him do believe in God, who raised him up from the dead, and gave him glory; that your faith and hope might be in God.

Revelation 13:8 And all that dwell upon the earth shall worship him, whose names are not written in the book of life of the Lamb slain from the foundation of the world.

These scriptures are an excellent example of the here a little, there a little collecting of information as God reveals men of character, His plan for mankind! Not the inspiration of one individual, but three different individuals and at different times. At the split-second Eve obeys a different voice, she is experiencing the free moral agency of choice God allows for all of mankind to experience.

This event is the very first lie ever heard by a human being. The serpent tells the woman the opposite of what God has already told both Adam and Eve. The consequences of disobeying God will be death. God says, "You will die!" The serpent says, "You will not die!" Satan tells the biggest lie of all time by telling God's new people they are immortal souls.

Lying catches on very quickly. Notice what Cain says to God after he murders his brother:

Genesis 4:8,9 And Cain talked with Abel his brother: and it came to pass, when they were in the field, that Cain revolted against Abel his brother, and slew him. (9) And the LORD said unto Cain Where is Abel thy brother? And he said, I know not: Am I my brother's keeper? Cain, lies to God when asked, "Where is Abel your brother?"

There are two huge lessons in this first story of lies and deceit. First, we cannot hide what we do from God. God is well informed of our actions whether they are good or bad. There is a record being kept in heaven continuously. Second, we are blessed and approved by God when we worship God in God's prescribed manner. If we don't, even though we think we are worshiping correctly, what we do in service or worship toward God is in vain.

Genesis 4:3-7 And in process of time it came to pass, that Cain brought of the fruit of the ground an offering unto the LORD. (4) And Abel, he also brought of the firstlings of his flock and of the fat thereof. And the LORD had respect unto Abel and to his offering: (5) But unto Cain and to his offering he had not respect. And Cain was very wroth, and his countenance fell. (6) And the LORD said unto Cain Why art thou angry? and why is thy countenance fallen? (7) If thou do well, shall thou not be accepted? if thou do not well, sin lies at the door. And unto thee shall be his desire, and thou shall rule over him.

This is the fundamental lesson for mankind. Good behavior begets blessings, bad behavior begets punishment. This event is the beginning of mankind coming to God with his own form of worship and not coming in God's prescribed way. Cain acknowledges God as the source of all natural good but rejects God's revealed way of worship; Abel, in conformity with that revelation, brings a blood offering, confessing himself a sinner.

In Cain begins all false religions, the essence of which is mankind coming to worship God in his own way. This theme will crop up over and over throughout this history of mankind. Man, has a problem with Divine authority. Man, wants to create his own God out of physical things to worship. Man, chooses his own things instead of what God the Creator of life is offering. Satan loves this behavior because it will defeat the reason mankind was created by God.

It is also the consequence of the Knowledge of Good and Evil. Choices must be made. Not long after the first family of mankind came into existence—Adam, Eve, Cain, and Abel—the land was stained with blood as brother killed brother. Jealous over the obedience and success of his own brother, Cain murdered Abel and began a long line of generational curses of bad behavior. God patiently watches as man becomes less and less what God intended. Evil and wickedness is everywhere He looks. As time ticked away, from His throne in heaven God saw all the evil and wickedness men did to each other until He was ready to destroy mankind completely.

The general condition of mankind before the flood was so depraved the Creator God considered a destruction of His created beings. Man degenerated to the point that every intent of the thoughts of his mind was to practice wickedness and evil. God was grieved in His heart and decided to destroy both mankind and beasts from the face of the earth!

Genesis 6:5-7 And GOD saw that the wickedness of man was great in the earth, and that every imagination of the thoughts of his heart was only evil continually. (6) And it repented the LORD that he had made man on the earth, and it grieved him at his heart. (7) And the LORD said, I will destroy man whom I have created from the face of the earth; both man, and beast, and the creeping thing, and the fowls of the air; for it repents me that I have made them.

BABYLON

abylon is the oldest civilization. Egyptian historians tried to make it appear otherwise by listing their King dynasties one after the other. This is not a true account of history. The kings of Egypt reigned parallel with each other in most cases. Egyptians wanted it to look like Egypt had the oldest civilization.

The truth is that all roads lead back to the Mesopotamian valley in today's northern Iraq and Babylon. All the generations of Noah settled in the Mesopotamian area that became known as Babylon. As the populace grew, so did the problems. The result was the Tower of Babel. Mentioned briefly in the bible, it was the first great dispersion of the tribes and clans from Noah to the other parts of the world. More about the Tower later.

Babylon as an ancient territory is the seat of false religion. It becomes more of a spiritual concept as time progresses. The Babylonian religion will be the force Christ comes to conquer upon His second return soon.

As my story progresses we will see that from Babylon the worldly influences upon people today originate from the philosophy of the generational line of one of Noah's sons, Ham. Cush, Ham's son, is the beginning of a long line of people who cause great concern in the post-flood era.

Another generational line of carnal thinking comes from the other two sons of Noah also. The paths are different, but the philosophies are similar. One of the twin sons of Shem, Assur, we will see the continuation of the Babylonian or Chaldean culture continued after the Tower of Babel event. Japheth's people migrate East and continue the philosophy for life of their cousin Cush. More about this world-changing event later.

NOAH

*H*is name means "comfort, consolation, rest or regeneration."

There is a similarity with Noah and Jesus Christ. Like Jesus, Noah is morally just, being an ethnic line walking with God. Noah and Jesus are both preachers of righteousness, examples of great faith in their obedience towards God. The world conditions in the time of Noah are in "Tribulation" condition. This will also be the condition of the world when Jesus returns in the near future.

The bible shows this man, Noah, caught God's attention. Noah was willing to respond to the Creator God and was instructed to build an Ark. This Ark would preserve Noah's family from the coming destruction. God told Noah about His plan to destroy all living creatures, including mankind. Suddenly, for the first time in all the writings of the Bible, we see the word grace.

Genesis 6:8 "But Noah found grace in the eyes of the LORD."

God promised to save Noah and his wife, three sons, and their wives. Noah was instructed to build the Ark from gopher wood and pitch, making it able to withstand the flood waters. It was to become the haven for his family and designated pairs of the various beasts of the earth for the duration of the coming disaster by flood. God gave Noah the details for the construction of an enormous ark. It figures to be Five-hundred-forty-seven feet long, Ninety-One feet wide, and Forty-Seven feet tall. Noah and his family were obedient to the voice of God and spend the next 120 years building this ship on dry land, far from any body of water that would support a ship of its size. Because he was building a ship far from any water to float it, Noah became a great attraction to the peoples of the land. Noah was persecuted and chided by the people. As word spread, the site became an attraction for the curious.

Then, in the six-hundredth year, on the seventeenth day of the second month of Noah's life, the fountains of the deep broke, and the windows of heaven opened with a deluge of water that eventually covered the highest mountain by Twenty-one feet. The earth was entombed in water!

One-hundred and fifty days later and on the First day of the first month in the year 2369 B.C., Noah turned the animals loose while he and his family left the ark for the first time in One-hundred and Fifty-Seven days! The first thing Noah built was an altar of uncut stones to worship the Creator God who saved him and his family. God presented Noah with a covenant. God sealed a promise to mankind, to never destroy the inhabitants of the earth again with water. This seal is reflected by the colors of the rainbow, which appears after huge rainstorms. In our present time, after a rain shower, the light often reflects this reminder of God's promise. This is a covenant between God and all flesh of the earth forever.

As time passed, the earth was repopulating, and mankind once again numbered in the hundreds of thousands. Noah was growing incredibly old. The people settled in various places along the Tigris and Euphrates rivers in Mesopotamia. Many of the offspring of third and fourth generations from Noah mixed into the main traits of the second generations. Present day anthropologists and archeologists have confirmed their special physical attributes down through time.

There are substantial records of the three main races of peoples since the flood. It is not my purpose to debate how they crossed the flood or the authenticity of ethnic cultures and where they are today. It really doesn't matter, because the three main racial strains and millions of mixed races in the world today.

One thing does matter about the subject of races today: the real issue of strife, prejudice, profiling, and debate between races is the personal choices of behavior by people, rather than skin pigment.

This is a story that has significance to mankind as a purposeful creation of God and how God has a plan of redemption for His creation if they are willing to surrender to it, regardless of race.

NOAH'S PRE-EMINENCE

*J*ust think about how people see Noah and his family. They are looked upon as gods! They were the only human beings to survive the flood! They carry all the information they have from the pre-flood days to pass on to their generations. The real separation of the characters of the three sons is more of a distinction of human proclivities.

As our story progresses, we see Shem promoting the way of life intended for mankind and the other two brothers doing their own thing. Not unlike Cain's doing his own offering his way. Mankind once again is looking to the things of creation rather than the Creator. There is a post-flood concept of Noah as the two-faced god of mankind from ancient history and folklore. The "two-faced" image is depictive of Noah having existed before and after the flood that destroyed all of mankind except Noah and his family. Later, the history of Noah is mixed into legends and myths of the god Janus. Janus, depicted by the "two-faced" image is considered the father of the world and the inventor of ships. No doubt this concept came from the history of Noah, and he evolved into a deity in the ideas of men.

Genesis 6:9 These are the generations of Noah: Noah was a just man and perfect in his generations, and Noah walked with God.

This great patriarch is a man, with a twofold life: before and after the flood. If you study the whole of mythology from Greece, Rome, and Asia, you will see the obvious parallel of the history and deeds of Noah. Even in India, their god Vishnu is a form of the Chaldean word Ish-nuh, meaning the man of rest or the man Noah. India's god of rain is Indra, god of the rains.

The god Janus is later referred to as Saturn, meaning the hidden one or man of the sea, a relationship to Noah while hidden in the ark upon the sea. This subject when pursued further leads into concepts held by any religions about regeneration and baptism mixed with myths and legends of pagan gods from many civilizations.

For this story, it is enough to say Noah is a powerful character because of his living through the worldwide flood. Noah's pre-eminence is eventually exploited by his three sons. They are kings in a fast-growing populace. This exploitation is what leads to the tower of Babel and the confusion of the languages.

The events leading up to the confusion at the Tower of Babel is the wolf in sheep's clothing for the generations up to present day. It is the desire of one person or one group of people to dominate and control their fellowman for their aggrandizement and service. This concept is all through the history of mankind.

A brief look at the behavior of being in charge of things will set the stage for the wars and strife between people of color and culture up to present times. Religion becomes the glue that holds the differences between peoples down through the ages.

I find that one of the keys to understanding the people of history is the Table of Nations found in Genesis 10. It is a master list of the 70 tribes that are scattered throughout the earth. There are 70 nations from a list of 16 basic family groups. These groups come specifically from the 16 grandsons of Noah. As we discover the wonderings and eventual location of the different families from the Tower of Babel, we see that they are settled in the climate and area best suited for their characteristics and human potential.

Science tells us that half of our personalities are genetics, and the other half is developed by our environment. Time, language change, corrupted traditions, and lies have aided in concealing the identity and legacy of the nations. This is shown by books I have read published in the early 30s that do not produce the influence of atheistic evolutionary historians. They openly try to deride the Biblical accounts of origin of nations. Their theories discredit and hide the fact of two major migrations of nations from the Middle East. They are afraid of the Bible narratives that document the classifications of nations.

The Bible also prophesies the future of these nations. This behavior is predictable because God made mankind and is very capable of knowing their proclivities for a will to survive and war over conflicting ideologies. As

I stated earlier in the introduction, historians ignore the Bible as a source of information guiding a person through the when, where, and why of motive or accuracy of the events of History.

The beginning of most academic history comes from Babylon after the flood and is found in the nations who begin to reckon their histories from their kings. The most complete secular record is found in the Akkadian Creation Epic. This account is full of myths and legends from pagan sources, but this does not mean it doesn't give us a good idea of the basic history from these times.

The epic account collaborates what is found in the bible about the Tower of Babel. Many scholars believe the Genesis account in the bible is an attempt to restore the truth of the Creator God as the omnipotent source of power in the universe. The Creator handles the existence of mankind as an alternative to created angelic spirit beings in the family of the Creator God; a theocratic system of hierarchy that keeps order in the vast universe.

I think as you progress with my story of why we are even born, you will come to see the bible is the more correct guidebook for what the Creator wants mankind to understand as our choices for one of two destinies.

JAPHETH

$\mathcal{N}$oah was 500 years old when he starts his family. Shem was 100 years old two years after the flood. The flood occurred in the 600th year of Noah's life. Japheth is 100 years old at the beginning of the flood. I mention Japheth first because he is the eldest of the three sons. These three sons of Noah are always listed in Sunday school and other studies as Shem, Ham, and Japheth out of habit I suppose.

Scholars have long wondered about such names as Magog and Gomer, Elisha, and others. These are found to be neighbors of the peoples in the Middle East and were in the region during the decades after the great flood of Noah's time. They are found in history to have migrated from the region for various reasons. The spirit of adventure is part of Japheth's character and therefore his generations have spread to the far corners of the world. He is also the father of billions of descendants. China, Indonesia, Thailand, and all the far East countries are his descendants. The term enlarges the tents of Japheth is an understatement.

God shall enlarge Japheth, and he shall dwell in the tents of Shem; and Canaan shall be his servant. (Genesis 9:27)

These eastern countries are crowded with millions of people today. Statistics show that 200 people die each day in China from auto accidents. They eventually disappear from the European areas in early history as they are forced out by the Anglo-Saxons and others. These are the Asian and Asian peoples of modern day. They too, like Ham get a strange form of religious order to control their people. These descendants of Japheth were to become very populous and expanded.

The very name Japheth is a play of the Hebrew word Yefeth, meaning to expand; Japheth's descendants account for more than one-third of the population of the world today.

The bible promise says it will enlarge Japheth. These are the peoples of China, Russia, Indonesia, and all the Far East nations today. They are truly the largest in population by far of all other races! As Abraham is noted as the father of the faithful, so Japheth can be noted as the father of billions of people.

SHEM

*S*hem means, man of distinction, the titled or noble race, Aryan. History bears out the fact that Shem has a Religious Primacy above Ham and Japheth. Shem is the father of the Europeans.

Genesis 9:26-27 And he said, blessed be the LORD God of Shem; and Canaan shall be his servant. (27) God shall enlarge Japheth, and he shall dwell in the tents of Shem; and Canaan shall be his servant.

These two verses of scripture set the precedent for the descendants of these three sons of Noah. Canaan as servant. Shem also becomes a mythological figure of the gods for the good side of good behavior versus bad behavior. Shem is also mentioned among the Egyptian dynasties of kings. He is also a contemporary of the bible patriarch Abraham. Sem-sem is Shem's Egyptian name. This is an interesting discovery for me. When I began to find that many characters of history are also recorded under different names, the story of their life becomes larger than the bible reveals.

This is true of many of the famous ancient people of the bible. As we move closer to our time in history this is true of the many kings of many nations. Especially the names of the gentile kings in the bible. These are sometimes the same people under a different name in Academic History records.

There is an interesting story in mythology of the Egyptians and later ancient Greece is about real people of the post-flood world as its civilizations flourished. Shem is the mythological character known as Hercules the Lamenter. He lives to see seven generations of his people suffer the wickedness and evil brought upon them from idolatry and treachery of the Babylonian system of religion. The myth is a story about a boar with tusks in his mouth that eventually destroys the horned boar. Horns or tusks have always been the biblical and mythological symbols for power and authority. Tusks in the mouth stands for a charismatic influence through speaking and declaration.

This is true of Shem. Shem is a Priest and King of many nations forming after the tower of Babel event. When the people find the people of like language they band together and migrate to other parts of the world. I see they still recognize their leadership from the post-flood world of Mesopotamia. Nimrod is the first King of Egypt.

His people migrate to Ethiopia and into modern day Africa eventually. Some of Nimrod's nephews are a line of black pharaohs in upper Egypt. Nimrod is called by the name Osiris in Egyptian records.

Shem is the great-uncle of Nimrod. Shem is also a king of many nations. Shem is a priestly king in Babylon, Palestine, Syria, Lower Egypt, and Canaan during his lifetime. He is also the famous priest of God who Abraham paid tithes to after the battle to free his nephew Lot. The order of Melchizedek is the Hebrew word to describe this righteous priest of God. Because of Shem's dedication to the Invisible God, he opposes Cush and Nimrod's new religion.

Shem's righteous line is continued through his other twin son Araxphad. Araxphad is the twin brother of Assur. Assur builds the great city of Nineveh in Babylon. As Hercules is known in mythologies as the son of Zeus, so he is in reality Shem son of Noah, the great one who lives before and after the flood. Zeus is one of the many name's mythology gives Noah. He is also known by many other names in legends and myths of many other civilizations down through time.

Shem lives over 500 years after the flood. He is contemporary with bible characters such as Abraham and Lot. Shem is a great kingly high priest of many nations, and he has great influence over the kings of the many provinces of Egypt and many associated nations.

Shem is what I would characterize as a national king. His charisma and righteousness are respected and recognized by all the nations. Shem is the righteous priest who supports the morality the Creator God expects from His creation, mankind. Shem is the person who eventually tracks down Nimrod and slays him. Shem is recognized among the nations as a great patriarchal king and priest of God.

It is fitting to talk about the patriarchal faith that is sustained through efforts of Shem. From Job's writings, we can understand that the patriarchal tribes adhered to the faith that was promoted by Shem.

This is due to the statements against idolatry in Job's writing. Idolatry of any form was held to be a sin and was visited with severe punishment on the heads of any who practiced it. This was long before Mt. Sinai event and Moses.

Job 31:26-28 If I beheld the sun when it shined, or the moon walking in brightness. (27) And my heart hath been secretly enticed, or my mouth hath kissed my hand: (28) This also were an iniquity to be punished by the judge: for I should have denied the God that is above.

This being the case in Job's Day, it surely was much more the case during the earlier period of history when the Babylonian Mysteries were conceived and promoted. I also noted that in the final testament of the bible, Babylon is mentioned as the final enemy system of false religion and domination to be defeated by the Christ. The main goal of the Babylon mysteries was to bind all mankind in a blind submission to a hierarchy dependent on the sovereigns of Babylon.

This philosophy is much like modern-day communism. The time in which Shem lived was the same time that patriarchal faith was still fresh in the minds of men. Therefore, Semiramis must introduce the Babylonian mysteries slowly and subtly to not arouse the true believers in a rebellion. Shem was the high priest of God who rallied the minds of the faithful for the truth and cause of the great invisible God and makes it hazardous for those who rebel against God.

INSET

We will see this system assume power once again after the coming of Jesus Christ the first time to earth. It is no coincidence the apostles are murdered during this time. More about that later. The Righteous-Line, as theologians call it, is a generational trait beginning with Adam. Abel is murdered by Cain, his brother. The Righteous-Line continues through Seth and his generations to Noah, from Noah through Shem and his generations to Abraham and so forth. The Unrighteous-Line begins with Cain through his generations to Noah, most notably Cush, Canaan, and

Nimrod, from Noah through Ham and his generations. Note the biblical reference in

Zechariah 14:21: Yea, every pot in Jerusalem and in Judah shall be holiness unto the LORD of hosts: and all they that sacrifice shall take of them and see therein: and in that day there shall be no more the Canaanite in the house of the LORD of hosts.

A prophetic reference to the unrighteous-line of Canaan. It is then carried through various mixed generations of Canaanites, Moabites, Hittites, and so forth. Shem is instrumental in quelling much of the Mystery Religion founded by Nimrod and Semiramis his mother/wife. Remember, God began dealing with mankind one on one before and after the flood. God continued to work with specific individuals up to the time of the Patriarchs. God stopped the specific process with Moses. Eventually forgiveness and salvation became available to all nations with the advent and sacrifice of the firstborn son of God, Jesus. God set up the Levitical Priesthood under Moses as He began to reveal His law and intentions for all of mankind through a specific people. More about that later.

HAM

The name Ham in Hebrew means Hot. Kemet is the ancient name for what the Egyptians refer to as their homeland. Kemet means Black Land. The Anthropologists figure out that Egypt is called Chemia, which means land of Ham. Ham also inherits the beautiful part of the wildlife reserves of Africa and the greatest array in complexity of animal species. These include the blessings of jungles, forests, seashores, and a variety of plant life exclusive to this part of the world. Most of academic history uses the grandson's name, Canaan, when referring to the generations of Ham. The Canaanites are a dark people; Cush was a Black man. (Ham's wife was a Black woman.)

He is later found to be the first King of the Chinese, referenced in their records as a Black man with bright-eyes. These descendants of Ham occupy most of Central Asia, Egypt, the Middle East, and Africa early on after migration from Mesopotamia. The epic account depicts the beginning of human government via a father and son. Cush, Ham's son, and Nimrod, Cush's son. These two were the first kings of Babylon. Shem and Japheth were also kings, but of a different nature in their influence of leadership. Later, Cush, Ham's and Cush's son, Nimrod, along with Shem's son Asshur, became the key players in the development of man's form of government and philosophy toward their neighbors. This eventually led to the Tower of Babel.

THE TOWER OF BABEL

The Tower of Babel was the beginning of mankind's government in the world and religious influence away from the Invisible God. Most all academic historical records reach back to this one event. When the whole story plays out, I find that it started with the rebellious acts against the source of mankind's existence, the Creator God. Interestingly all the ancient civilizations date their kings back to this one event in world history.

There are two ancient accounts of the Tower. One is from the Bible. The other is from the Akkadian Creation Epic. The two main characters are found in the biblical account. Genesis 10:8-10 And Cush begat Nimrod: he began to be a mighty one in the earth. (9) He was a mighty hunter before the LORD: wherefore it is said, Even as Nimrod the mighty hunter before the LORD. (10) And the beginning of his kingdom was Babel, and Erech, and Accad, and Calmer, in the land of Shinar. The chronology of all the near east civilizations begins from this point. By back tracking through the list of the kings the true date of the tower event is proven. This is possible because of the exact record keeping of the Romans. From the time of Rome's conquering of Philip, king of Macedonia, and the reign of Ninus, King of the Assyrians is 1995 years. Remember, Ninus is one of Nimrod's many names. Phillip was conquered in 197 B. C. Nimrod's reign began in 2192 B. C. This is the sum of 197 and 1995 years. Nimrod's sole reign begins after the sixty-two years of joint reign with Cush, Nimrod's father. This sets a date for the tower event at 2256–2254 B.C. This is where comparing academic history with the bible helps to confirm the dates.

The Akkadian Creation Epic reveals it took two years to construct the tower. The bible speaks of the general condition of earth's peoples as being divided. (Genesis 10:25) This passage must be referring to the people, for the earth is not in two pieces. The final confirmation is found in the Chinese authentic history records. These are called the Annals of the bamboo books. These records start the beginning of the Chinese civilization in the year 2254. It speaks of their king, Shun; he is a Black man. The account says Shun's eyes shown with double brightness. This is an academic term for a theological term, demon owned. His name is spelled several different ways, Chusou or Kusou. He can be no one else but Cush!

The account even mentions Cush's wife, Semiramis. She is referred to as the queen mother of the king of the west. This made no sense to me at first because I thought Babylon was in the east, not the west. I wasn't thinking this through deep enough. The whole populace of the world was at Babylon until the confounding of the languages by the Creator God. When the languages were confused, the groups of people who could understand each other banded together and moved away from Babylon to other parts of the world. This was the purpose God caused the languages to be confused. Instead of a flood, as promised to never be an event again, God caused the peoples to separate because of communication difficulties.

Shun was the first king of the Chinese speaking people because He was King of Babylon. The Chinese migrated to the east and their civilization continued to increase. It is noteworthy that as the people were separated by language they still paid homage to their original kings. Therefore, the kings of Babylon at the time of the Tower event appear in the different languages that God separated the people with.

Thus, to the Egyptians the Nimrod of the bible becomes the god Osiris, to the Phoenicians he is Baal, to the later Babylonians he is Marduk, and to the Semites he is Tammuz. Nimrod became a king to the people who had forsaken the Creator God. It gets confusing at times to keep the names connected. Nimrod and his mother/wife are both called by many different names because of their power and position in Babylon before the tower event.

The first major manmade religious order was born in Babylon and has changed faces many times down through history and to the present day. This Mystery Religion is traced to days of a Babylonian Queen named Semiramis. She comes to power just a few centuries after the great flood of Noah's time. Her influence reaches the point of worship. She is worshipped as Rhea, the great Mother of the gods. She is the Venus of impurity and the mother and eventually wife of Nimrod, the son of Cush.

Genesis 10:8-12 And Cush begat Nimrod: he began to be a mighty one in the earth. (9) He was a mighty hunter before the LORD: wherefore it is said, Even as Nimrod the mighty hunter before the LORD. (10) And the beginning of his kingdom was Babel, and Erech, and Accad, and Calneh, in the land of Shinar. (11) Out of that land went forth Asshur, the builder Nineveh, and the city Rehoboth, and Calah, (12) And Resen between Nineveh and Calah: the same is a great city.

When this scripture is compared with academic history of this time period, there are two lines of genealogies characterized in the bible. One is from Noah's son, Ham.

The other is from Shem. Nimrod and Assur are popular characters of these times also. The great city of Nineveh in the bible was built and run by Assur. Assur was one of the twin sons of Shem. Some scholars believe he may have been the famous Sargon II. From each of these generations of peoples there is a representation in the beginnings of the post flood predatory, imperialistic, and militaristic fascism. The basic principles of banking, large corporations, radically centralized governments, and authoritarianism can be traced back to one of these men called Sargon in Academic history. His Biblical identity is Assur. Sargon the Great is the twin brother of Araxphad. These are the sons of Shem. It is through the generations of Araxphad that the righteous line is carried up to the creating of the nation of Israel.

NIMROD

$\mathcal{N}$imrod was the first to change from the ancient manners of people. He incites a new passion—conquest. Nimrod was the first to wage war against his neighbors. He conquered all the nations from Assyria to Libya, as they were not yet acquainted with the arts of war. Nimrod appeared at a time when wild beasts multiplied faster than the restored human race. These beasts caused great terror among the sparse populations. The exploits of Nimrod, in hunting down these beasts and ridding the world of these savage monsters, certainly granted him power in the eyes of the populations.

This activity plus his training an army of men to war against his neighbors was how he gained power and pre-eminent dictatorship over the masses of people. For them, he became like a savior from terror and their obligation to an invisible God. He afforded them the carnal comforts of carnal living and a conscience that was not responsible to One Invisible God, as promoted by Noah and Shem. Slowly and steadfastly He and his mother/wife steered the masses of people away from the Invisible Creator.

Nimrod eventually married his own mother Semiramis, Cush's wife. Nimrod was the emancipator of people who looked only to walk after the sight of their own eyes and the imaginations of their own hearts. His power and strength among the masses of people caused them to rally around his free lifestyle he promotes.

This separated people from the influences of the Invisible God and put God and the strict spirituality of His law at a distance, creating a huge gulf between heaven and earth. This was the beginning of Humanism replacing the belief in a higher calling to a better destiny for mankind. Ancient history states that Nimrod, the mighty hunter, was the first king to war against his neighbors.

Nimrod's Egyptian name is Osiris, and his Assyrian name is Ninus. See, here are three different names from history being the same individual. He was the first to breed dogs with leopards for hunting. He was also the first to break horses to ride while hunting wild animals. People feared these wild animals, and Nimrod soon became their deliverer from these beasts. It is no coincidence that he is depicted as the Centaur or man-horse with the bow and arrow in the stories and mythologies carried on through history down to and through Greece.

Nimrod, the son of Cush and Ham's grandson, was a major player in the spreading of the Babylonian religion to Egypt and other parts of the world as the languages were confused at Babel. He also became a large figure in mythology of the gods and later in the stories of mythology penned by the Greeks and Romans. The Romans kept strict records of the kings of all the nations from the time of Ninus or Nimrod, up to the time of their conquest of Phillip of Macedonia. Roman records reflect Nimrod was the first ruler of the Assyrians.

When Nimrod fled to Egypt, Assur became the king of the Assyrians, staying in Babylon. His people eventually migrated into modern-day Europe. I should tell you I have found this highly informative down through academic history to my lifetime, in the sense that the Germans are direct descendants of the Assyrians, a fact they have purposely tried to hide from the world for centuries. From the time of Nimrod to Rome's conquering Macedonia is an interval of 1,995 years, the skills of war became awesome in these nearly two-thousand years of these tribes.

Remember that many of the characters of the Bible are found in academic history under different names. They are names from the language of that particular culture and nation after the confounding of the languages at the tower Babel. This is when the first duplication of one famous individual's name starts much of the confusion found in academic history. Cush begets Nimrod and is known as the ringleader of apostasy during these times.

In the Egyptian writings, Cush is named Hermes or Mercury. This is an Egyptian synonym for the son of Ham. Cush is the original prophet of Idolatry. In the writings of Hyginus he is characterized as the grand agent in the confounding the languages at the Tower of Babel. This is because

Cush created his own version of God and convinced the people to build this huge tower.

Cush became known as the confounder because he was the reason God confounded the languages and scattered the people all over the earth! There is no doubt these names and titles were given to these characters of ancient history by the Pagans whom they worshipped as their deliverer or Messiah just as adversaries were stigmatized as giants who we now understand were the real giants or Mighty Ones, of which Nimrod was the leader.

These are giants of evil, not giants of size. Hebrew word: n ephîyl n ephil pronounced, nef-eel,' nef-eel;' properly, a feller, that is, a bully or tyrant: - giant confirms this as a fact. Cush, Nimrod, and Semiramis were mighty leaders against the principles of the Creator God.

It becomes obvious that Shem became the opposition to the apostasy from the patriarchal faith brought through the flood by Noah. Therefore, Shem being named Hercules the lamenter in mythology makes perfect sense. Hercules is the avenger against the Giants, not by mere force but also with the power of the Invisible God of creation with him. This of course was a special influence of the Holy Spirit power of the invisible God on Shem. This entirely agrees with the historical character of Shem, the righteous high priest of God. Shem's affiliation and loyalty to the invisible creator God is supported by Egyptian accounts of the death of Osiris or Nimrod.

The Egyptian account about the death of Nimrod says that the grand enemy of their god overcame Nimrod, not by violence first, but through conspiracy with seventy-two of the leading rulers of Egypt. I will make this brief as possible. Once the death sentence was passed on judicially against Nimrod, the 72 judges of Egypt made a horrific sentence to be carried out. They were so influenced by the power and charisma of Shem or Sem (his Egyptian name) that they feared what Nimrod had created would bring great destruction to their nation. They ordered Nimrod should be killed and cut into seventy-two pieces. Then each piece of Nimrod's slain body was to be delivered to the ruler of each of the seventy-two provinces of Egypt as a reminder of what would happen if they ever sought to follow Nimrod's evil ways.

This punishment is used later by the Judges of Israel when they dismembered the Levite's concubine and sent one piece to each of the twelve tribes of Israel.

Judges 19:29-30 And when he was come into his house, he took a knife, and laid hold on his concubine, and divided her, together with her bones, into twelve pieces, and sent her into all the coasts of Israel.(30) And it was so, that all that saw it said, there was no such deed done nor seen from the day that the children of Israel came up out of the land of Egypt unto this day: consider of it, take advice, and speak your minds.

Long story short, this Levite's concubine was rebellious and left for four months, whoring among the men of nations. Her punishment was an example to the tribes not to be rebellious to the laws of God taught by the Levites. There were no kings in Israel in those days. All civil and religious matters were passed on judicially by the Levitical Priesthood.

History and the bible are very bloody at times! I come to see in my years of reading and studying history and religion that all roads of deceit and apostasy lead back to Babylon. It becomes the center of the wrong culture and God disrupts it quickly. This system of worship and religious order shows up in the history of mankind to the present and into the future as prophesied in the Bible. This Babylonian Mystery Religion is not set up at once. It comes in quietly at first so as to not arouse the attention of the patriarchal faith of Noah. We must remember this patriarchal faith has nothing to do whatsoever with the institutions set up through Moses, for he is not yet on the scene of history.

It is a pure faith of the patriarchs and idolatry in any form is held as a crime with severe penalties for its practice. Even during the time of Job, it is still looked upon as evil and pagan to practice any form of worship of idols.

Job 31:26-28 If I beheld the sun when it shined, or the moon walking in brightness; (27) And my heart hath been secretly enticed, or my mouth hath kissed my hand: (28) This also were an iniquity to be punished by the judge: for I should have denied the God that is above.

Semiramis and Nimrod are smart enough to not introduce their religion all at once so as to not raise the wrath of the patriarch Noah and Shem. It had to be done stealthily and in secret. Even though they were powerful people, they were aware that the incorruptible people would put their religion down, especially if it were forced upon the masses too quickly. This would certainly defeat their intent to bind all mankind in blind and absolute submission to a hierarchy entirely dependent on the sovereigns of Babylon.

By these means all knowledge, sacred and profane, came to be monopolized by the priesthood. They continued this mystery religion after the Tower of Babel in Egypt, where they took up leadership once again. This took four hundred years. The result is the people who were slowly converted to their system became bound to the priests, because they were the only depositories of religious knowledge. They had the only true traditions by which the symbols and rituals of public religion could be interpreted.

Therefore, without blind implicit submission to them, the things necessary for their salvation could not be known by the masses of people. This is exactly what I find happens later on in history with the early Papacy and the times of no public printing or distribution of the Holy Scriptures.

I have come to understand that the great men of the bible have become the affection of the myths, folklore, and paganism of the post flood world. The seeds of rebellion toward the Creator God planted by Nimrod, Semiramis, and others were eventually watered and nurtured by all nations of the world. The many stories of many nations were laced with the similarities of the post flood righteous leadership.

The Greeks and Romans were the primary sustaining cultures for these pagan aspects of a corrupt religious influence upon the world. The narrative of the Bible is all about the conflict of man's system of religions and governments versus what God intends for man to understand about Him and mankind's destiny.

Remember the bible is a guidebook that documents the activities of men and nations God begins to deal with as populations increase. God uses many individuals to promote and keep His intended way of living. The principle of how to pay respects to and worship the Invisible Creator God and how to treat properly our fellowmen, of all ethnic backgrounds and culture. There came a time when God chose a nation of people to stand for His ways of life in the world.

Contained in the Bible is the story of how they were just as human as every other nation and had to learn to stand up for what God taught them and not be persuaded by the false religions of the pagan nations. They became an example of how God deals with disobedience from His chosen people while eventually extending the same redemption plan to all the peoples and nations of the world.

THE PATRIARCHS

ABRAHAM (Father of the Faithful) Abraham was a descendant of Shem through Araxphad. He was the son of Terah, who was the 8th son from Shem. Terah had three children: Haran, Nahor, and Abram or Abraham. Haran died at an early age. Haran's son was Lot of the bible. Abraham was Lot's uncle. He was of Chaldean descent, though Jews often make the mistake of thinking Abraham was a Jew.

Abraham lived before the term Jew was placed upon a people. Now modern historians would like us to believe that Abraham is a Semite, or an Arab-type. However, this is not true. Abraham's original ethnic race is Chaldean or white.

Genesis11:28 And Haran died before his father Terah in the land of his nativity, in Ur of the Chaldees.

Genesis11:31 And Terah took Abram his son, and Lot the son of Haran his son's son, and Sarai his daughter in law, his son Abram's wife; and they went forth with them from Ur of the Chaldees, to go into the land of Canaan; and they came unto Haran and dwelt there.

Genesis15:7 And he said unto him, I am the LORD that brought thee out of Ur of the Chaldees, to give thee this land to inherit it.

Hebron in the land of Canaan and is where the term Hebrew originates. Ur is in Chaldea, in Mesopotamia. This is where Terah, Abraham's father, dwelt with his three sons. So, Abraham was a Chaldean from the line of Shem, Arphaxad, and so forth. These people are white Aramean. The Arab line, as related to Abraham, comes through Hagar, Sarah's handmaid. She is Egyptian or Semite.

Genesis16:1 Now Sarai Abram's wife bare him no children: and she had a handmaid, an Egyptian, whose name was Hagar.

Genesis12:11 And it came to pass, when he was come near to enter Egypt, that he said unto Sarai his wife, behold now, I know that thou art a fair woman to look upon:

Genesis 12:14 And it came to pass, that, when Abram was come into Egypt, the Egyptians beheld the woman that she was very fair.

This is a reference meaning that Abraham is not a dark Semite or of Arab nature, and neither is Sarah his wife. It has been said that Abraham is the father of the faithful. He is indeed a man of courage and determination to follow the invisible God. His faith is the expression of the things he hopes will come to pass as he lives his life in a different manner than other people. He is 75 years old when he leaves Chaldea at the command of God. He is a Chaldean and comes from the Babylonian culture. Though others of his family worship manmade gods, Abraham is a wise man and not afraid to question the things of life around him. He sees manmade gods as obedient only to the men who create them. They produced no power of themselves and any benefit from them is only by men who believe in those gods.

It is fair to say that the certain existence of an invisible God and the uncertainty of His mode of existence causes men to have an enormous amount of error in their interpretation of the Invisible God. It is natural that they find His existence in the material things surrounding them, such as the heavenly bodies they can see above them. They accept these as the attributes of His manifestation.

The fact is, most ancient records of idolatry deify the heavenly bodies as the Sun, being the brightest, the moon the lesser, stars and so forth. It is no wonder the natural ignorance of man is to worship the Sun as the dominant evidence for an invisible God.

The sun is the main emblem of worship by the people of the lands of Chaldea and Egypt for centuries. Even Abraham, upon his first impression of a certain star sees it as the God of the universe. But when the star is diminished by the light of the rising sun, Abraham knowing that God is an unchangeable force of creation, feels deceived, yet he believes God is identifiable somewhere out there.

Abraham is the 10 th generation from Noah and is known as someone who does not believe in the gods set apart by men. Abraham is a great leader and influential teacher of men. He goes to Canaan and becomes quite wealthy as a leader and person of notoriety. When a famine threatens his livelihood, he moves his family to Egypt.

The Pharaoh of that time hears of the fair-looking beauty of Sarah. This is why Abraham fears to let it be known she is his wife. Circumstances eventually produce the truth. However, Abraham's charisma intrigues the Pharaoh and his advisors. They learn many things from Abraham and respect his intelligence and wisdom. Abraham is Chaldean and very smart about things the Egyptians know truly little about. Abraham teaches them Arithmetic and Astronomy, quite convincing them of the art of learning.

This is new information passing from the Chaldeans to the Egyptians, and later on to the Greeks. Abraham is a great leader and soldier. He marshals an army from his own people and sets out to deliver his own nephew Lot, and the Sodomites in a battle with the Assyrians. Even though his army is outnumbered, Abraham shows how the power of readiness and courage can overcome a great enemy. He surprises the Assyrians by attacking at night and wins a victory over them, delivering the King of Sodom, and Lot his nephew. This event is found in the bible.

Genesis 14:14-24 And when Abram heard that his brother was taken captive, he armed his trained servants, born in his own house, three hundred and eighteen, and pursued them unto Dan (15) And he divided himself against them, he, and his servants, by night, and smote them, and pursued them unto Hobah, which is on the left hand of Damascus. (16) And he brought back all the goods, and also brought again his brother Lot, and his goods, and the women also, and the people. (17) And the king of Sodom went out to meet him after his return from the slaughter of Chedorlaomer, and of the kings that were with him, at the valley of Shaveh, which is the king's dale. (18) And Melchizedek king of Salem brought forth bread and wine: and he was the priest of the High God. (19) And he blessed him, and said, blessed be Abram of the High God, possessor of heaven and earth: (20) And blessed be the high God, which hath delivered thine enemies into thy hand. And he gave him tithes of all. (21) And the king of Sodom said unto Abram, give me the persons, and take the goods to thyself. (22) And Abram said to the king of Sodom, I have lift up mine hand unto the LORD, the High God, the possessor of heaven and earth, (23) That I will not take from a thread even to a shoelace, and that I will not take anything that is thine, lest thou should say, I have made Abram rich:(24)

Save only that which the young men have eaten, and the portion of the men which went with me, Aner, Eshcol, and Mamre; let them take their portion.

Abraham is a good man, and he is favored by the High Priest of the land of Canaan and surrounding territories. This is significant because later in the narrative of the Bible, Melchizedek is the typology of the type of High Priest that will someday become an eternal existing High Priest of God for all of mankind. God bestows a lifechanging promise upon Abraham because of his faithfulness to the Invisible God. Abraham is tested by God in many areas of life and is found to be a man faithful to the commands of the Invisible God. These tests may seem strange to us in modern times.

There are many things that happen to these patriarchs which foreshadow the future in understanding how God is developing a people an inheritance from Him. As I have said in the beginning of this book, the bible is the guide for lessons of life revealing a higher level of understanding for people of the end times in the times we are born. One of these tests is the promise from God to Abraham that is told in the bible.

Genesis 13:14-17And the LORD said unto Abram, after that Lot was separated from him, lift up now thine eyes, and look from the place where thou art northward, and southward, and eastward, and westward: (15) For all the land which thou see, to thee will I give it, and to thy seed forever. (16) And I will make thy seed as the dust of the earth: so that if a man can number the dust of the earth, then shall thy seed also be numbered. (17) Arise, walk through the land in the length of it and in the breadth of it; for I will give it unto thee.

Just before this promise is made Abraham sees the land cannot support all of his cattle and Lot's. So, Abraham gives Lot the choice of which land he will live on, and Lot chooses Jordan.

Genesis 13:10-13 And Lot lifted up his eyes, and beheld all the plain of Jordan, that it was well watered everywhere, before the LORD destroyed Sodom and Gomorrah, even as the garden of the LORD, like the land of Egypt, as thou come unto Zoar. (11) Then Lot chose him all the plain of Jordan; and Lot journeyed east: and they separated themselves the one from the other. (12) Abram dwelled in the land of Canaan, and Lot dwelled in the cities of the plain, and pitched his tent toward Sodom. (13) But the men of Sodom were wicked and sinners before the LORD exceedingly.

Abraham cannot understand how his generations will be so many since his wife Sarah is barren and cannot conceive a child. God promises Sarah will have a son for Abraham, even though she is 90 years old. She laughs when told the news. Then she does what most people do with little faith and belief in God and tries to help God by giving Hagar her Egyptian handmaid to Abraham as a means of producing him a son.

This is typical of carnal nature, to try to outguess God and help God out. The end result is Ishmael, father of the Arabs. Jealousy ensues as often happens with human nature.

Genesis 16:11-12 And the angel of the LORD said unto her, Behold, thou art with child, and shalt bear a son, and shalt call his name Ishmael, because the LORD hath heard thy affliction. (12) And he will be a wild man; his hand will be against every man, and every man's hand against him; and he shall dwell in the presence of all his brethren.

God does not abandon Hagar and her child. Instead, He promises to make a great nation from her son. His name is Ishmael, father of the Arabs. He is a race mix of Chaldean and Egyptian, resulting in chiseled dark features. The Arabs will appear later in this story as religious supremacy is sought after by the nations. Eventually, Sarah is blessed with a child by God's miracle, and his name is Isaac.

Genesis 21:2-7 For Sarah conceived, and bare Abraham a son in his old age, at the set time of which God had spoken to him. (3) And Abraham called the name of his son that was born unto him, whom Sarah bare to him, Isaac. (4) And Abraham circumcised his son Isaac being eight days old, as God had commanded him. (5) And Abraham was one-hundred years old, when his son Isaac was born unto him. (6) And Sarah said, God hath made me to laugh, so that all that hear will laugh with me. (7) And she said, who would have said unto Abraham, that Sarah should have given children suck? for I have born him a son in his old age.

Many times, we as carnal humans do not have the patience to wait and see the marvelous acts of God that can have an effect on our lives. Our life is often the victim of time and chance.

INSET TIME and CHANCE:

Our Physical lives are a series of events occurring in irreversible succession. These events are the effects of the unexpected, random, and unpredictable nature of our world in the universe. A universe revealed as space, stars, planets, moons, asteroids, and galaxies of gaseous phenomenon that is ever expanding. The Bible says we are a creation of God that is subject to Time and Chance.

Ecclesiastes 9:10-12 Whatsoever thy hand finds to do, do it with thy might; for there is no work, nor device, nor knowledge, nor wisdom, in the grave, where thou go. (11) I returned, and saw under the sun, that the race is not to the swift, nor the battle to the strong, neither yet bread to the wise, nor yet riches to men of understanding, nor yet favor to men of skill; but time and chance happens to them all. (12) For man also knows not his time: as the fishes that are taken in an evil net, and as the birds that are caught in the snare; so are the sons of men snared in an evil time, when it falls suddenly upon them.

Time is a non-spatial continuum of events occurring in irreversible succession from the past, through the present, and into the future. Chance is the abstract nature shared by unexpected, random, or unpredictable events. Circumstance can have an effect on Time and Chance. Circumstance: The condition or power in our life, attending an event and having bearing on it, as a determining factor, causing intervention or change. The circumstance for many of these bible characters is the divine intervention of the Invisible God in their lives. Later in history this type of circumstance can be an influence in all men's lives if they choose to believe in the Invisible God.

ISAAC

The circumstance for Abraham and Sarah was the miracle of being able to conceive and bear a child as promised by the angel of the Lord. Isaac was born and when he was 25 years old, God told Abraham to sacrifice Isaac to Him. Abraham followed the command, and he and Isaac journeyed up a mountain to perform a sacrifice.

There Abraham told Isaac what God had commanded him to do. Isaac did not express anxiety at the situation but told his father that he was willing to obey his father, and if it was God's request, he was willing to be the sacrifice.

Now, if I were Isaac, I would have tried to negotiate my way out of this situation. It is impressive to me that Isaac was quite willing to trust his dad heard God correctly. Being of such an inquiring mind, I would have asked for some kind of proof of such a command. Isaac was a very loyal son to his dad and Abraham's teachings certainly showed in Isaac's faith. Remember, Abraham was a Chaldean and highly intelligent about the world around him.

As I said before, Abraham taught the Egyptians many things they knew extraordinarily little about. This was an obvious test of faith for both Abraham and Isaac. Abraham obeyed the command and Isaac complied up to the very second before his throat was slashed. God stopped Abraham from the act of sacrificing Isaac. God told him it was not His desire to kill Isaac, but this request was to test the temper of Abraham's mind. A ram was supplied for the sacrifice, and Isaac and Abraham both came down the mountain that day.

Genesis 22:11-18 And the angel of the LORD called unto him out of heaven, and said, Abraham, Abraham: and he said, here am I. (12) And he said, lay not thine hand upon the lad, neither do thou anything unto him: for now, I know that thou fears God, seeing thou hast not withheld thy son, thine only son from me. (13) And Abraham lifted up his eyes, and looked, and behold behind him a ram caught in a thicket by his horns: and Abraham went and took the ram and offered him up for a burnt offering in the stead of his son. (14) And Abraham called the name of that place Jehovah: as it is said to this day, In the mount of the LORD it shall be seen. (15) And the angel of the LORD called unto Abraham out of heaven the second time, (16) And said, by myself have I sworn, said the LORD, for because thou hast done this thing, and hast not withheld thy son, thine only son: (17) That in blessing I will bless thee, and in multiplying I will multiply thy seed as the stars of the heaven, and as the sand which is upon the sea shore; and thy seed shall possess the gate of his enemies; (18) And in thy seed shall all the nations of the earth be blessed; because thou hast obeyed my voice.

Abraham's faith is referred to by the writers of the New Testament. There are 70 scriptures in the New Testament that refer to the belief, obedience, and faith of Abraham. It is an interesting study to just look up all the New Testament scriptures referring to Abraham. They actually tell his story of belief, obedience, and faith in God. These are the 3 main requirements to begin to understand the Bible and the Plans of God for all of mankind. Abraham's obedience and Isaac's readiness to comply confirms the choice of Abraham and Isaac as the fathers of many peoples. They will be the fathers of many nations and peoples like as the number of the stars and sand of the beaches.

All of this is leading up to God using a chosen people to spread His laws and ways of living to the rest of the nations.

Matthew 1:17 So all the generations from Abraham to David are fourteen generations; and from David until the carrying away into Babylon are fourteen generations; and from the carrying away into Babylon unto Christ are fourteen generations.

INSET

I think it is noteworthy that the promise God makes to Abraham is also prophetic to the fact that eventually the salvation process is opened to all the nations of the earth. The Spiritual salvation of ancient Israel will be a special time in the future. Israel's spiritual salvation is revealed through the prophets and the visions of John the Apostle. There is a hint of this time in the book of Ezekiel also. It is part of the mysterious story of the valley of dry bones. When studied thoroughly it is showing a time when the whole house of Israel will be given a chance to enjoy the redemption process pioneered by Jesus Christ. It is a time set for the future.

The house of Israel becomes divided before Christ comes the first time as the savior. Their spiritual salvation will begin when they are resurrected as one nation. It is a whole subject of prophecy that can be studied. The process of time is slowly leading up to the coming of the very first begotten son of the Invisible God. He is begotten through the power of the Holy Spirit into the womb of a selected human host named Mary. JACOB (Israel)

The next person in this line of descendants is Jacob. Jacob is the twin brother of Esau. Esau is not as a responsible person as Jacob and foolishly gives his birthright to Jacob. Isaac is told to pronounce a blessing over his son and God allows both Isaac and Esau to be tricked by Jacob and his mother. It's one of many Sunday school stories we have all heard. Because of contentions between Jacob and Esau, Jacob is forced to flee for his life. Isaac has now become alive to the real destiny of Jacob. He therefore calls for him to bless him and give him a command. The command is to take a wife, not from Kenaan but from the kindred of his parents. The blessing comes from God Almighty

(Genesis17:1). It is a blessing belonging to the chosen seed—the blessing of Abraham. It embraces a many offspring, the land of promise, and all that is included in the blessing of Abraham. A congregation of peoples. This is the word congregation which is afterward applied to an assembled people of God, and to which the Greek word ekklēsia, corresponds.

Jacob follows his mother's advice and his father's command and at the same time reaps the bitter fruit from his deceitful action toward his brother. It results in the hardship and treachery of an exile of twenty years away from his family. He travels a long day's journey from Beersheba to Bethel, about forty miles. Providence brings him to a convenient place, shaded with trees to rest himself that night.

Jacob uses stones for his pillows, and the heavens for his canopy and curtains. In his time, this was not as bad as it would seem for us today. He lays very cold, the cold ground for his bed. Who can know which one would make the matter worse, a cold stone for a pillow, or exposed to the cold air. Solitude affords time for reflection, and it is the time God begins to bring Jacob under a course of religious instruction and training. To dispel his fears and steady the inward confusion of his mind, nothing was better fitted than a vision of a gigantic ladder reaching from himself to heaven. Upon this ladder the angels were continually ascending and descending from God Himself performing their benevolent errands. Jacob sees what he thinks is a ladder extending from earth to heaven and persons descending up the ladder—persons that are more excellent than humans.

At last, he sees a bright image of someone standing above the ladder and calling to him by his name. God then speaks to Jacob with these next words (I will paraphrase them):

"It is not fit for you, who are the son of a good father, and grandson of one who has obtained a great reputation for his eminent virtue, to be dejected at your present circumstances, but to hope for better times; for you shall have great abundance of all good things by my assistance; for I brought Abraham

here, out of Mesopotamia, when he was driven away by his kinsmen, and I made your father a happy man; nor will I bestow a lesser degree of happiness on you. Jacob, be of good courage and under my conduct continue on this journey for the marriage you go to look for. You shall have children of good character, their multitude will be many, and they will leave what they have to a still more many posterity, and to whose posterity, will receive the dominion of the lands. Their posterity will eventually fill the entire earth and sea, so far as the sun beholds them. This is a clue to why the Israelites were a "scattered" peoples after they became a nation. Do not fear any danger, nor be afraid of the many labors you must undergo, for by my providence I will direct you what you are to do in the time present, and still much more in the time to come."

Genesis 32:27-28 And he said unto him, what is thy name? And he said, Jacob. (28) And he said, your name shall be called no more Jacob, but Israel: for as a prince hast, thou power with God and with men and hast prevailed.

This is a distant clue to the success and blessings of the descendants of Israel as they are eventually scattered and dispersed over the world because of their sins, down through time. One needs only look at the nations of northern Europe, Great Britain, and America to see the great natural resources and prosperity they enjoy. The place where Jacob rests on stones for a pillow and sees the vision is now modern-day Jerusalem. The Jacob's Stone has perpetual meaning as will be clear as our story continues. It becomes known as the Stone of Scone in modern day history. It is the coronation stone resting under the throne of England. Many kings and queens have been crowned while sitting on that throne with the ancient Jacob's pillow stone under the chair. This stone is symbolic of the promise to king David that his generations would be the perpetual people of God before the nations. (read *2Samuel 7:1-17*)

Psalms 89:3-4 I have made a covenant with my chosen, I have sworn unto David my servant, (4) Thy seed will I set up forever and build up thy throne to all generations.

Jeremiah 33:17 For thus says the LORD; David shall never want a man to sit upon the throne of the house of Israel.

Yes, on the throne of England reigns a descendant of king David. A dynasty that has ruled Ireland, Scotland, and England for over 2500 years. All of them were crowned over that stone of destiny, Jacob's pillow stone.

JOSEPH

$\mathcal{A}$s I said earlier in the book, I will spend more time with some characters than others because of how their stories and historical lives influenced my understanding of how mankind's knowledge of God progresses down through time.

If we did not have the Bible account of Joseph, you would have no idea why Joseph is even in Egypt, much less why he became second in command of the whole nation. Academic history doesn't recognize him because they do not know his Egyptian name. Joseph becomes a Pharaoh in Egypt!

The Bible supplies reasons and motives for many of the events of history. It reveals a reason Joseph was so successful and his whole family moved to Egypt. God used Joseph and his family to educate the Egyptians in many areas of living. This is how the bible character Job arrived. He was Joseph's nephew, the son of Issachar, one of Joseph's 11 other brothers. More about him later.

Genesis 46:26 All the souls that came with Jacob into Egypt, which came out of his loins, besides Jacob's sons' wives, all the souls were threescore and six.

Joseph is the favorite son of Jacob, or Israel. We have all heard the story of Joseph in Sunday school. Joseph is a very pivotal character in the history of how God moved toward using a nation of people to spread God's knowledge to the rest of the nations.

Genesis 37:5-8 And Joseph dreamed a dream, and he told it his brethren: and they hated him yet the more. (6) And he said unto them, Hear, I pray you, this dream which I have dreamed:(7) For, behold, we were binding sheaves in the field, and, lo, my sheaf arose, and also stood upright; and behold, your sheaves stood round about, and made obeisance to my sheaf. (8) And his brethren said to him, Shalt thou indeed reign over us? or shalt thou indeed have dominion over us? And they hated him yet the more for his dreams, and for his words.

Joseph told his dream to his brothers, and they were offended because it depicted them bowing down before him. I will try to be brief because most everyone knows the Sunday School Version of Joseph and how his brothers hated him, sold him, and told Jacob that Joseph was killed by a wild beast.

Joseph found himself a slave and prisoner in Egypt and was tested in many ways. He was about seventeen years old when his brothers sold him to a passing caravan of nomads. He found himself in Egypt where he becomes the slave of a wealthy Egyptian.

The man's wife propositioned him, but Joseph was a loyal worker. He knew it would not be right. This is an example of the known code of moral laws long before a public declaration from God at Mount Sinai. Joseph refused her and she was enraged. She falsely accused him to her husband, and Joseph's boss tossed him into prison, believing his wife to be telling the truth.

While Joseph was in prison, the king of Egypt was troubled by a dream. He sought answers, but the king's wise men could not seem to interpret the dream, so he searched for different interpreters. God revealed the meaning of the Pharaoh's dream to Joseph.

It is important to note that this Pharaoh or King reigning over Egypt is found in the third Dynasty of the Egyptian Kings documented in the Turin Papyrus scrolls. The third Dynasty of Memphis, Egypt, compared with the writings of Manetho, an Egyptian historian, along with the Palermo Stone reveals many of these Dynasties of Pharaohs reigning parallel with each other.

This is an important discovery for the placing of many biblical characters in the timeline of ancient history. The modern historians list Egyptian Dynasties of Pharaohs one after the other. The truth is there are many Pharaohs ruling in Egypt simultaneously in different Dynasties during the same time period. There are five successive kings who dominate this third dynasty.

The First king is called Zoser, also spelled Djoser. I mention this because in all of the historical records of Pharaohs, there are only seven years of famine in Egypt mentioned. Now, look at the vision that the Pharaoh wanted Joseph to interpret:

Genesis 41:15-32 And Pharaoh said unto Joseph, I have dreamed a dream, and there is none that can interpret it: and I have heard say of thee, that thou canst understand a dream to interpret it. (16) And Joseph answered Pharaoh, saying, It is not in me: God shall give Pharaoh an answer of peace. (17) And Pharaoh said unto Joseph, In my dream, behold, I stood upon the bank of the river: (18) And, behold, there came up out of the river seven cows, fat fleshed and well favored; and they fed in a meadow: (19) And, behold, seven other cows came up after them, poor and very ill favored and lean fleshed, such as I never saw in all the land of Egypt for badness: (20) And the lean and the ill-favored cow did eat up the first seven fat cows: (21) And when they had eaten them up, it could not be known that they had eaten them; but they were still ill favored, as at the beginning. So, I awoke. (22) And I saw in my dream, and behold, seven ears came up in one stalk, full and good: (23) And behold, seven ears, withered, thin, and blasted with the east wind, sprung up after them: (24) And the thin ears devoured the seven good ears: and I told this unto the magicians; but there was none that could declare it to me. (25) And Joseph said unto Pharaoh, the dream of Pharaoh is one: God hath shewed Pharaoh what he is about to do. (26) The seven good cows are seven years; and the seven good ears are seven years: the dream is one. (27) And the seven thin and ill-favored cows that came up after them are seven years; and the seven empty ears blasted with the east wind shall be seven years of famine. (28) This is the thing which I have spoken unto Pharaoh: What God is about to do he showed unto Pharaoh. (29) Behold, there come seven years of great plenty throughout all the land of Egypt: (30) And there shall arise after them seven years of famine; and all the plenty shall be forgotten in the land of Egypt; and the famine shall consume the land; (31) And the plenty shall not be known in the land by reason of that famine following; for it shall be very grievous. (32) And for that the dream was doubled unto Pharaoh twice; it is because the thing is set up by God, and God will shortly bring it to pass.

You don't find this story in the academic history because historians reject the bible as a credible account of history. The interpretation of the dream shows a coming famine upon the land of Egypt. This is documented both in academic history and the bible's narrative. This vision from the bible happens at the same time of King Zoser's time when ruling Egypt.

From Egyptian records, here is the translated account of this seven years' famine in Egypt as written by King Zoser, during the eighteenth year of his reign!

Following is an excerpt from the historical writing of Zoser during his time.

"Year eighteen. I was in distress on the Great Throne, and those who are in the palace were in Hearts affliction from a very great evil since the Nile had not come in my time for a space of seven years. Grain was scant, fruits were dried up, and everything which they eat was short. The infant was wailing; the youth was waiting; the heart of the old man was in sorrow... the courtiers were in need. The temples were shut up.... Everything was found empty."

I wish not to bore you to tears with the recorded Dynasties that are parallel to each other in the timeline of ancient history. Egyptian Dynasties III, IV, & V are all greater and lesser Pharaohs ruling over the many provinces of Egypt at the same time.

Historians will have us believe the Pharaohs are rulers one after the other. This is not true. These three Egyptian Dynasties are contemporary. They are not Kings or Pharaohs ruling in succession. The time span of these three Dynasties covers the years 1737 to 1487 B.C.

Historians purposefully screw up the timeline by placing these Pharaohs in series, not parallel as they appear in the actual ancient dates and writings. This is done as an attempt to make Egyptian history appear older than Babylonian history.

It is actually Manetho's prejudice that causes the confusion—carnal-minded men wishing to make Egypt's culture appear as the oldest civilization! During these specific years there are two Pharaohs listed in the Turin Cannon and in Manetho's list that are named Suphis and Souphis. One of the ruler's names is Suphis (or Souphis or Saophis).

These different Greek spellings are from Manetho's abstractors. Historians list this Pharaoh as an unknown ruler. Why? Because of what I said about the Modern Historic Method: they do not recognize the bible as a legitimate historical document.

Therefore, I think it is a great injustice to historic information to reject the writings of the bible as beneficial explanation for a lot of academic history. The bible stories of various people God worked with down through history can give us a better understanding of academic history. It also fills in the places historians simply write down people of history as unknown.

Suphis is the Greek name for Joseph! The name Suphis is in the Pharaoh list of all three Dynasties! This discovery of ignored biblical history intrigued me, so I began comparing ancient academic history with biblical history. This comparison study of academic history with biblical history is no more outrageous than some of the myths and legends that have been fabricated about real people. When both sources of history are compared and then fit into the proper timeline, history makes better sense.

The bible gives academic history motive. Moving on with the story, we see Joseph coming into a position of power and recognition because of the interpretation of the vision. This was the first step in the fulfillment of the promise God made to Abraham, Isaac, and Jacob. Remember, God told Abraham that his generations would populate and cover the world in huge numbers!

The dream he told his brothers about became a reality when Joseph was made a Pharaoh under Amenemhet III. Twenty years had passed since Joseph's brothers sold him into slavery. Now Joseph's brothers bowed to Pharaoh/Joseph not knowing he was their blood brother. Joseph forgave his brothers and explained that it was God's providence that caused him to end up in Egypt for a greater purpose than herding cattle.

Joseph soon moves his father Jacob to Egypt during the great famine. Amenemhet III is the Pharaoh who dominates all Egypt in Joseph's day. He is a Pharaoh of positive vision. Under him, Lake Moeris and the large Faiyum for the storage of water were created.

He handles the construction of a canal or secondary river along the Nile to the lake Moeris. It is called to this day the Bahr Yusuf or the River of Joseph.

It is interesting to note that Amenemhet III is associated with 12 rulers under him, called Dodecarchy. One could guess the 12 brothers of Joseph were these rulers.

Joseph was very admired by the Egyptians during his time for he saved Egypt from the worst famine of their history. Joseph was 30 years of age when he became ruler in Egypt under Amenemhet III. He served Egypt for 96 years as a Pharaoh!

Genesis 41:43-47 And he made him to ride in the second chariot which he had; and they cried before him, Bow the knee: and he made him ruler over all the land of Egypt. (44) And Pharaoh said unto Joseph, I am Pharaoh, and without you shall no man lift up his hand or foot in all the land of Egypt. (45) And Pharaoh called Joseph's name Zaphnathpaaneah; and he gave him to wife Asenath the daughter of Potipherah priest of On. And Joseph went out over all the land of Egypt. (46) And Joseph was thirty years old when he stood before Pharaoh King of Egypt. And Joseph went out from the presence of Pharaoh and went throughout all the land of Egypt. (47) And in the seven plenteous years the earth brought forth by handfuls…

JOB

$\mathcal{A}$n interesting story reveals itself when Dynasty IV is compared with Dynasty III. These are parallel reigns of Egyptian pharaohs. The Pharaohs of Memphis belong to a different line than those of Thebes.

Among the Memphis Pharaohs is one named Khufu or Cheops. In the Turin Canon, Cheops is said to have suffered the death of all his family at the same time. This coincides with the story of Job in the bible!

Job 1:18-22 While he was yet speaking, there also came another, and said, thy sons and thy daughters were eating and drinking wine in their eldest brother's house: (19) And behold, there came a great wind from the wilderness, and smote the four corners of the house, and it fell upon the young men, and they are dead; and I only am escaped alone to tell thee. (20) Then Job arose, and rent his mantle, and shaved his head, and fell down upon the ground, and worshipped, (21) And said, Naked came I out of my mother's womb, and naked shall I return thither: the LORD gave, and the LORD hath taken away; blessed be the name of the LORD. (22) In all this Job sinned not, nor charged God foolishly.

Remember me saying the books of the bible are not in chronological order? <u>This is why the Book of Job is not obvious to historians that it is written during the time of Joseph</u>! The story of Joseph was written by Moses in the first five books of the bible, but modern historians refuse to recognize the bible as a legitimate source of information. These two Pharaohs, Joseph, and Job are contemporaries. They are relatives! Cheops 1726–1663 B.C.—this is Khufu or Job! Suphis 1734-1668 B.C.— this is Joseph. Job is Jacob's grandson and Joseph's nephew. Job's father is Issachar, one of Joseph's 12 brothers.

The story gets better when we look at what academic history says about Joseph and his admiration by the Egyptians he saves during the seven years of famine. Josephus, Jewish historian, says when the Egyptians ran out of money to buy the stored grain from Joseph, they began to sign over title of their land to Joseph for grain.

Later, when the famine ended, Joseph returned their land to them. He commanded them to pay a fifth of their income to the pharaoh's treasury. The people were so overjoyed to have their land returned to them, they built a monument to Joseph because of his great kindness. By the end of the Great Famine, Joseph and his family were rulers of the land of Egypt, from the mid part of Egypt to the southern part of Egypt.

Egyptians are known to not be shepherds or keepers of cattle, so when Jacob and his family come to Egypt they are welcomed as shepherds to take charge of the Egyptians' cattle. In the writings of the historian Herodotus, he talks about the closing of pagan temples of the Egyptians. Cheops or Job is a worshipper of the One God. The God whom Job serves is called the Amen.

The Egyptian rulers know of the Invisible God in the days of Joseph; it is not until the days of Moses that gross idolatry spreads throughout all of Egypt. Cheops was a contemporary of King Zoser of Egypt. Ancient Egypt was a confederation of small city states. Amenemhet III 1741-1692 B.C. was king of upper Egypt and Pharaoh over all of Egypt. Under him were lesser kings, among who were Zoser, Cheops, and Suphis.

Historians note that a man named Souf, another spelling of Souphis, helps Khufu or Cheops, Job, build the Labyrinth for Amenemhet III. This man is none other than Joseph, Job's uncle. Manetho the Egyptian historian, wrote of Cheops:

"He was arrogant toward the gods, but repented and authored the sacred book… A work of great importance."

This is the book of Job, preserved from the days of Egypt. Herodotus obviously writes from his pagan prospective, characterizing Job as arrogant and opposed to the many gods of the Egyptians.

Remember Cush and Nimrod were the first Babylonian influence on the people who migrated with them after the confounding of languages at the Tower of Babble or Babel. Think about it. The book of Job in the Bible is the oldest book of the bible. Job lives and writes of his encounter with the Invisible God. Job authored his book long before Moses was even born.

Moses wrote the first five books of the bible years after Joseph and Job died. All bibles say the Book of Job's author is unknown. This is a good example of how comparing academic history with the timeline of the bible can enhance our understanding of both worlds of history. If the translators knew Job's Egyptian name, Khufu or Cheops, or Suphis in the Greek, they would know Job authored this book about himself. Job's story fits right in between Genesis 48 th and 50 th Chapters, time-wise. Job wrote his autobiography.

It is not a sacred book for the Egyptians because Cheops or Job closed their pagan temples and forbade pagan worship of idols. In the conclusion of his writing, Job acknowledged the awesome power and omnipotence of the Invisible God. I will paraphrase Job's conclusion: *"Then Job answered the Lord, and said, I know that thou can do everything. I know and acknowledge your omnipotence, which you have set forth so magnificently before me. It is brought home to me by the grand review of your works which you have made, and the details into which you have condescended to enter. I know also and acknowledge that no thought can be with-held from you. I also confess your omniscience—that you know even the thoughts of all created beings. I have heard of you by the hearing of the ear. Hitherto, I have had nothing but hearsay knowledge of you; I have not known you in any true sense; but now—now that you have revealed yourself—my eye sees you; my spiritual eye is open, and I begin to see you in your true might, your true greatness, your true inscrutableness. Now I recognize the distance which separates us and feel how unreasonable it is that I should contend with you, argue with you, I assumed myself to be competent to pass judgment on your work."*

Job is a book that is often overlooked even by theologians because of its information about life and death. It has always been a curious thing to me how people fear death and as such tend to ignore the subject. Job was most certainly ahead of his time with his understanding of death. He recognizes the difference between the <u>biological soul</u> and the <u>spirit in man</u>.

One stays and decays and the other goes back to God. These very passages of scripture are used in funerals by ministers.

Job 7:9 As the cloud is consumed and vanishes away: so, he that goes down to the grave shall come up no more. Job 14:10-14 But man dies, and wastes away: yea, man giveth up the ghost, (spirit in man) and where is he? (11) As the waters fail from the sea, and the flood decays and dries up: (12) So man lies down and rises not: till the heavens be no more, they shall not awake, nor be raised out of their sleep. (he is emphasizing the permanent end of the physical body, the mortal man) (13) O that thou would hide me in the grave, that thou would keep me secret, until thy wrath be past, that thou would appoint me a set time, and remember me! (14) If a man die, shall he live again? (Job asks the question and then answers it) all the days of my appointed time will I wait, till my change come. (changed into a spirit being in the kingdom of heaven)

Job 30:22-23 Thou lift me up to the wind; (I'll fly away) thou cause me to ride upon it and dissolve my substance. (the mortal body) (23) For I know that thou wilt bring me to death, and to the house appointed for all living. (the mansion in the kingdom of God)

The Pioneer of Salvation, Jesus Christ, is at this point in the story, centuries away. Yet Job's writings and his understanding of the salvation process are dead on (no pun intended).

Job full well understands there is an appointed time for the resurrection of the dead to be started. More on this subject later in my book.

Even as far back as Adam and Eve, God addresses the subject of death at once with His new humans.

Genesis 2:16-17 And the LORD God commanded the man, saying, of every tree of the garden thou may freely eat: (17) But of the tree of the knowledge of good and evil, thou shalt not eat of it: for in the day that thou eat thereof thou shalt surely die. Satan put a spin on what God said by saying:

Genesis 3:1-5 Now the serpent was subtle than any beast of the field which the LORD God had made. And he said unto the woman, Yea, hath God said, Ye shall not eat of every tree of the garden? (2) And the woman said unto the serpent, we may eat of the fruit of the trees of the garden: (3) But of the fruit of the tree, which is in the midst of the garden, God hath said, Ye shall not eat of it, neither shall ye touch it, lest ye die. (4) And the serpent said unto the woman, you shall not surely die: (5) For God doth know that in the day ye eat thereof, then your eyes shall be opened, and ye shall be as gods, knowing good and evil.

Satan uses the oldest come on in the book. God isn't telling you everything. He is keeping you in the dark. He is holding back something you don't have yet. Satan cons Eve into disobeying the only voice she has ever heard before that day. He tells the biggest lie of all time: Humans can't die. Oh yes, they can and do. More about this later. Back to Job.

We know Job built the Great Pyramid, but do we know why he built it? Job was a very devout man toward the Invisible God. When you read the book of Job in the bible, you see that Job was a proud and arrogant man who engineered and built great things—things such as the great Pyramid.

The monument was a tomb and a marker of the Southern border of the territory ruled by Joseph. It was a monument to Joseph. The monument is the Great Pyramid designed by Khufu also known as Cheops. Per the historian, Herodotus, the Great Pyramid took 20 years to build.

No doubt Job was a great man and engineer designer of the Great Pyramid which still stands today as a testament to the greatness and goodness of Joseph, and a wonder to the world. The name inscribed over the original passageway is Khufu. It is Joseph's tomb until his bones were carried out of Egypt at the Exodus.

When Caliph Mamoon in the 9 th century A.D. searched for the entrance of the Great Pyramid, he accidently cut into a passage leading to the tomb chamber. He found no treasures or mummy. Why? Probably because, as the bible says, the Israelites took Joseph's bones with them when they left Egypt during the Exodus.

Exodus 13:19 And Moses took the bones of Joseph with him: for he had straightly sworn the children of Israel, saying, God will surely visit you; and ye shall carry up my bones away hence with you.

I wish to spend a few paragraphs about this man Job because he is a good example of how the Israelites were such a profound influence on the Egyptians.

The Egyptian records of the kings of the many provinces in Egypt show that the children of Israel, specifically the brothers of Joseph, taught the Egyptians many important things, especially things like mathematics, astronomy, and agriculture. Though they learned a lot from the sons of Israel, they also forgot a lot after the 110 years of Suphis and Cheops or Joseph and Job.

The Father of History, Herodotus, says the Egyptian priests make the following statements about Job: When Cheops succeeds the throne He plunges into wickedness and closes all the temples. He then forbids sacrificing to the gods. The priests say the affliction of Job's rule in Egypt lasts 106 years, the whole of which the pagan temples are shut up, not to be opened. They so detest the memory of these two kings (Joseph and Job), they refuse to mention their names.

They, like Manetho, are prejudiced pagans who dislike the men who worship the Invisible God. When I add up the contemporary reigns of Joseph and Job, I produce approximately 106 years. To me there is no doubt that these kings are Joseph and Job. Their actions reflect an allegiance to the One Invisible God. Years later the rebellious son of Job restores pagan temple worship and is warned by an Egyptian oracle his life will end in 7 years. He ignores the oracle's insight. The oracle replies, *"The two kings on the throne before you understand this… You do not understand."* These Egyptian Oracles serving God are ignored and eventually Egypt falls back into Pagan Idolatry as before.

Cheops is known by another name from Egyptian history. He is called Saaru of Shaaru. Saaru is another name for the inhabitants of Mt. Seir. These are Mountains of Seir. Biblical Mount Sinai portrays God as having dwelt at Mount Seir and seems to suggest that this equates with Mount Sinai; Mount Seir names the mountain range separating the Land of Canaan from the Arabian Desert. Cheops is an Asiatic Pharaoh whose domain extends from Mt. Seir to Lower Egypt. This is during the time of Joseph or Souphis, Pharaoh under Pharaoh Amenemhet III, who is ruler over all of Egypt.

Job 3:11-15 Why died I not from the womb? why did I not give up the ghost when I came out of the belly? (12) Why did the knees prevent me? or why the breasts that I should suck? (13) For now, should I have lain still and been quiet, I should have slept then had I been at rest, (14) With kings and counsellors of the earth, which built desolate places for themselves; (15) Or with princes that had gold, who filled their houses with silver: While Job is being tested, he cries out that he wishes he had died. It is a historical fact that Job is buried with the other Pharaohs of Egypt. Proof, Job is Pharaoh of Egypt.

Job 29:21-25 Unto me men gave ear, and waited, and kept silence at my counsel. (22) After my words they spoke not again; and my speech dropped upon them. (23) And they waited for me as for the rain; and they opened their mouth wide as for the latter rain. (24) If I laughed on them, they believed it not; and the light of my countenance they cast not down. (25) I chose out their way, and sat chief, and dwelt as a king in the army, as one that comforted the mourners.

Job 18:4 He tears himself in his anger: shall the earth be forsaken for thee? and shall the rock be removed out of his place?

This scripture is an obvious reference the Great Pyramid. Job is the engineer of the great Pyramid. It is a monument to behold. A rock structure that stays to this day. One of the Wonders of the world.

Job 38:1-6 Then the LORD answered Job out of the whirlwind, and said, (2) Who is this that darkens counsel by words without knowledge? (3) Gird up now thy loins like a man; for I will demand of thee and answer thou me. (4) Where was thou when I laid the foundations of the earth? Declare, if thou hast understanding. (5) Who hath laid the measures thereof, if thou know? or who hath stretched the line upon it? (6) Whereupon are the foundations thereof fastened? or who laid the corner stone thereof; God in this passage of scripture dresses Job down to size, causing Job to repent of his arrogance and vanity expressed because of knowledge.

Job 22:15-17 Hast thou marked the old way which wicked men have trodden? (16) Which were cut down out of time, whose foundation was overflown with a flood (17) Which said unto God, Leave from us: and what can the Almighty do for them?

The flood was still on people's mind in Job's time.

Job 1:5 And it was so, when the days of their feasting were gone about, that Job sent and sanctified them, and rose up early in the morning, and offered burnt offerings according to the number of them all: for Job said, It may be that my sons have sinned, and cursed God in their hearts. Thus did Job continually.

Job worshipped and sacrificed in the same manner as all the patriarchs did before the disposition of the law to Moses and the nation of Israel. Notice that none of the conversations in the book of Job refer to the exodus or Moses; Job lived before the law was given to Moses and the Israelites.

Job rose to the throne in 1726 B.C. This was the same year Jacob came to Egypt by Joseph's invitation. Israel did not come to Egypt as slaves. The sons of Jacob or Israel was influential and respected by the Egyptians because of Joseph's leadership and favor of the Pharaoh. Job was Jacob's grandson, and the son of a very smart man named Issachar. He was a mathematician.

Genesis 46:13 And the sons of Issachar; Tola, and Phuvah, and Job, and Shimron.

The things Joseph and Job did for Egypt and the intelligence with knowledge shared by his brothers, the Israelites, are the reason for such a huge monument. It is the boundary marker signifying the Egypt of Joseph. It is a great story about the families of men and their contributions to the other peoples of the world. The righteousness of Job is remarkable and well known. No wonder in the writings of the prophet Ezekiel he mentions the goodness of three main characters of righteousness in these men.

Ezekiel 14:14-16 Though these three men, Noah, Daniel, and Job, were in it, they should deliver but their own souls by their righteousness, says the Lord GOD. (15) If I cause noisome beasts to pass through the land, and they spoil it, so that it be desolate, that no man may pass through because of the beasts: (16) Though these three men were in it, as I live, says the Lord GOD, they shall deliver neither sons nor daughters; they only shall be delivered.

This speaks volumes about the Godly character of these men. Before I introduce Moses, I would like to explain how certain people of the bible are often not named within the period of academic history:

They appear in Egyptian and other nations of history, but they are not found by their Hebrew names. Likewise, Joseph and Job are not shown by their Hebrew names. They are listed in Egyptian history under their Egyptian names Khufu or Cheops. Their Greek names are Suphis or Souf. This is not any great revelation of intellect on my part. It is found to be the case in the Bible in the book of Daniel. Nebuchadnezzar, King of Babylon, gives the four Hebrew children with Babylonian names to replace their Hebrew names:

Daniel 1:3-7 And the king spoke unto Ashpenaz the master of his eunuchs, that he should bring certain of the children of Israel, and of the king's seed, and of the princes; (4) Children in whom was no blemish, but well favored, and skillful in all wisdom, and cunning in knowledge, and understanding science, and such as had ability in them to stand in the king's palace, and whom they might teach the learning and the tongue of the Chaldeans. (5) And the king appointed them a daily provision of the king's meat, and of the wine which he drank: so, nourishing them three years, that at the end thereof they might stand before the king. (6) Now among these were of the children of Judah, Daniel, Hananiah, Mishael, and Azariah: (7) Unto whom the prince of the eunuchs gave names: for he gave unto Daniel the name of Belteshazzar; and to Hananiah, of Shadrach; and to Mishael, of Meshach; and to Azariah, of Abednego.

This is a clue to how these bible characters are overlooked in Academic Secular History, along with the fact that historians ignore the Bible. The same is true of the great kings from Noah, Shem, Ham, and their children. Cush and Nimrod, Babylonian names, or their Egyptian names, Menes and Athothis who came and united Upper and Lower Egypt into one kingdom under their authority for over 30 years. The seventh king in Dynasty I is named Semempses or Semsem. Semsem in Egyptian means the Great Sem or Shem. The hieroglyphics depict Shem as an Asiatic, not Egyptian. He appears as a white-bearded old man in priestly garb. Shem is about 430 years old.

The truth of the matter is Shem came to Egypt to divide up the country into various provinces in order to prevent the rise to power of one kingdom over the entire world. Shem sets up a confederation of territories, with headquarters at Thebes in Northern Egypt and Memphis in Southern Egypt. Several civil wars ensue as struggles for power in Thinis, and later Elaphantine.

Remember, Cush and Nimrod tried this one kingdom in Mesopotamia at the tower of Babel. It is during this time that eventually Egypt is under one overall Pharaoh named Amenemhet III. He was the one in charge during the time of Joseph. He had several lesser Pharaohs, like Joseph and Job, under him who were Pharaohs over many confederate territories.

MOSES

Moses is one of the most dynamic individuals of the Old Testament writings and Egyptian history. Most of our impressions of this man have been influenced by the movie, THE TEN COMMANDMENTS. There is a lot more to this man Moses than Cecile B. De Mille could ever portray in the three hours' epic film.

However, his choice of Charlton Heston to play the part of Moses is excellent. This was the time in the progression of God's varied encounters with mankind that He was moving from a one-on-one relationship to a national encounter. Moses was the person God used to lead the people of Israel through a process of national reform, moving them to Canaan Land. After the Exodus from Egypt, God made a covenant with the chosen people. He promised to bless them for obedience and punish them for disobedience to His standard as an educational process for the other nations of the world.

In our world of political correctness, people look at this as unfair and prejudiced. Who do we think we are to tell the creator of all we can experience who He can choose for His purposes? Starting with Israel, God is teaching a government of oversight coupled with moral laws to sustain a nation for generations to come.

It is a democracy based on choosing obedience or disobedience to the covenanted moral standard. Like God allowed the nation of America to be created by overpowering the native inhabitants to create a freedom for all peoples, Israel is backed by the power of God to drive out the Gentiles to set up a nation of example for a better way of life.

Ancient history speaks of Moses as a decisive man with a striking stature and handsome, chiseled features. The bible doesn't give us as much detail as Egyptian history does. Moses was charismatic and brilliant.

Putting both together makes quite an interesting story about this man God chose to lead the children of Israel out of Egypt.

As we study Moses, we will see why God used him to deliver the offspring of Jacob as a nation of people to spread God's way throughout the earth. As Israel's current Prime Minister said recently, Israel has been a nation of scattered people for centuries, but never again. I believe God purposefully used Israel's dispersions and captivities to promote information to other nations during the ancient times.

Moses was born after the Egyptians persecuted the Israelites through slavery for many years. The Egyptians began to fear the Israelites because of their success and diligence in labor and wealth. History tells us that the Egyptians forgot what Joseph did: prepared them for the coming famine. They became lazy and jealous of the prosperity and wealth of the Israelites. Much like the prophecy of the coming Messiah to deliver the Jews, the Egyptian soothsayers predicted a deliverer who would arise from among the Israelites. They foretold how this deliverer would bring the Egyptians low and raise the Israelites to great power. They said this man would be of great stature and be long remembered for his leadership and power over the Israelites.

When the ruling Pharaoh heard this news, he at once ordered the murder of all Israelite male babies in an effort to diminish the hope of the Israelites and squelch any chance of a deliverer being born among them.

Moses's father, Amram, prayed for his son's life to be spared. God heard Amram's prayer and visited him in his sleep. God told him his child would be concealed from those who wished to destroy him. He would be brought up in a surprising way and would eventually deliver the nation of Israel from bondage, and he would be remembered for as long as the earth shall live.

Amazingly when Amram's wife gave birth to the child, her pains of labor were so mild that no one was aware of the birth. Trusting that God would make good on His promise to keep the child safe; they fashioned a basket like a cradle and set it adrift in the Nile. The child's sister followed along the bank to see where the basket's journey would end.

The bible narrative tells us Moses was about 3 months old when he was discovered by Pharaoh's daughter.

Exodus 2:2-10 And the woman conceived and bare a son: and when she saw him that he was a goodly child, she hid him three months. (3) And when she could no longer hide him, she took for him an arc of bulrushes, and daubed it with slime and with pitch, and put the child there; and she laid it in the flags by the river's brink. (4) And his sister stood afar off, to wit what would be done to him. (5) And the daughter of Pharaoh came down to wash herself at the river; and her maidens walked along by the river's side; and when she saw the ark among the flags, she sent her maid to fetch it. (6) And when she had opened it, she saw the child: and behold, the babe wept. And she had compassion on him, and said, this is one of the Hebrews' children.

As my timeline progresses, you will see that Israelites were just as human as the other peoples of the world. They eventually disappointed God with their behavior of disobedience towards the covenant they agreed to honor. God used their apostasy as an example and to educate the other nations about His intentions for mankind's behavior toward each other. During the process, God allowed Israel to eventually move the authority from the Priesthood to the civil aspects of authority in the spirit of His moral laws.

(7) Then said his sister to Pharaoh's daughter, Shall I go and call to thee a nurse of the Hebrew women, that she may nurse the child for thee? (8) And Pharaoh's daughter said to her, Go. And the maid went and called the child's mother. (9) And Pharaoh's daughter said unto her, take this child away, and nurse it for me, and I will give thee thy wages. And the woman took the child and nursed it. (10) And the child grew, and she brought him unto Pharaoh's daughter, and he became her son. And she called his name Moses: and she said, Because I drew him out of the water.

The basket found its way into the hands of one of the Pharaoh's daughter, Thermuthis. She noticed the basket being carried along in the current and sent her handmaid to grab for it. She opened the basket, and it was love at first sight, for God fashioned the child with astonishing stature and beauty. Then, as only God can arrange things, Thermuthis requested a Hebrew woman be brought to the palace to nurse the child. Moses's sister Miriam was there to tell them she would bring a Hebrew woman to nurse the child.

It was an opportunity for Moses's mother to take care of her own child! The Egyptians did not know Jochebed was the child's mother. Egyptians call water Mo, so Thermuthis named the child Moses, meaning *"one drawn from the water."* Having no child of her own, Thermuthis adopted the child. She perceived the child was remarkable. It is recorded she felt the child was sent to her by the gods of the Nile river. She saw him as divine in form and of a generous mind. She told her father that her son was a suitable heir to the throne of Egypt. Moses was brought up and educated in the king's palace and was taught the attributes for Kings of Egypt.

He was a natural, being a descendant from the tribe of Levi. This was the tribe God eventually selected to perform the priestly duties for Israel's national religion. By the time Moses reached maturity, the Ethiopians were warring with Egypt on a regular basis and carrying away many of their treasures. They killed many of Egypt's soldiers and people. They did not leave off persecuting the Egyptians and eventually come as far as Memphis with their destructive wars.

The Egyptians consulted their Oracles and prophecies about this sad oppression from the Ethiopians, and they concluded that the gods wanted them to make use of Moses as a general to lead their army against the Ethiopians.

Remember: actual history is different from the movie 10 Commandments. The Egyptians were well aware Moses was not an Egyptian. It was no problem for them because of Joseph and his family successes in Egypt. This pleased the king, and he made Moses a general of the Egyptian army to lead the Egyptians to war.

It surprised me to learn that the Egyptian Pharaoh would even know about Moses. This is where the influence of the epic film, The Ten Commandments has left such an impression on me. Drama is often created by directors. They call this artistic liberty. Truth is, the Egyptians were not prejudiced toward the Asiatic. Joseph was the first to be adopted into the realm of Pharaohs. Moses was no exception.

Thermuthis was the daughter of a Pharaoh and an only child. Moses became an adopted heir to her father's throne if her father should die. Furthermore, only kings could command an Egyptian army. Moses was made a king when the decision was made to use him to fight the Ethiopians.

His Egyptian name was Mermeshoi Semenkhkare. He was the 17 th king listed in the Turin Cannon catalog of Egyptian kings, of the 13th Dynasty. Mermeshoi is Egyptian name for English words the general.

This name appears on two large statues found in the Delta at Tanis. Mermeshoi is the first non-Semite to appear on the list of the 13 th Dynasty. Logic dictates to me this must be the man Moses, a descendent of Levi, because the king or Pharaoh listed before Mermeshoi was named Userkare Khendjr. He was the Egyptian Pharaoh over the eastern lower Delta (Joseph's territory years before).

A pyramid was discovered at South Saqqara with Userkare Khendjr's inscription upon it. No descendant of this Pharaoh is known to have succeeded his particular throne. He had no male child. This points to him as probably the Pharaoh whose daughter is Thermuthis. She is mentioned in the Bible finding Moses in the basket on the Nile. She is not named in the bible narrative, but academic history enables us to find out her name.

Again, cooperation between the bible and academic history! As I said earlier, historians aid the secular unbelievers in trying to discredit the bible as a true source of history and information.

Exodus 2:5 And the daughter of Pharaoh (Thermuthis) came down to wash herself at the river; and her maidens walked along by the river's side; and when she saw the ark among the flags, she sent her maid to fetch it.

MOSES THE GENERAL

Moses proved his military strategy by leading a surprise attack upon the Ethiopians. The Ethiopians used the river as the means of entering the land of Egypt because of their fear of vipers in the swamps. Moses developed a strategy that allowed the Egyptians to cross the serpent-filled lands unharmed and surprise the enemy. He had baskets fashioned to hold Ibes. Ibes are tame birds and enemy only to serpents, chasing them relentlessly until they attack and devour them.

Moses turns the birds loose on the land ahead of the army to clear away the serpents. This allows the army to surprise the Ethiopians and conquer them. The Ethiopians never thought an army would attack from the swamp land. They counted on the swamp as protection from their enemies. Egypt's successful attack against the Ethiopians caused them to fear being overpowered and indentured into slavery like the Israelites (Israel had been in slavery over 300 years at this point).

Most of the Ethiopians retreated to Saba, the capital city of Ethiopia. Then a strange thing happened. The daughter of the king of Ethiopia saw Moses near the city walls as he led the Egyptians to them with great valor and courage.

The Ethiopian king's daughter was so struck by his beauty and stature she fell in love with him and sent her most trusted servant to negotiate for mercy upon the impending conquering of her people. Her father, the king, offers a peaceful surrender and no further tries to wage war upon Egypt. The conditions of surrender were incredibly unique. Surrender only if Moses would marry his daughter, Tharbis, and make her happy as his wife.

Ethiopians are Black people, the descendants of Cush. There are actually two branches from Cush; modern India is one of those branches.

Years later in the wilderness, after the exodus, Moses's brother, and sister ridiculed Moses because he married a Black woman.

Prejudice is an old behavior that still gets in the way of things. The bible account shows how harshly God deals with racial prejudice and disrespect for His chosen servants.

Numbers 12:1-2 And Miriam and Aaron spoke against Moses because of the Ethiopian woman whom he had married: for he had married an Ethiopian woman. (2) And they said, Hath the LORD indeed spoken only by Moses? has he not spoken also by us? And the LORD heard it.

Numbers 12:3-10 (Now the man Moses was very meek, above all the men which were upon the face of the earth.) (4) And the LORD spoke suddenly unto Moses, and unto Aaron, and unto Miriam, Come out ye three unto the tabernacle of the congregation. And they three came out. (5) And the LORD came down in the pillar of the cloud, and stood in the door of the tabernacle, and called Aaron and Miriam: and they both came forth. (6) And he said, hear now my words: If there be a prophet among you, I the LORD will make myself known unto him in a vision, and will speak unto him in a dream. (7) My servant Moses is not so, who is faithful in all mine house. (8) With him will I speak mouth to mouth and not in dark speeches; and the similitude of the LORD shall he behold: wherefore then were ye not afraid to speak against my servant Moses? (9) And the anger of the LORD was kindled against them; and he left. (10) And the cloud left from off the tabernacle; and behold, Miriam became leprous, white as snow: and Aaron looked upon Miriam, and behold, she was leprous.

The Bible doesn't tell us why Moses married a Black woman, but academic history does. <u>Another example of enhanced information when both sources are consulted</u>. The Bible says Moses was against the Egyptians' cruel treatment of the Israelites. He saw an Egyptian overseer beating an Israelite slave mercilessly, and Moses killed the overseer. He then hid the body. Pharaoh found out about the murder and was set on killing Moses.

The Pharaoh who wanted to kill him was not Moses's stepfather. It was the Pharaoh over all of Egypt who wanted to kill Moses, Pepi II also known as Unis and Onnos. He was a contemporary Pharaoh of the Pharaoh Merenre II who perished in the red sea. Pepi II or Unis was cannibal.

After Moses fled Egypt, Pepi II began the practice of eating the firstborn of his enemies. A possible reason God chose the slaying of the firstborn as the final plague against Egypt.

Because the movie The Ten Commandments was such an influence on me, I wondered why the name of the Pharaoh I found in history was not called Rameses, like in the movie. The answer comes back to what I discover about the method of modern history and how it is taught. It is taught without the Bible considered as a source of history.

The bible is a guide to history. It is not a textbook of history. Moses wrote the history from Adam to Joshua's succession as leader of Israel. It does not have as much detail as can be found in the Babylonian and Egyptian academic history.

The academic history of civilizations is obviously more detailed than the combined writings of one man. It was compiled by many people as a specific job in an established nation. Israel was not yet a nation.

Another epic event since the Tower of Babel was the Exodus. Israel was about to become a chosen nation to promote the Invisible God of Creation to the rest of the world in a national sense.

Before the event at Mt. Sinai, God worked through individuals, not a specific nation of people. Bible history is the story of people who met the invisible Creator known as Elohiym, pronounced El – o – heem. This is the Hebrew word for the English word, God.

Moses wrote of these specific Pharaohs using their official title, not their given names. There are Pharaohs with variations of the name Rameses living during the time of Ham. Ham's son, Cush, is the father of Mizraim. Remember, Cush was a Black man.

Genesis 10:6 And the sons of Ham; Cush, and Mizraim, and Phut, and Canaan.

The line of kings from Mizraim were the first Pharaohs in the land of Egypt after Cush and Nimrod fled the confusion at the tower of Babel. This part of Noah's family settled in Egypt after the language differences at Babel caused the population to disperse into the other parts of the world.

These were the first black Pharaohs. Moses used the name Rameses to describe the Delta of Egypt as a province or territory, not a specific Pharaoh. The line of kings in Egypt listed in academic history begins at 2254 B.C. and ends at 525 B.C. with the coming of the Persians to Egypt.

Mizraim separated from Cush and Nimrod and formed his own dynasty near the provinces of his father and his nephew. In 1744 B.C. the eighteenth Pharaoh listed in this line of kings is Rameses. Remember, the Egyptian dynasties are sequential in numbers and contemporary in timeline.

When Dynasty IV is compared with the time Joseph is a Pharaoh in Egypt, there is a Pharaoh named Rameses of the Mizraim or Menes dynasty. When Moses was born in Egypt about 1528 B.C., the Pharaoh of the Rameses territory, named Rameses Uaphru (1588-1559 B.C.), died about 60 years before Moses.

This could be why the writings of Moses refer to the land of Rameses, not a specific Pharaoh of the land. Genesis 47:11 And Joseph placed his father and his brethren and gave them a possession in the land of Egypt, in the best of the land, in the land of Rameses, as Pharaoh had commanded.

Exodus 12:37 And the children of Israel journeyed from Rameses to Succoth, about six hundred thousand on foot that were men, beside children.

Numbers 33:3 And they left from Rameses in the first month, on the fifteenth day of the first month; on the morrow after the Passover the children of Israel went out with a high hand in the sight of all the Egyptians.

Numbers 33:5 And the children of Israel removed from Rameses and pitched in Succoth.

The movie, The Ten Commandments, calls the Pharaoh in the time of Moses Rameses. No big deal, but history does tell us who this Pharaoh is. Dynasties V and VI reveal the Pharaohs that Moses dealt with in the Land of Rameses. Pharaoh Pepi II is listed in Dynasties V and VI.

Remember, these Dynasties overlap each other because Egypt was a confederation of provinces ruled by many Pharaohs under Pharaohs.

Picture these many Pharaohs as presidents over several provinces and the governors, lieutenant governors, over their own specific province. These dynasties would be records of who was President of the USA and who are the governors and the lieutenant governors in specific states during that specific time of history.

Pepi II or Neferkare was the longest ruling Pharaoh in Egyptian history. This Pharaoh was a greater king who ruled over all the Deltas in Egypt. He is also listed in Dynasty V as Unis.

This is Pepi II, or Neferkare, the Pharaoh who turned to cannibalism not too long after Moses fled to Midian. This Pharaoh was known as the Magician King and is mentioned with his son, Menthesuphis or Merenre Antyemzaef. They are mentioned in the writings of the Apostle Paul. We can know this because their names in the Greek language are Jannes and Jambres and are mentioned with Moses.

II Timothy 3:8 Now as Jannes and Jambres withstood Moses, so do these also resist the truth: men of corrupt minds, reprobate concerning the faith.

Pepi II was out to kill Moses for the murder of the overseer, and Merenre Antyemzaef would not let the Israelites leave Egypt.

The Apostle Paul simply made a comparison with the evil behavior of these men because he remembered the Old Testament scripture from his education. Remember, Paul studied under Gamaliel the Jewish Pharisee. Being a Jewish scholar, he knows this story from the Pentateuch. It was the Jewish textbook of those days. This can also be a confirmation that the older copies of the Pentateuch were a little more detailed than what came down to the King James translators in 1611 A. D. How else would Paul have known the names of these two Pharaohs?

(Speculation on my part.) Moses fled through the desert to the land of Midian. There he met a man named Jethro and married his daughter Zipporah. Moses was content to shepherd sheep and work in the land of Midian while raising his flocks and family.

One day while moving the herd, he came across a burning bush. The odd thing was that the bush was not being consumed by the flame. As he moved closer, a voice came from the bush! Moses, remove your shoes, you are standing on Holy ground. Now what I am relating to you sounds like something out of science fiction. The bible says the flame was an angel and the voice was God. Moses was fascinated and listened to the voice of God from the burning bush.

The bush was not God; the bush was illuminated by the power of an angel to cause Moses to stop and listen. It was a focal point for Moses to experience for the first time with personal awareness the forces in this world he could not see. The same watching and overseeing that guides the basket down the Nile over forty years before, when he was just a baby.

An angel. Everyone has seen the movie, The Ten Commandments. Therefore, I will move on with the academic history. The biblical history of Moses had a huge impression on me as a child and later as I began to feel doubt in the reality of an invisible God. The words coming from the flame in the bush, I AM THAT I AM. seem strange to me. It is because my carnal mind cannot relate the power of those words in print.

Moses heard a voice. All the encounters with God from Adam to Moses have been a voice from an invisible source or an angel. Moses was familiar with the stories about the Invisible God who was with Abraham, Isaac, and Jacob. He was puzzled why God would speak with him.

He became fearful and hid his face from the flames of the bush. God continued to tell Moses that He heard the cries of the Israelites. He chose Moses to deliver a message to the elders of Israel. Moses was reluctant to accept the mission. He felt inadequate and predicted the elders would not believe him. God assured Moses that great signs and wonders would go with Moses to convince the elders God would deliver Israel from Egypt.

The Burning Bush event happens about 1488 B. C. We know this because of what we see in Egyptian's academic history about the Pharaohs. Pepi II dies in 1488 B. C. He is the king of Egypt that died, in the scripture.

Exodus 2:23 It came to pass in process of time, that the king of Egypt died: and the children of Israel sighed by reason of the bondage, and they cried, and their cry came up unto God by reason of the bondage.

Exodus 4:19 And the LORD said unto Moses in Midian, Go, return into Egypt: for all the men are dead which sought thy life.

Exodus 14:4-7 And I will harden Pharaoh's heart, that he shall follow after them; and I will be honored upon Pharaoh, and upon all his host; that the Egyptians may know that I am the LORD. And they did so. (5) And it was told the king of Egypt that the people fled: and the heart of Pharaoh and of his servants was turned against the people, and they said, why have we done this, that we have let Israel go from serving us? (6) And he made ready his chariot and took his people with him: (7) He took six hundred chosen chariots, and all the chariots of Egypt.

Exodus 14:13 And Moses said unto the people, Fear ye not, stand still, and see the salvation of the LORD, which he will show to you today: for the Egyptians whom ye have seen today, ye shall see them again no more forever.

Exodus 14:26-30 And the LORD said unto Moses, stretch out thine hand over the sea, that the waters may come again upon the Egyptians, upon their chariots, and upon their horsemen. (27) And Moses stretched forth his hand over the sea, and the sea returned to his strength when the morning appeared; and the Egyptians fled against it; and the LORD overthrew the Egyptians in the midst of the sea. (28) And the waters returned, and covered the chariots, and the horsemen, and all the host of Pharaoh that came into the sea after them; there remained not so much as one of them. (29) But the children of Israel walked upon dry land in the midst of the sea; and the waters were a wall unto them on their right hand, and on their left. (30) Thus, the LORD saved Israel that day out of the hand of the Egyptians; and Israel saw the Egyptians dead upon the seashore.

Merenre II was next in line in this dynasty of Pharaohs and is recorded as ruling for one year, 1488-1487 B.C., showing he died suddenly. As the scriptures tell us, Merenre II died in the Red Sea! He was succeeded by his wife, Nitocris, 1487 – 1475 B.C. She was then succeeded by their second born son, Neferka the Younger, 1475 – 1454 B.C. This is because their "first born" son died at the hands of the "death angel" during the Passover of 1488 B.C.!

At this juncture in Egyptian history, records show a total collapse of the Egyptian governments and foreign invaders enter the land, Ethiopians, and others.

Moses was at this point in charge of more than 600,000 Israelites. They journeyed to Mount Sinai and camped below the mountain. Moses followed the suggestion of his father-in-law Jethro and formed a captain's system of communication and government for the tribes.

I have personally seen this system in practice as a small boy in the late '50s at a church festival I attended in Big Sandy Texas. There were thousands of people from many different states. We were all camping in a large pine forest on the church grounds. Different men were assigned as captains of 1,000, 100, and 10s in charge of the respective number of people assigned to them. Each captain of a lower number of people was responsible to the captain with the larger number of people in his assigned group. This system is used to relay information and emergency notices to any one family of campers who needs to be found and notified. It works beautifully.

It was about three months after the Israelites arrived at the base of Mount Sinai. Moses was instructed by God about the national relationship between God and the children of Israel. Moses was one of the mightiest agents affecting human affairs the world has ever known. Just as prophesied, Moses and his accomplishments have never been forgotten all down through the history of nations! Moses holds a unique position in all of history.

Moses was directed by God to frame the constitution of a nation that would survive for over 2,500 years; Moses stamped a people with the mark of nationalism which time itself has not obliterated. His writings have imparted the saving knowledge and laws of the Invisible Creator to the saving and preservation of many nations who have adopted their divine principles for moral conduct in their nations. In the first sentence of his writing,

Moses lays the foundation for a religion practiced by millions: In the beginning, God created the heavens and the earth. Think about the impact of this one event at Mount Sinai. Mankind is so prone to worship the things seen rather than the unseen invisible God, who has made everything.

The world is continually sinking into the debasement of Idolatry and bad behavior. The public expression of the Ten Commandments from the invisible God to the nation of Israel was the first depository of true moral law for religious participation, codified and documented on stone with the letters invented by mankind and understood by mankind.

The Ten Commandments are the basic moral code of worship toward God and relationship with mankind. The first four commandments deal totally with how to respect and acknowledge God. The last six commandments are a moral code for the relationships between neighbors of mankind. One of the six holds a promise. The fifth command, to honor father and mother, our creators of physical life, states that a person's days upon this earth enjoy a certain amount of longevity when proper respect and care is acknowledged toward the parents of the individual. God places a high significance on the creation of human life and the preservation of human life.

What a pity in our present time these moral commands are unwelcome in public display in many areas of our nation. With the first public declaration of these 10 commands from God for the code of moral behavior toward Him and our fellow humans, the children of Israel were struck with tremendous fear as the voice of God thundered out the commands.

The bible account says they did not wish to hear directly from God. They insisted that Moses be the "intercessor" between them and God. History attests to how difficult it is to help as "intercessor" between God and mankind without carnal prejudice for centuries. The power of speaking with authority from the Creator God is dangerous territory for any mortal person to partake of. It has long been the reason for many false concepts and mistaken information about the will of God for mankind to understand the truth of God's will for mankind.

The bible itself warns of being a teacher of the invisible God. It is an awesome responsibility to teach and explain the words of God.

James 3:1 Brethren, be few teachers, knowing that we shall receive the greater condemnation.

The Ten Commandments are known by many individuals long before the event at Mount Sinai. This event at Sinai is the first time this code of conduct is publicly assigned and covenanted with an entire nation of people. God engraves on the tablets of stone His testimony against the great and all polluting sin of mankind, the worship of idols. You shall have no other gods before Me. You shall not make any graven image nor any likeness to anything that is in heaven above or on the earth beneath to stand for Me. You shall not bow down to them or serve them. You shall not use My name in vain. This covenant agreement was sealed by the sprinkling of animal blood upon the people.

GOD CHOOSES A NATION

Exodus 24:3-8 And Moses came and told the people all the words of the LORD, and all the judgments: and all the people answered with one voice, and said, All the words which the LORD hath said will we do. (4) And Moses wrote all the words of the LORD, and rose up early in the morning, and built an altar under the hill, and twelve pillars, according to the twelve tribes of Israel. (5) And he sent young men of the children of Israel, which offered burnt offerings, and sacrificed peace offerings of oxen unto the LORD. (6) And Moses took half of the blood and put it in basins; and half of the blood he sprinkled on the altar. (7) And he took the book of the covenant and read in the audience of the people: and they said, all that the LORD hath said will we do, and be obedient. (8) And Moses took the blood, and sprinkled it on the people, and said, Behold the blood of the covenant, which the LORD hath made with you concerning all these words. (This is a physical blood covenant sealing the agreement, later in timeline Jesus lets His blood be poured out for Spiritual salvation for all mankind)

Ironically, in less than 40 days after this monumental agreement, the Israelites made a golden calf to worship while Moses was away on the mount, receiving detailed instructions from God.

Exodus 32:7-8 And the LORD said unto Moses, Go, get thee down; for thy people, which thou brought out of the land of Egypt, have corrupted themselves: (8) They have turned aside quickly out of the way which I commanded them: they have made them a molten calf, and have worshipped it, and have sacrificed thereunto, and said, these be thy gods, O Israel, which have brought thee up out of the land of Egypt.

God was ready to destroy Israel and start over with only Moses.

Exodus 32:9-10 And the LORD said unto Moses, I have seen this people, and behold, it is a stiff-necked people: (10) Now therefore let me alone, that my wrath may wax hot against them, and that I may consume them: and I will make of thee a great nation.

Moses here became a type of intercessor like the future Messiah. Moses reasoned with God and saved the Israelites from total destruction.

Exodus 32:30-35 It came to pass on the morrow, that Moses said unto the people, Ye have sinned a great sin: and now I will go up unto the LORD; peradventure I shall make an atonement for your sin. (31) And Moses returned unto the LORD, and said, this people have sinned a great sin, and have made them gods of gold. (32) Yet now, if thou wilt forgive their sin—; and if not, blot me, I pray thee, out of thy book which thou hast written. (33) And the LORD said unto Moses, whosoever hath sinned against me, him will I blot out of my book. (34) Therefore, now go, lead the people unto the place of which I have spoken unto thee: behold, mine Angel shall go before thee: nevertheless, in the day when I visit I will visit their sin upon them. (35) And the LORD plagued the people because they made the calf, which Aaron made.

Notice the phrase, "My book." This will be addressed later in my story. It is a metaphor for how God keeps records. From this time forward Israel became a national and public lesson for all other nations to see. Soon God added to the agreement with Israel certain rituals needed from the people when they committed sin.

There were rituals requiring the sacrifice of different animals by a priesthood system standing for God's agreement to forgive and allow physical life to continue.

The times before Christ were all about physical salvation from sin to avoid the death penalty for disobedience. As the chosen people of the Invisible God, the Israelites were under a covenant to obey and be prospered or disobey and suffer all types of consequences as a nation among the other nations of the world.

Israel prospered as a nation and became a force to be reckoned with. God intervened on their behalf as they conquered nations. They eventually had their own king and a priestly government based on the institutions Moses set up. They even built a permanent temple to house the relics and sacraments of their power. God fought their battles for them with awesome power!

The original relics from Moses were placed in an Ark housing the items and covenant. For hundreds of years, their temple vessels were housed in the humble trappings of tents and booths. But the establishment of a significant permanent temple to house their vessels for worship and tablets of laws was no match for their insatiable weakness to worship and create physical objects.

God eventually saw fit to allow their temple to be destroyed and sent the people into captivity for seventy years under the domination of the Babylonians. This 70 years of captivity was predicted by Jerimiah over 100 years before the event.

Jeremiah 25:11 This whole land shall be a desolation, and an astonishment; and these nations shall serve the king of Babylon seventy years.

The second prediction from Jeremiah was that the king of Babylon too would also be eventually conquered.

Jeremiah 25:12 And it shall come to pass, when seventy years are carried out, that I will punish the king of Babylon, and that nation, says the LORD, for their iniquity, and the land of the Chaldeans, and will make it perpetual desolations.

The third prediction was that God would restore Israel to its land.

Jeremiah 29:10-14 For thus says the LORD, that after seventy years be carried out at Babylon I will visit you, and perform my good word toward you, in causing you to return to this place. (11) For I know the thoughts that I think toward you, says the LORD, thoughts of peace, and not of evil, to give you an expected end. (12) Then shall ye call upon me, and ye shall go and pray unto me, and I will hearken unto you. (13) And ye shall seek me, and find me, when ye shall search for me with all your heart. (14) And I will be found of you, says the LORD: and I will turn away your captivity, and I will gather you from all the nations, and from all the places whither I have driven you, says the LORD; and I will bring you again into the place whence I caused you to be carried away captive.

How could Jeremiah predict the captivity, its duration, and then Israel's restoration 100 years before? Jeremiah was a Prophet. The answer is obvious to anyone who has the belief that things seen are controlled and directed by the unseen hands of an invisible God.

Amos 3:7 Surely the Lord GOD will do nothing, but he reveals his secret unto his servants the prophets.

There is no question that Moses was a great tool in the hands of God to constitute the righteous way of life into the nation of Israel. From the time of Moses until present day, the concepts of God, law, and morality were taught and preserved through the nation of Israel and all nations who adopted these foundational principles and judgments given through Moses from God.

Our laws in America were founded on the Judgments and Precepts of the writings of Moses in Exodus chapters 20-24. Such laws as parapets or banister rails being a requirement to prevent a person from just walking off a balcony or high platform is just one simple example of these laws to protect individuals as part of our laws today. Compensation laws and civil laws are all variations of the great judgments of God given through Moses to Israel.

As Israel was ruled by various kings good and bad, they eventually were split into two nations. Judah and Benjamin remained in Jerusalem and the other 10 tribes dispersed throughout the other lands of the surrounding areas.

JOSHUA

*J*oshua was commissioned by God to lead the Children of Israel into the Promised Land.

Joshua 1:1-2 Now after the death of Moses the servant of the LORD it came to pass, that the LORD spoke unto Joshua the son of Nun, Moses' minister, saying, (2) Moses my servant is dead; now therefore arise, go over this Jordan, thou, and all this people, unto the land which I do give to them, even to the children of Israel.

The word servant, as applied both to Moses and Joshua, is to be understood in a very peculiar sense. It signifies God's prime minister, the person by whom God Issues His orders, and by whom He carries out all His purposes and designs. No person ever bore this title in the like sense but Jesus Christ, the Redeemer of Mankind, for whom Moses and Joshua were prototypes. Joshua led the Children of Israel in the Laws that God gave Moses, and the conquest of the enemies of Israel became known throughout the lands. Many of the great bible stories come from this book, the saving of the spies by Rahab and other stories of the Sunday School days.

Like Moses, Joshua got old, and the time came for him to leave Israel to themselves in the appointed lands of their inheritance. He reminded them of their deliverance and protection from God as long as they obeyed.

Joshua 24:21-31 And the people said unto Joshua, nay; but we will serve the LORD. (22) And Joshua said unto the people, Ye are sees against yourselves that ye have chosen you the LORD, to serve him. And they said, we are witnesses. (23) Now therefore put away, said he, the strange gods which are among you, and incline your heart unto the LORD God of Israel. (24) And the people said unto Joshua, The LORD our God will we serve, and his voice will we obey. (25) So, Joshua made a covenant with the people that day, and set them a statute and an ordinance in Shechem. (26) And Joshua wrote these words in the book of the law of God, and took a great stone, and set it up there under an oak, which was by the sanctuary of the LORD. (27) And Joshua said unto all the people, Behold, this stone shall be a witness unto us; for it hath heard all the words of the LORD which he spoke unto us: it shall be therefore a witness unto you, lest ye deny your God. (28) So, Joshua let the people leave, every man unto his inheritance. (29) And it came to pass after these things, that Joshua the son of Nun, the servant of the LORD, died, being a hundred and ten years old. (30) And they buried him in the border of his inheritance in Timnathserah, which is in mount Ephraim, on the north side of the hill of Gaash. (31) And Israel served the LORD all the days of Joshua, and all the days of the elders that outlived Joshua, and which had known all the works of the LORD, that he had done for Israel.

JUDGES

Not long after their promise to obey God, the Israelites fell into the bad behavior of their enemies and began to backslide and worship idols. They began to forsake the laws of God.

Judges 2:11-17And the children of Israel did evil in the sight of the LORD and served Baalim:(12) And they forsook the LORD God of their fathers, which brought them out of the land of Egypt, and followed other gods, of the gods of the people that were round about them, and bowed themselves unto them, and provoked the LORD to anger. (13) And they forsook the LORD and served Baal and Ashtoreth. (14) And the anger of the LORD was hot against Israel, and he delivered them into the hands of spoilers that spoiled them, and he sold them into the hands of their enemies round about, so that they could not any longer stand before their enemies. (15) Whithersoever they went out, the hand of the LORD was against them for evil, as the LORD had said, and as the LORD had sworn unto them: and they were distressed. (16) Nevertheless, the LORD raised up judges, which delivered them out of the hand of those that spoiled them. (17) And yet they would not hearken unto their judges, but they went a whoring after other gods, and bowed themselves unto them: they turned quickly out of the way which their fathers walked in, obeying the commandments of the LORD; but they did not so.

Next, God raised a system of Judges to rule Israel and turn them back to God.

Judges 2:18 And when the LORD raised them up judges, then the LORD was with the judge, and delivered them out of the hand of their enemies all the days of the judge: for it repented the LORD because of their groaning by reason of them that oppressed them and vexed them.

Though they returned, it was not long before they once again turned to evil and idolatrous ways. God allowed them to become victims of their enemies to test them whether they would return and obey Him.

Judges 2:19-23 And it came to pass, when the judge was dead, that they returned, and corrupted themselves more than their fathers, in following other gods to serve them, and to bow down unto them; they ceased not from their own doings, nor from their stubborn way. (20) And the anger of the LORD was hot against Israel; and he said, because that this people hath transgressed my covenant which I commanded their fathers, and have not hearkened unto my voice; (21) I also will not henceforth drive out any from before them of the nations which Joshua left when he died: (22) That through them I may prove Israel, whether they will keep the way of the LORD to walk therein, as their fathers did keep it, or not. (23) Therefore, the LORD left those nations, without driving them out hastily; neither delivered he them into the hand of Joshua.

God let this go on for 40 years until they became captives of the Philistines. As was in the case of Abraham and Sarah, God allowed a barren woman to become the mother of a special person to lead Israel out of captivity. We all know the story of Samson.

Judges 13:3-5 And the angel of the LORD appeared unto the woman, and said unto her, behold now, thou art barren, and bear not: but thou shalt conceive, and bear a son. (4) Now therefore beware, I pray thee, and drink not wine nor strong drink, and eat not any unclean thing: (5) For, lo, thou shalt conceive, and bear a son; and no razor shall come on his head: for the child shall be a Nazarite unto God from the womb: and he shall begin to deliver Israel out of the hand of the Philistines.

This too is another great bible story of the Sunday school days. I remember seeing the movie version as a young man. It was well done for those days; I remember the horror of Samson's eyes being put out with a red-hot poker rod. Eventually Israel was on its own again.

Judges 21:24-25 And the children of Israel left thence at that time, every man to his tribe and to his family, and they went out from thence every man to his inheritance. (25) In those days there was no king in Israel: every man did that which was right in his own eyes.

Next is the era prior to Israel's first King. The Elders of the people were instrumental in trying to bring their respective tribes back to the ways of the invisible God. This is where we get the great stories of David, Goliath, and Israel's first King, King Saul. They wanted a King like the other nations had, and God allowed it.

SAMUEL

$\mathcal{E}$lkanah was an inhabitant of Bethlehem and of the territory of the tribe of Ephraim. He was the father of Samuel and stood for the fifth generation of settlers in Canaan. Samuel was born about 130 years after the entrance into Canaan four complete generations or 132 years, and about 40 years before King David. As Israel developed their national status, God used the Priests as the wise men and moral leaders of the people.

The story of Samuel left a huge impression on me as a young man assigned by my dad to read it. Hannah's prayer for a child is one of the most beautiful texts of prayer. She promised, I will give him unto the Lord. Samuel, as a descendant of the house of Levi, is the Lord's property from twenty-five years of age till fifty, but the vow Hannah made implied that he was consecrated to the Lord from his infancy to his death, and that he was not only a Levite, but as a Nazarite, on whose head no razor should pass.

Samuel was the last priestly judge in Israel and his whole life was spent in service to God. He was a huge influence on the young man, David. After the people chose Saul, Samuel handled preparing David to become the King of Israel.

SAUL FIRST KING OF ISRAEL

The story of Saul is a quick lesson in what not to do if you are chosen by God and then do not follow God's commands and instructions for leadership. Saul amended the command from God to completely destroy the Amalekites. Samuel was commissioned to go to Saul and tell him that God has rejected him as King of Israel because of his blatant disobedience.

1Samuel 15:11 It repents me that I have set up Saul to be king: for he is turned back from following me, and hath not performed my commandments. And it grieved Samuel; and he cried unto the LORD all night.

1Samuel 15:23 For rebellion is as the sin of witchcraft, and stubbornness is as iniquity and idolatry. Because thou hast rejected the word of the LORD, he hath also rejected thee from being king.

Leadership needs impeccable standards of obedience to the power that is granted to the individual, especially when the Invisible God has specifically chosen that person.

DAVID

avid is the next character that helps me understand a lot about how God can work through men and lead nations in the ways of God. From the times of Moses, God used the nation of Israel, 12 tribes, to be an example before the other nations and spread His ways. When they backslid into idolatry and wickedness, they were eventually split, and only the tribes of Judah and Benjamin returned to Jerusalem eventually until the time of Christ.

The other ten tribes were scattered among the other nations by the Babylonians during the 70 years of captivity prophesied by Jeremiah. From whatever side we view the life of David, it is remarkable. The man Abraham excelled David in the aspect of faith in God, and Moses was superior in the power of a concentrated fellowship with God. Moses was persistent, until he convinced God to show him His glory. David also was many-sided and richly-gifted. David had a special power with God and mankind. This power was accounted for his behavior. David, like Moses, is known to have been very handsome. The beauty of his features, his rare gifts, and talents, were enhanced by the Spirit of the Lord.

The spiritual power is a remarkable attribute of his heart. It is said, The Spirit of the Lord came mightily on David. Jesse, David's father, and his sons regarded David as simply someone selected to be trained in Samuel's schools.

Samuel, a priest, gave David long and careful training, and David profited by this training. David perfected his skills, not only in reading and writing but in poetry and music. Saul and David were both men of extraordinary natural ability.

David was noticeably young when he was summoned to Saul's presence to fight with Goliath long before he was prepared for kingship. It was a testament to his courage and faith in God to deliver him from his enemies.

The story of David and Goliath is one of the cherished stories of childhood Sunday schools. The Spirit of God came upon David from that day forward as he fearlessly assaulted Goliath. In modern language we would say that David's character grew and developed nobler in both the intellectual and moral responses he showed in his growth toward kingship. David's ethical truth was seen by the Israelites. This was recognized in the high qualities he displayed with his acts and words, projecting the presence, and working of a Divine Spirit as a great king.

It was a breathing of God which moved David onward and fostered in him all that is morally great and good. As a young teenager, David is an example of faithful trust in the Invisible God. His very first recorded act is one of everyone's favorite bible story. It is the standard for the actions of courage, bravery, and the will to trust God for deliverance.

1Samuel 17:45-46 Then said David to the Philistine, you come to me with a sword, and with a spear, and with a shield: but I come to thee in the name of the LORD of hosts, the God of the armies of Israel, whom thou hast defied. (46) This day will the LORD deliver thee into my hand; and I will smite thee and take thine head from thee; and I will give the carcasses of the host of the Philistines this day unto the fowls of the air, and to the wild beasts of the earth; that all the earth may know that there is a God in Israel.

Samuel, God's priest, gives his youthful pupil something better than accomplishments—he carefully educates him in the law of God, and leads his mind to all that is good.

Prophecy and Monarchy are both of his institutions, as orderly elements of the Jewish state. David embodied the ideal of the theocratic king and was to Israel the type of their coming Messiah. It was Samuel's wisdom in teaching his young men music which gave David the skill to be the sweet singer of the sanctuary; and David is notable as the arranger of the worship service in the house of God. He assigned priests and Levites their appointed duties which is the model the Jews have continued to follow for centuries.

As a man after God's heart and the captain of the people of God, David fulfilled the will of God. The great type and the earthly progenitor of the Messianic King became the author of Israel's greatness, powered by God's Spirit.

David was a poet and sang his own Hebrew melodies to his tuneful harp. His writings were called the Psalms of the Bible. He was Godly and dedicated his music to the praise of God. He was profoundly acquainted with the word of God. This enabled him to portray many of the bible's heroes of faith and their grace to music. They became holy attributes to the volume of inspiration, The Psalms.

David and eventually his son Solomon created the apex of Israel's influence upon the nations of the world. Sadly, the prosperity and blessings of Israel led them once again to backslide, committing sins that consumed them and caused their demise and eventual captivity. God's promise of blessings for obedience or cursing for disobedience are lasting promises.

David and Solomon were both blessed with wisdom and knowledge from the Invisible God. They both described things in the language of their day, even the discoveries medical scientists have found and named in the later centuries. For example:

Psalms 139:13-16 For thou hast possessed my reins: thou hast covered me in my mother's womb. (14) I will praise thee; for I am fearfully and wonderfully made marvelous are thy works; and that my soul knows right well. (15) My substance was not hiding from thee, when I was made in secret, and curiously wrought in the lowest parts of the earth. (16) Thine eyes did see my substance yet being imperfect; and in thy book all my members were written, which in continuance were fashioned, when as yet there was none of them.

Think about it, this is long before the invention of the Microscope! Is verse 16 speaking of DNA and chromosome structure?

Ecclesiastes 3:18-21 I said in mine heart concerning the estate of the sons of men, that God might manifest them, and that they might see that they themselves are beasts. (19) For that which befalls the sons of men befalls beasts; even one thing befalls them: as the one dies, so dies the other; yea, they have all one breath; so that a man hath no preeminence above a beast: for all is vanity. (20) All go unto one place; all are of the dust, and all turn to dust again. (21) Who knows the spirit of man that goes upward, and the spirit of the beast that goes downward to the earth?

The essence of the pineal gland in the brain stem, found by scientists as invisible energy—enough to light a 25-watt light bulb. Once again, I come back to the understanding of Job. His understanding of our living spirit was as dead on as his understanding of death. Scientist discovered and proved what Job knew about centuries before it was checked and proven in a scientific laboratory.

Job 27:3 All the while my breath is in me, and the spirit of God is in my nostrils.

Job 32:7-10 I said, Days should speak, and multitude of years should teach wisdom. (8) But there is a spirit in man: and the inspiration of the Almighty giveth them understanding. (9) Great men are not always wise: neither do the aged understand judgment. (10) Therefore, I said, hearken to me; I also will shew my opinion.

Job 32:17-18 I said, I will also answer my part, I also will shew my opinion. (18) For I am full of matter, my spirit within me constrained me. Job 34:11-16 For the work of a man shall he make unto him and cause every man to find according to his ways. (12) Yea, surely God will not do wickedly, neither will the Almighty pervert judgment. (13) Who hath given him a charge over the earth? or who hath disposed the whole world? (14) If he set his heart upon man, if He (God) gather unto Himself his (mankind) spirit and his breath; (15) All flesh shall perish together, and man shall turn again unto dust. (16) If now thou hast understanding, hear this: hearken to the voice of my words.

Job7:11 Therefore I will not refrain my mouth; I will speak in the anguish of my spirit; I will complain in the bitterness of my soul. (Note: soul and spirit are two different phenomena; the soul is what mirrors the spirit in man. More about this later in the book.)

Psalms19:7 The Law of the LORD is perfect, converting the soul: the testimony of the LORD is sure, making wise the simple.

Psalms33:19 To deliver their soul from death, and to keep them alive in famine. (Note: the soul of a person can die, more about this later in the book)

These men understand what we now understand: how the brain is the soul, and <u>the breath of life perpetuates the spirit in man's brain cells.</u> I will address a very touchy subject later in this book about Life, Death, and what happens after physical death. God blessed David with knowledge and prophetic insights that revealed much of His plan.

The writings of David are very poetic, yet prophetic in advancing the will of God for mankind. His life's experiences are an open book for all to learn from his successes and mistakes. David's feet of clay are obvious from his bad behavior. His sins and poor judgment were documented for us to learn from.

David's position in the coming kingdom of God is well proven, and his throne is occupied at present and is named down through history.

Both the book of Psalms and Proverbs are excellent sources of information. These two books are a great place to start if you have never read the bible and wish to learn the greater principles and wisdom helpful in living life. They are great books to teach young people how to get a grip on the things of importance and value.

There is proof from the bible and history that the Throne of David is set up by God as a perpetual Throne of authority. It is a long story and is not that important to this story. It does have significance with the Lost Ten Tribes because Brits are descendants of Ephraim—one of Joseph's two sons of the 12 tribes of Israel.

However, would you believe that Queen Elizabeth, Prince Charles, and Prince William are all direct descendants of King David? It is true, and a proven fact. I think I know why the British Monarchy is still in place. It is the Throne of King David, still in existence as God promised. The story of David influenced my life with his consistent worship and praise of the Invisible God. As David became old and stricken with years, certain things happened which are always associated with the death of great men.

There are always people who are wondering who will succeed the throne. Can we understand all that is going on in the minds of our friends when we ourselves are approaching the hour and article of death? Would we be surprised by some revelations of character which we have little suspected of people close to us? This is certainly the norm for men in power and kingship.

SOLOMON

$\mathcal{S}$olomon succeeds his father David as king of Israel. His ascension to the royal throne of Israel was made under the happiest auspices. Born after his father became monarch of the whole kingdom, his claim, per the notions of Asian people, is preferable to all, even his older brothers.

The Hebrew kingdom enjoyed internal prosperity; it was respected and renowned abroad, and Solomon knew how to improve these advantages. Solomon did not come by his great discernment and wisdom by accident.

He did something most people don't think to do. He asked for Wisdom. Solomon embraced wisdom to appropriate his knowledge. I have learned using wisdom to appropriate knowledge is an important quality for leadership and good living.

It has been said, Knowledge without understanding and wisdom is the sister of folly. God gave Solomon wisdom and understanding generously, and largeness of heart — that is, high powers of mind, great capacity for receiving, as well as aptitude for communicating his acquired knowledge. Solomon's wisdom excelled the wisdom of all the children of the east country —the Arabians, Chaldeans, and Persians and all the wisdom of Egypt.

Egypt is renowned as the seat of learning and sciences. The existing monuments clearly describe the ancient state of society and the arts. These monuments show the high culture of the Egyptian people existing down to Solomon's time from what the Egyptians learned from the sons of Israel!

It is interesting to note that Solomon's fame and wisdom attracted the other nations and their leaders. Not unlike his brethren, Solomon too, often fell to idolatry and bad behavior.

1Kings 4:29 And God gave Solomon wisdom and understanding exceedingly much, and largeness of heart, even as the sand that is on the seashore. 1Kings 4:32-34 And he spoke three thousand proverbs: and his songs were a thousand and five. (33) And he spoke of trees, from the cedar tree that is in Lebanon even unto the hyssop that comes out of the wall: he spoke also of beasts, and of fowl, and of creeping things, and of fishes. (34) And there came of all people to hear the Wisdom of Solomon, from all kings of the earth, which had heard of his wisdom.

I wish to point out that Solomon's affinity for the daughter of one of the Pharaohs of Egypt. I mention this as an example of how Egyptian ancient history parallels the history of Israel in the bible. This parallel supplies a timeline that helps us show the names of certain people in the Bible. It also gives us an approximate year certain events happen, the timeline of events not specifically called out in the bible narrative.

1Kings3:1 And Solomon made affinity with Pharaoh king of Egypt, and took Pharaoh's daughter, and brought her into the city of David, until he had made an end of building his own house, and the house of the LORD, and the wall of Jerusalem round about.

There are some clues in this verse of scripture that show more information than appears in the bible. As I mentioned earlier in this section, biblical information is compiled by those who are directly involved with the Creator God. Other nations are progressing at their own rate without knowledge or acknowledging the Creator God.

This is how academic history, documented by other nations and governments, can fill in the blanks about people only briefly mentioned in the biblical narrative. We can actually name certain people in the bible who are only referred to by their position of power or territory as they meet the named characters of the bible. People may say, who cares what their names are, so what, or it makes no difference to the present. It does, doesn't. I will tell you what it does for a believer of the bible like me!

It made me understand the unseen hand, invisible force, making the bible the most important guide for understanding our purpose and destiny! I envy people who can believe or accept information with blind faith. It is the easiest way to have hope and move on without a lot of digging and searching for answers to confirm something you can't see. But when I see how certain information can be combined as I search for validation, it confirms my faith and hope.

Bear with me while I wade through a couple of detailed examples of validating information. It is important to understand the conditions of the political air in Egypt at different times.

The Pharaohs who ruled Egypt during the Eighteenth Dynasties were not the Shepherd Kings; they were the Black Pharaohs. Why? Because during the time of Solomon, Egypt was united with and dominated by the Ethiopians! The Pharaohs were Ethiopians. These kings ruled from 1076 to about 906 B.C. Pharaoh Ahmose came to power in 1076 B.C. His wife, Nofreteroi, is depicted in the monuments and records as being of a black countenance.

The next Pharaoh who ruled twenty-five years later is known to be a Black man. This is because Egypt and Ethiopia were a United Kingdom. This eighteenth Dynasty of Thebes began a few years after the overthrow of Egypt. This happened while Saul was King of Israel. For the next 196 years the Egyptian Pharaohs were Black Ethiopians who ruled the eighteenth dynasty of Pharaohs. The Egyptian royal family for this time period were of Ethiopian blood.

Bible history and academic history become parallel during the time of Solomon. This synchronism begins when Solomon becomes allied to the Pharaoh of Egypt by marriage. Solomon takes Pharaoh's daughter to wife and brings her to the city of David:

1Kings 3:1 And Solomon made affinity with Pharaoh King of Egypt, and took Pharaoh's daughter, and brought her into the city of David, until he had made an end of building his own house, and the house of the LORD, and the wall of Jerusalem round about.

Who is Solomon's father-in-law as Pharaoh of Egypt? The bible does not say his name, but logic and clues of information from the bible compared to historical information do. This is what I find interesting about comparing the two sources of information, bible, and academic history.

We can figure out the name of this Pharaoh by combining the bible timeline with the academic history of Egyptian Dynasties. For example:

1Kings 6:1 And it came to pass in the four hundred and eightieth year after the children of Israel were come out of the land of Egypt, in the fourth year of Solomon's reign over Israel, in the month Zif, which is the second month, that he began to build the house of the LORD.

The clue is the phrases, <u>four-hundred and eightieth year</u> after the Exodus of Israel from Egypt and fourth year of Solomon's reign as king over Israel. The Exodus happened in the spring of 1487 B.C. It was 480 years to the 4 th year of Solomon's reign over Israel, 1008–1007 B.C.

In the Egyptian Dynasty Eighteen, Thutmose II reigned from, 1017–997 B.C. Thus, nine years into Thutmose II's reign was 1008 -1007 B.C., which was the 4 th year of Solomon's rule over Israel. The result is: Thutmose II was Solomon's Pharaoh father-in-law.

This same logic can be used to figure out other names and places of people not specifically named in the bible accounts. For example, the Queen of Sheba. Most everyone only knows her by this phrase of scripture. The Queen of Sheba is mentioned in just a few places in the bible. Does this queen have a name? Can she be found in academic history? Yes, she can.

When the movie character, Indiana Jones, finds clues to uncover where some important artifact of history is found, it becomes a great story or movie of entertainment. This is what comparing and sorting out academic history with the bible does also for people like me! With a few tools, such as logic, timelines, and facts from history, we can conclude about certain people and times with a lot lighter on what, when, where, and even what their name is during their short time in history.

The name of the "Queen of Sheba" requires some other clues. *1Kings_10:1 And when the Queen of Sheba heard of the fame of Solomon concerning the name of the LORD, she came to prove him with hard questions.*

First, we must figure out when she comes to visit Solomon. The time factor must relate to the year of Solomon's reign when he is visited.

1Kings 6:37-38 In the fourth year was the foundation of the house of the LORD laid, in the month Zif: (38) And in the eleventh year, in the month Bul, which is the eighth month, was the house finished throughout all the parts thereof, and according to all the fashion of it.

So was he seven years in building it. We have already proved that the 4 th year of Solomon's reign was 1009 B.C. It took him 7 years to build it. Subtract 7 from 1009; this is 1002 B.C. With the Lord's house finished, he began construction on his own house.

1Kings 7:1 But Solomon was building his own house thirteen years, and he finished all his house. Subtract 13 years from 1002; this is 989 B.C. Now as we read on in I Kings we see verification of this timeline:

1Kings 9:10 And it came to pass at the end of twenty years, when Solomon had built the two houses, the house of the LORD, and the king's house.

1Kings 10:1 And when the Queen of Sheba heard of the fame of Solomon concerning the name of the LORD, she came to prove him with hard questions.

Solomon started construction of these two buildings in the 4 th year of his reign; it was the 24 th year of his reign, because of the 7 + 13 = 20 years of construction. The year was 989 B.C. We now know the time this specific queen came to see Solomon, but we cannot specifically name her until we find a place called Sheba.

There is a clue in Daniel's writings about future events ahead of his time that will help show what territory Sheba is during ancient history.

Daniel 11:5-8 And the king of the south shall be strong, and one of his princes; and he shall be strong above him and have dominion; his dominion shall be a great dominion. (6) And in the end of years they shall join themselves together; for the king's daughter of the south shall come to the king of the north to make an agreement: but she shall not retain the power of the arm; neither shall he stand, nor his arm: but she shall be given up, and they that brought her, and he that begat her, and he that strengthened her in these times. (7) But out of a branch of her roots shall one stand up in his estate, which shall come with an army, and shall enter into the fortress of the king of the north, and shall deal against them, and shall prevail: (8) And shall also carry captives into Egypt their gods, with their princes, and with their precious vessels of silver and of gold; and he shall continue more years than the king of the north.

The term King of the South has long been proved to be referring to the king or queen of Egypt, not the lower Arab states. The compact here is one formed between Berenice, the daughter of Ptolemy Philadelphus, king of Egypt, and Antiochus Theos, king of Syria. Ptolemy, in order to bring the war in which he was engaged to an end and restore peace, gives his daughter in marriage to Antiochus in hopes of setting up a permanent peaceful alliance between the two kingdoms.

Jesus used this term as He spoke of the royalty of Egypt when He referred to the known history of His time.

Matthew 12:42 The queen of the south shall rise up in the judgment with this generation and shall condemn it: for she came from the uttermost parts of the earth to hear the wisdom of Solomon; and behold, a man greater than Solomon is here.

This reference to the time of Solomon about the "queen of the south" is referring to the Queen of Sheba. As calculated, the time is 989 B.C., a time when Egypt and Ethiopia were united.

The word Sheba in Hebrew means one of the three tribes of Ethiopia, descendants who go as far back as Cush, who was of the Black race. The only Black Pharaoh Queen of the Egyptian Dynasty of 989 B.C. was named, Hashepsowe. She ruled from 996 to 975 B.C. One striking proof of this is in the archeological finds at Deir el Bahari, Egypt, in the ancient temple. The inscription says, <u>The queen went to visit God's Land.</u> The year was 988-989 B.C., the very year when Solomon's palace was completed.

1Kings 10:1-4 And when the queen of Sheba heard of the fame of Solomon concerning the name of the LORD, she came to prove him with hard questions. (2) And she came to Jerusalem with a very great train, with camels that bare spices, and very much gold, and precious stones: and when she was come to Solomon, she communed with him of all that was in her heart. (3) And Solomon told her all her questions: there was not anything hid from the king, which he told her not. (4) And when the queen of Sheba had seen all Solomon's wisdom, and the house that he had built....

It is a lot of scattered pieces of information and of no particular value to most people. But it helps me to see the authenticity of God's preserved word and how History is tangled up writers of History do not include the timeline and history of the Bible. They refuse to believe God intervenes at times in the course of man's existence, yet science has many projects such as SETI, the Search for Extra Terrestrial Intelligence. Millions of hours and dollars are invested to look for other life in the universe.

Mankind feels there is an Invisible Intelligence out there, just can't accept it as the bible reveals it. All Jesus needs when He comes to earth is Belief in Him and the Father.

THE PSALMS, PROVERBS, & ECCLESIASTES

The Psalms, Proverbs, and Ecclesiastes celebrate the creation and history of mankind. They also reflect the wisdom of both David and Solomon in the matters of human relationships with God and the processes of life itself. These books are rich in the knowledge of creation, the sovereignty of God, and the application of knowledge with wisdom and understanding, specifically the book of Psalms, rich in context relating to prophecy.

I recommend these books as a starting place for introducing young adults to biblical principles and wisdom. These include the coming Messiah and His suffering for the sins of mankind.

Prophecy is another mystery and rejected agent of Modern Historians.

THE IMPORTANCE OF PROPHETS

This is my understanding of what we call prophets and prophesies. Remember, the Babylonians and Egyptians, two of the main civilizations, had their version of prophets or oracles to turn to for advanced information. God used the prophets to warn and prepare His people for events that will affect the future of time and chance.

Even in our modern times we have academic prophets. Many believe the man, Nostradamus, was such a person. Prophets must always pass the test of time. They are mostly a wait and see proposition.

I believe there are no new prophets of any credibility since the prophecy Jesus gave to the Apostle John while he was in prison on the Island of Patmos. The bible is very plain about how God is warning people today. Note the following scripture:

Hebrews 1:1-2 God, who at sundry times and in different manners spoke in time past unto the fathers by the prophets, (2) <u>Hath in these last days spoken unto us by His Son</u>, whom He hath appointed heir of all things, by whom also He made the worlds.

This is very plain to me that in the past God spoke about future events through prophets to the patriarchs. But since the time of Jesus, God speaks through Jesus when it comes to the future just ahead of our time. Jesus is the last and final prophet to speak for God.

Revelation19:10 And I fell at his feet to worship him. And he said unto me, See thou do it not: I am thy fellow servant, and of thy brethren that have the testimony of Jesus: worship God: for the testimony of Jesus is the spirit of prophecy.

Jesus speaks to John, in visions, the various details of how things will eventually be settled after He returns the next time. The spirit of prophecy is a general testimony concerning Jesus, for He is the scope and design of the whole Scripture; to Him all the prophets give witness. Take Jesus, His grace, Spirit, and religion out of the Bible, and it has neither scope, design, object, nor end.

To prophesy is to understand and proclaim the truth concerning God. This is clear in the face of prevalent ignorance or opposition to biblical history. The understanding of God through prophecy is what is meant by holding the testimony of Jesus.

We who believe in Jesus carry the Testimony of Jesus; to testify of the Lord Jesus, by the same Spirit which inspires the prophets of old. The language does not mean of course that this is the only design of prophecy, but that this is its great and ultimate end.

Jesus prophesied to His disciples before the crucifixion. All of Matthew the 24 th chapter is a dual prophecy from Jesus concerning the time just ahead of the Apostles and then the future ahead of those living in the time upon Jesus's return to earth.

Even the writings of the Apostle Paul have various references to prophecy that Jesus teaches him personally during a vision. It has been said that lightening does not strike twice in the same place This is not true when the events of a prophecy take place. Prophecy is dual, it strikes twice in the same place but not at the same time, especially when it concerns Jerusalem.

Do we think, as a nation, we can let non-Christian religions build their temples and teach their ways to our children and God will just let it be? The history of God's people teaches that God will punish His people for allowing other religions and cultures to infect the things God has set forth for His people.

The Bible is full of warnings against doing away with the things of God. Prophecy is a major proof of the Bible is the inspired word of God. It is not too late for us to repent. Jonah is sent to prophecy against Nineveh to change their ways. They repent and God does not destroy them. Our country today is far removed from the principles and reasons the Pilgrims came to America.

I understand that freedom of religion is what we have in our constitution. There is nothing wrong with freedom of religion. Choices are what we are supposed to be making and there is no better place in the world to do it than America. It is time for the Christian to listen to the preacher, study the Bible, and search out the truth about the faith once delivered.

Proverbs 2:3-5 Yes, if you cry after knowledge, and lift up your voice for understanding, (4) If you seek her as silver, and search for her as for hidden treasures; (5) Then shall you understand the fear of the Lord and find the knowledge of God.

As we seek knowledge from God, sound wisdom and understanding can sustain us in times of confusion and tribulation. Proper attitude and approach with the knowledge from God are needed for the Holy Spirit to work in us. One of the most interesting prophecies concerning salvation and the church is written in the book of Daniel. Because of the comprehensive and structural nature of Daniel's prophecies, both for the other nations and for Israel, the study of Daniel's prophesies are the keys to understanding the prophetic Scriptures in the other books of the Bible.

Prophecy is a tool of God, giving humanity insight to events of the future. Prophecy predicts circumstances that will bless or befall us when our behavior is changed from good to bad or bad to good. One third of the Bible is "prophecy." These prophecies of the Bible confirm the actions of God.

Amos 3:7 surely, the Lord GOD will do nothing, but he reveals his secret unto his servants the prophets.

God is pleading with His people down through time to listen to the preachers He sends to warn them of the consequences that will come upon them for their bad choices. With the information available to us in these end times, we have no excuse not to find out, within a small margin of speculation, what is going to happen in the world when God makes a choice to intervene in the affairs of mankind.

As we study the Scriptures, it becomes plain there is a profound unity between the Old and New Testaments. For example, this unity is proved by the fact that over one third of the New Testament is made up of quotes from the Old Testament. In truth, many Old Testament passages simply cannot be understood without the New Testament.

Consider the many prophecies referring to Jesus Christ, such as those in Psalms 22 and Isaiah 53. Without the writings of the New Testament, we would never realize that Old Testament texts are Messianic in nature. Similarly, dozens of Old and New Testament prophecies about the end time cannot be understood without the book of Revelation. Through knowledge of the ancient Holy days given to ancient Israel to remind them of the Invisible God, a general prophetic time for the fulfillment of the plan of God is revealed.

These examples show the unity of Scripture and are proof of God's inspiration of the entire Bible as the complete Word of God. In the book of Isaiah, God supplies us the "standard" by which to seek Him and understand His word, as well as discern those who speak the truth: *"To the law and testimony! If they speak not according to this word, it is because there is no light in them."*

Isaiah 8:20. Verse 16 of this same Chapter 8 is a prophecy telling us Jesus and the Apostles will be the heart and soul of the books of the New Testament.

Isaiah 8:13-16 Sanctify the LORD of hosts himself; and let him be your fear and let him be your dread. (14) And he shall be for a sanctuary, but for a stone of stumbling and for a rock of offence to both the houses of Israel, for a gin and for a snare to the inhabitants of Jerusalem. (15) And many among them shall stumble, and fall, and be broken, and be snared, and be taken. (16) Bind up the testimony, seal the law among my disciples. All scripture is God-breathed and is profitable for doctrine, for conviction, for correction, for instruction in righteousness so that the man of God may be complete and fully equipped for every good work.

The Bible is a Priestly Document. Daniel is used by God to present the outline of the history of the Gentile Kingdoms. Prophets were used by God to warn mankind of certain consequences that can result from the wrong choice for how we live as individuals and as a nation.

The prophets supply divine inspired information for mankind to foresee the need to make right choices in this life. Prophecy gives mankind the ability to make the right choices based on probable consequences or blessings related to behavior and moral standards.

Unfortunately, it is a subject that is left untouched in most churches of today. The prophets open our understanding to the bigger picture of what the Plan of God for mankind is. They connect lifestyle and culture to nations and the world considering what God knows will be the best for mankind's life. They supply a heads up to people and nations to change their ways before consequences overtake them.

ISAIAH, JERIMIAH, & EZEKIEL

*P*rophets become the next dominant people of the Old Testament as Israel and Judah are losing power and making huge mistakes as a nation, eventually leading them into 70-year captivity. This was predicted by 3 incredibly famous prophets: Isaiah, Jerimiah, and Ezekiel. All three of these books are quite lengthy and require a lot of study and background information for interpretation.

Isaiah, whose name means, _salvation of the Lord_, is one of the greatest writing prophets. His writings were penned over a period of 60 years just prior to the first captivity of the Jews by Babylon. His prophesies cover many subjects of God's intervention with mankind. He predicts things such as the coming Messiah, how Jesus would suffer, and many of the end-time scenarios of the coming kingdom of God.

Jeremiah and Ezekiel are the two prophets who warned the 10 tribes of Israel who split away from Judah and Benjamin that they would become captives of the Assyrians and then the Babylonians. (I do not wish to elaborate on these three books now. I will refer to the information of these books relating to the predictions of the Messiah and then the end time events ahead of our immediate future from time to time in this story.)

I will use one example from Jeremiah's writings that forewarned the nation of Israel that they were headed for demise and captivity because of their straying away from the laws and principles God taught them as a nation.

Jeremiah 25:4-9 And the LORD hath sent unto you all his servants the prophets, rising early and sending them; but ye have not hearkened, nor inclined your ear to hear. (5) They said, turn ye again now everyone from his evil way, and from the evil of your doings, and dwell in the land that the LORD hath given unto you and to your fathers for ever and ever: (6) And go not after other gods to serve them, and to worship them, and provoke me not to anger with the works of your hands; and I will do you no hurt. (7) Yet ye have not hearkened unto me, says the LORD; that ye might provoke me to anger with the works of your hands to your own hurt. (8) Therefore thus says the LORD of hosts; Because ye have not heard my words, (9) Behold, I will send and take all the families of the north, says the LORD, and Nebuchadnezzar the king of Babylon, my servant, and will bring them against this land, and against the inhabitants thereof, and against all these nations round about, and will utterly destroy them, and make them an astonishment, and a hissing, and perpetual desolations. The warning from the prophets is specific.

Jeremiah 25:11 And this whole land shall be a desolation, and an astonishment; and these nations shall serve the king of Babylon seventy years.

DANIEL

*G*od is My Judge Daniel, whose name means God is my judge was taken at the young age of 17 during the first deportation of the Jews under the Babylonian king, Nebuchadnezzar. This was in the year 604 B.C. As I stated earlier, this captivity was predicted 100 years before by the prophet Jeremiah.

Jeremiah 25:11,12 And this whole land shall be a desolation, and an astonishment; and these nations shall serve the king of Babylon seventy years. And it shall come to pass, when seventy years are done, that I will punish the king of Babylon, and that nation, says the LORD, for their iniquity, and the land of the Chaldeans, and will make it perpetual desolations.

Jeremiah 29:10 For thus says the LORD, that after seventy years be done at Babylon I will visit you, and perform my good word toward you, in causing you to return to this place.

The book of Daniel was written by himself, one of the most beloved prophets of the bible. His life was like that of Joseph's in the sense that God used him to educate the Babylonians about the invisible God. This is a unique event in the history of Israel because their captivity introduces the ways and power of the invisible God to the pagan nations. It is another huge transformation in the history of God's people influencing the rest of the worldly nations.

Daniel is the only prophet that has a one-on-one encounter with the King of Babylon. Daniel's behavior and God's favor with him educated the King in the power and plan of the Invisible God. The effect was carried on to the empire of Persia. For a short time, the Persians were sympathetic and responsive to the Jews' religion and way of life. Daniel and his three friends revealed a way of life that is superior to the futility of putting trust and confidence in manmade gods of the earth who have no power.

The book of Daniel is one of the most important prophecies of the Old Testament. The writings of Daniel are a testimony to the power of the word of God as it is applied specifically to a life lived with integrity. Daniel and his three companions were powerful witnesses to the word of God as it is applied specifically to a life with consistent loyalty to God. In their devout worship and trust in the Invisible God, they were powerful examples to the Babylonian Empire for the behavior God wanted to see in mankind. As a teenager, I was impressed by Daniel's complete reliance on the Invisible God. He was a victim of the Jewish culture. There was truly little time to choose his own way in the world. Yet he found courage and was chosen to bring the knowledge of the Invisible God to the pagan King of Babylon. He was the most positive influence for the Babylonians since the times of Shem.

Because Israel had become so corrupt and arrogant, God used Daniel as a one-on-one person to educate the King of Babylon in the intended behavior for mankind to reach the ultimate destiny. The book of Daniel holds the only nutshell timeline of future events from Daniel's time to the second coming of Jesus Christ.

The book of Daniel is about the rise and fall of the Kingdoms of Mankind. It introduces us to the first of the kingdoms of men that oppress His chosen people and influence the people of the world with military force. The book of Daniel was written by Daniel and is a record of the events during the captivity of the Jews. This captivity was carried out by the Babylonian armies as they began a world conquest of the lesser nations.

It is admirable how the Jewish people are so dedicated to preserving their religious beliefs, even though they are prone to backsliding and abandoning their own credence about their religious behaviors. Even while being taken captive and scattered into other nations they supported their beliefs strong in their hearts. Although Jerusalem was overthrown and the temple reduced to rubble, the Jews carried the true Jerusalem in their hearts.

They said, *"Even though our holy city is no more, and we are dispersed, and many are sold into slavery, the holy temple of our God lives and will continue to live within our hearts! Wherever we go or are dispossessed, whether in the splendid cities of the East, or amid the fascinations of Egypt, the tents of wandering shepherds, our affections will be in the holy land, and we will turn our faces toward the land where our fathers worshipped the invisible God of the heavens."*

The story of Daniel begins with the deportation of him and three of his friends from Jerusalem. Among the great prophetic books of Scripture, the Book of Daniel supplies the only sequential timeline for the world ruling kingdoms of men and both advents of the Christ. I believe the book of Daniel is key to the great themes of prophecy from the Old Testament. It is key to the Mount of Olives Prophecy from Jesus to his disciples. Also, it connects the Revelation of Jesus to John the apostle in 100 A.D. to Matthew 24.

The book of Daniel is a unique marker for prophetic events surrounding the Jews and Gentile nations. It is introducing the influence of dominating Empires influencing the peoples of the world as each nation is conquered. The prophetic symbolism describes predicted behaviors and strengths of these empires. The symbolism is expressed in animal and physical things to characterize the spirit of behaviors and strengths.

Daniel's writings give the only prophesied outline of world history from Babylon of 600 B.C. to the second advent of Christ. It includes the Gentile nations influencing the Jews during their seventy years of captivity. It predicts the rise of carnal men and their empires of influence ruling the known world down through the ages.

Daniel's story is different from other prophets in the bible. This is because of his personal influence of the kings of these Gentile governments from his position of authority sanctioned by these governments. These governments are based on the ideals of men and paganism. Israel's government is based on God's design for all nations of mankind to understand God's will and plan for the posterity of humanity. Similar to Joseph's and Job's purpose to influence Egyptian government, Daniel was called, prepared, matured, and blessed by God to influence the King of Babylon and his government.

By the identical circumstance, Daniel was appointed second in command of the first world-ruling empire. This was done by the King after an interpreted dream. Daniel was instrumental in educating Nebuchadnezzar, king of Babylon, about the one true, all- powerful Invisible God. The God above all the manmade gods! Daniel reveals the greatness of the Gentile kingdoms, beginning with Babylon, and reveals other kingdoms to rise and fall.

Please remember, the bible is our guide to these events of history. The facts of history do not automatically organize themselves into a scenario of unmistakable truth and answers. Geology and artifacts do not answer the questions such as when and why certain events became a fact of truth.

Ancient Historical records often do not supply motive, or accuracy in transmission of facts and information, but the bible does give us some answers, if we are looking for and willing to listen to what the bible can tell us.

This story from Daniel influences my understanding of many of the events of world history and prophesies from the bible. I am inspired by Daniel's integrity and witness before the people and Kings of Babylon.

As I said before, Daniel is about seventeen years old when he and his friends Hananiah, Mishael, and Azariah are carried away from their families to Babylon. Then Daniel and his companions at once find favor in the eyes of the authorities. The reason for such favor is not explained. It may be presumed, however, that it was because of the attractiveness of his person and manners.

Whatever the reasons, two things are worthy of notice: The effect of this favor upon Daniel was to him a great advantage. By the friendship of a man named Melzar, Daniel was enabled to carry out the purposes of temperance and religion which he had. He did this without coming in conflict with those who were in high positions of power in the Babylonian government. I think God was the author of the favor which was bestowed upon Daniel.

It was an influence Daniel felt and unashamedly acknowledged before all people. It is something God would like for all His people to acknowledge. Daniel 1:7 unto whom the prince of the eunuchs gave names: for he gave unto Daniel the name of Beltshazzar; and to Hananiah, of Shadrach; and to Mishael, of Meshach; and to Azariah, of Abednego. It is the common practice of Gentile captors to change the names of their captives to promote the Babylonian culture in them. The names of the idols worshipped by Babylonians were incorporated into their captives' new names. This change was to serve as remembrances of the manmade divinities. We have already noted these influences on Abraham and others called away from Chaldea, later called Babylon.

It was the post-flood area and civilization dominated by Ham, Cush, and Nimrod. Their religion turned people from the Invisible God worshipped by Noah, Shem, Japheth, and their sons.

Daniel 1:3-4 And the king spoke unto Ashpenaz the master of his eunuchs, that he should bring certain of the children of Israel, and of the king's seed, and of the princes; (4) Children in whom was no blemish, but well favored, and skillful in all wisdom, and cunning in knowledge, and understanding science, and such as had ability in them to stand in the king's palace, and whom they might teach the learning and the tongue of the Chaldeans.

Israel was not a nation distinguished for science in the sense this term is now commonly understood—embracing astronomy, chemistry, geology, and mathematics. Their science extended chiefly to music, architecture, natural history, agriculture, morality, theology, war, and the predicting of future events; in all this information they occupied an honorable distinction among the other nations.

In many of these respects they were, doubtless, far more advanced than the Chaldeans, and it became the purpose of the Chaldean monarch to avail himself of what they knew. We should also remember Abraham, their forefather, migrated from Ur of the Chaldeans.

Daniel 1:18-20 Now at the end of the days that the king had said he should bring them in, then the prince of the eunuchs brought them in before Nebuchadnezzar. (19) And the king communed with them; and among them all was found none like Daniel, Hananiah, Mishael, and Azariah: therefore, stood they before the king. (20) And in all matters of wisdom and understanding that the king enquired of them, he found them ten times better than all the magicians and astrologers that were in all his realm.

THE IMAGE Here is the first mention of the overall outline for the Gentile Kingdoms being introduced to mankind. It is presented in the dream as an Image of different precious elements. This interpretation from the invisible God is for all nations of mankind to understand, not just Israel or the Jews.

I remember my dad teaching me this chapter as a young teenager. I would ask him how he knew this information is related to world kingdoms. He said I needed to pay more attention in school when my history class was talking about various governments in history. And he reminded me that the bible is more than a book about religion and history. It is a book of events relating to mankind and its relationship with God.

Daniel 2:26-28 The king answered and said to Daniel, whose se name was Belteshazzar, Art thou able to make known unto me the dream which I have seen, and the interpretation thereof? (27) Daniel answered in the presence of the king, and said, the secret which the king hath demanded cannot the wise men, the astrologers, the magicians, the soothsayers, show unto the king; (28) But there is a God in heaven that reveals secrets, and makes known to the king Nebuchadnezzar what shall be in the latter days. Thy dream, and the visions of thy head upon thy bed, are these; This is superior behavior from Daniel. He takes no credit for the interpretation by revealing an invisible source of power, the God of creation, as the One supplying the answers for the king through Daniel. Daniel 2:31-35 Thou, O king, saw, and behold a great image. This great image, whose brightness was excellent, stood before thee; and the form thereof was terrible. (32) This image's head was of fine gold, his breast and his arms of silver, his belly, and his thighs of brass, (33) His legs of iron, his feet part of iron and part of clay. (34) Thou saw till that a stone was cut out without hands, which smote the image upon his feet that were of iron and clay, and brake them to pieces. (35) Then was the iron, the clay, the brass, the silver, and the gold, broken to pieces together, and became like the chaff of the summer threshing floor; and the wind carried them away, that no place was found for them: and the stone that smote the image became a great mountain, and filled the whole earth.

This is where the bible becomes an outline that parallels academic history before it happens. Even though it is written in 500s B.C., it predicts events that have become history preceding our time. These verses of scripture were a mystery when I first studied them as a young man. But through years of study and comparing academic history, the verses began to make sense. When I studied the New Testament writings of Jesus and John, I began to see the meaning of this Image the old king dreamed about.

Only a supernatural being can look far into the future and predict the events eventually brought to life by the behavior of mankind. I believe these nine verses of scripture present a thumbnail sketch of these kingdoms setting up their influence upon the people of the world. They outline man's governments and empires, beginning with Babylon up through the time of the Roman Empire. They include prophetic glimpses of Roman influence upon people until the second return of Jesus Christ.

Daniel 2:36-45 this is the dream; and we will tell the interpretation thereof before the king. (37) Thou, O king, art a king of kings: for the God of heaven hath given thee a kingdom, power, and strength, and glory. (38) And where so ever the children of men dwell, the beasts of the field and the fowls of the heaven hath he given into thine hand, and hath made thee ruler over them all. Thou art this head of gold. (39) And after thee shall arise another kingdom inferior to thee, and another third kingdom of brass, which shall bear rule over all the earth. (40) And the fourth kingdom shall be strong as iron: forasmuch as iron break in pieces and subdue all things: and as iron that break all these, shall it break in pieces and bruise. (41) And while thou saw the feet and toes, part of potters' clay, and part of iron, the kingdom shall be divided; but there shall be in it of the strength of the iron, forasmuch as thou saw the iron mixed with miry clay. (42) And as the toes of the feet were part of iron, and part of clay, so the kingdom shall be partly strong, and partly broken. (43) And while thou saw iron mixed with miry clay, they shall mingle themselves with the seed of men: but they shall not cleave one to another, even as iron is not mixed with clay. (44) And in the days of these kings shall the God of heaven set up a kingdom, which shall never be destroyed: and the kingdom shall not be left to other people, but it shall break in pieces and consume all these kingdoms, and it shall stand for ever. (45) Forasmuch as thou saw that the stone was cut out of the mountain without hands, and that it breaks in pieces the iron, the brass, the clay, the silver, and the gold; the great God hath made known to the king what shall come to pass hereafter: and the dream is certain, and the interpretation thereof sure.

This great Gentile King didn't even realize he was the ruler of a world empire until Daniel enlightened him. Daniel lived to become the influence upon the Kings of the next world empire after the demise of Babylon— The Persian Empire. I do not wish to wade knee deep into the prophetic rhetoric at this time in my story. I will get into the details of all of Daniel's part of revelation from God about the overall plan of God for the world later in this book.

For now, I will press on to general historical facts about the relationship between Israel and the worldly system of government. When I was a young man, this was the first time I truly became interested with the boring subject of history. Reading about four world-ruling kingdoms and comparing their characteristics with the bible language is an interesting task. It is often like a crossword puzzle.

I believe the Jew's captivity, for seventy years, was providential as the means for God to show His intentions for mankind, as a universal understanding among the different nations of the world. God's chosen people were forced to learn and express their values in a language not their own. They learned Aramaic and Chaldean and used by them during their captivity with the Babylonians. If we consider the geography of Israel's country, we will see divine providence at work. The territory during the times of Abraham through the life of Moses in the Land of Canaan was not the established focal point for the Israelites. The territory was overrun by wandering tribes and fixed boundaries were scarce. There were only the older territories of Chaldea, a cradle of mankind and Egypt, a type of womb for birthing learning skills. As the peoples migrated south and north, they accumulated and exchanged knowledge, creating a better world for all peoples.

Only after the fact do we see the wisdom of God showing the nation of Israel in Canaan Land, later to become known as Judea, or Palestine and the city of Jerusalem.

This is where Jacob's pillow rock and hand-dug well refreshed him on his journey. It is a tract of land midway between the three major territories—Asia, Africa, and Europe. It was the unavoidable route of trade, commerce, and conquest for all of the known world at that time, accessible by both land and sea for moving product and information. It became a filter for the refining of information concerning commerce and culture mixing of the nations. It was an international place of congregating and combining information.

The writings of Daniel reveal a new era for the infusion of knowledge throughout the expanding civilizations and nations of the world. The dominant influence of specific cultures, such as Chaldean, Persian, Greek, and Roman, nationalized the exclusive knowledge the Creator God gave the Israelites. This did not impede the weakness for Idolatry in them.

God allowed the tribes of Israel to be scattered into other nations, enacting His tough love policy with them for their idolatry and disobedience of the Ten Commandments. Israel's captivity can be found in academic history as the main reason for their captor's attaining knowledge of the One True Invisible God.

At this time in history most all of the major nations of the world are void of the knowledge of the Invisible God. The Jews were the people God used to make Himself known to all of mankind. It wasn't hard for other nations to see that Israel, while leaving Egypt, were backed by an invisible force as they conquered territory after territory in their quest to set up their nation in the world. Israel wanted a king like the other nations and God provided.

They wanted wealth and prosperity, and God provided. They eventually paid a price for their power: power often corrupts. Israel lapsed into apostasy and God punished them by allowing the Babylonians to destroy their cities and make them captive. Then they (the Babylonians) dispersed the Israelites to their country and others. God sent the prophet Jeremiah to warn them to mend their ways, but they did not heed the warnings. The seventy years of captivity in the time of Daniel was the beginning of a long journey for Israel.

This was their first major defeat, captivity, and scattering, as promised if they disobeyed God. History shows us they were a conquered people and scattered all over the world time after time. Only as late as 1948 did they become a sovereign nation owning territory once again. Present-day conditions for Israel garner persecution and total destruction of their country. This is the cry from Iran and other ancient enemies.

Looking back, I see Israel's habits and customs were so carnal and ancient; they reflected truly little spiritual life. Looking at the overall history of the Jews, I see God makes selections of certain men to relieve others. Though the individuals God chooses may not be good, those for whom he is chosen must be good, or they can receive no favor from God. For example, Moses. He was chosen as an infant; he could neither be good or bad.

But the nation of Israel at that time was good, and because of their goodness Moses was selected to deliver them. This is free moral agency in action. God created mankind. He gave us all the necessary power to choose to be good. When mankind refused, we then bore the responsibility personally. Mankind is to blame and not God. These actions of bad and evil by mankind is what caused the worldwide flood. The drowning of the Egyptians. The cremation of the Sodomites and the Canaanites destroyed.

This protection and deliverance were drastically changed by the captivities and scattering of the Israelites among the conquering nations. Israel was now exposed to the thinking of other nations. Beginning with Daniel, God revealed His existence, intent, and purpose to the pagan King of the world, Nebuchadnezzar.

As I have told you God started working with individuals and eventually a chosen people, teaching them to govern themselves under His Laws as His people.

But their improprieties and propensity for Idolatry caused them to lose their freedom as a chosen people under the protection of the Invisible God. I see God using Israel's punishment to express His purpose for mankind among other nations, first by the universal diffusion of the Greek language, and then by the conquest of the world by the Romans. The interpretation of the Four World Ruling Empires revealed to Daniel supplies a knowledge of future events and changing conditions of the world.

Ten of the twelve tribes are scattered all over what is now Europe. As of 1948 A. D., the remaining tribes of Judah and Benjamin remain to promote the worship of the Invisible God as a nation from the land of Israel.

THE GENTILE KINGDOMS

*D*aniel gives us an outline of the coming Gentile Kingdoms that will dominate and influence the nations of the world as knowledge and information increases through accumulating cooperation.

This is how God allows the knowledge of Israelites and the Gentile nations to mix and complement each other. What the bible calls the Gentile Kingdoms exposes the prejudice of God's chosen people. Gentile is an English word meaning one who speaks Greek.

The term has come to be interpreted as any nation or person who is non-Jew. People who do not practice Judaism are lumped together under the term Gentile. These Gentile people over power the Jews with their cultures and education. The Gentile influence will dominate world conditions from the time of the Babylonian, Persian, Greek, and Roman kingdoms till the end of mankind's governments. This is the interpretation of the outline in the prophecy of Daniel.

I found it quite amazing that the visions of Daniel about the four world ruling kingdoms are described in analogy that fits the very character of these kingdoms when I look at their history. For example, Greece is compared to a leopard. Alexander the Great conquered more of the known world than the preceding kingdoms at lightning speed. His armies were swift and implemented new tactics and resources never before used.

How could Daniel have made up these analogies that match the character of Greece and Rome before they ever became known to the world? Only God could predict such information. Gentile domination of the world began 557 years before God shows up as a human being. God developed His plan slowly over six millenniums of mankind's activities and choices for living life. Looking back on the history of the World Ruling

Kings and their Empires, I see the God-given right of choice and free moral agency being taken away by the governments of men.

America, the Pilgrims—these are just a few of the struggles for people to remain free to choose their destiny. As these Gentile Kingdoms rose and fell, their influence produced different choices for nations to accept or reject.

This is why I say in the beginning of this story that more wars are fought in the name of religion and political power than for any other reason. We are living near the end of the Divine Plan for mankind to live, make choices, and reach their attainable goals for life. The chaos created by the carnal thinking of men is going to be stopped by the Return of Jesus Christ in the near future.

Look around you. The governments of men are continuing to fail in the Way of Life God intended for His creation. America has lost their moral compass to give proper direction to the other nations of the world. Our currency says, In God We Trust, but our courts are saying The Ten Commandments are now a violation of Civil Rights. America has become a cesspool of immorality, greed, hypocrisy, and spineless leadership slowly diminishing free spirit.

We have allowed foreign religions to infect our Judeo-Christian values. America's civil laws are based on the laws of God, not the sharia law of Muslims. Freedom of Religion is not forcing your religious convictions onto the status quo of a nation founded on Christian ethics. Our Christian ethics tolerate differences, but that does not give the people with differences the right to force their laws upon the establishment.

Ezekiel 22:30 And I looked for a man among them, which should make up the hedge, and stand in the gap before me for the land, that I should not destroy it: but I found none.

There are seventeen people running for the GOP presidential nomination for 2016. Why would anyone want to be president of a nation that is 21 trillion dollars in debt, with more people in prison than in churches, and justices that crumble to political correctness instead of supporting the Laws and Precepts this nation is founded upon?

America looks a lot like Ancient Israel and is on a path to self-destruction from within. The second World Empire, the Medes, and Persians, were like their neighbors the Arabians; they had not completely forsaken the patriarchal religion. They did not practice idolatry, and a tolerance and respect for Israel's faith developed.

The first restoration of the Jewish nation was financed by their conquerors. This began after the Babylonian Empire fell to the Persians. The Persians were influenced by the Faith of the Jews and were against idolatry for a time. The fact that the book of Esther is placed books ahead of the prophets causes some people to miss the significance of its content related to history. It is after the fall of Babylon and during the Persian Empire the Story of Esther takes place.

Similar to the story of Joseph, Esther, a Jewish woman, ends up marrying King Xerxes of Persia and saves Israel from a conspiracy for destruction. There is a temporary relationship between the Gentile nations and the Jews. This cooperation was achieved because of the influence of God's way of life on the Gentiles.

Again, God worked through human beings to keep His chosen people within His concern for them down through history.

Esther 1:1-5 now it came to pass in the days of Ahasuerus, (this is Ahasuerus which reigned, from India even unto Ethiopia, over an hundred and seven and twenty provinces) (2) That in those days, when the king Ahasuerus sat on the throne of his kingdom, which was in Shushan the palace, (3) In the third year of his reign, he made a feast unto all his princes and his servants; the power of Persia and Media, the nobles and princes of the provinces, being before him: (4) When he showed the riches of his glorious kingdom and the honor of his excellent majesty many days, one hundred and fourscore days. (5) And when these days were expired, the king made a feast unto all the people that were present in Shushan the palace, both unto great and small, seven days, in the court of the garden of the king's palace.

Remember, I told you that the Hebrew names of the same kings is different in academic history. King Ahasuerus (Xerxes is his Persian name) was in the third year of his reign, which was 484-483 B. C.

ZOROASTOR

*D*uring these times, a man named Zoroaster became an influence of reform, his attempt at enhancing the influence of the Jews on the Gentiles. Zoroaster was a type of Moses. Zoroaster fought to merge Jewish doctrines for acceptance into Gentile culture.

However, he was not called by God to this mission; it proved to be his own carnal attempt at reform. Zoroaster availed himself of the true revelation for his version of the true principles of faith in an Invisible God.

He did this with a mixture of base and noble motives, to help the Empire and reflect glory upon himself. His success is teaching a simple and sublime theology based on the theology of Moses.

Remember, sheep in wolves clothing has been an operation of carnal men for centuries. Deriving from Moses, the concept of One Living God as Invisible Creator of heaven and earth, Zoroaster's doctrines appealed to the Jews.

The doctrines are corrupt and end up sanctifying crimes and follies of carnal men. The end result is a religion of Judaism combined with Persian religion. This is what happened to Christianity after the time of Jesus.

The Persian Empire's king, Cyrus, was influenced by Zoroaster's teachings. Therefore, Cyrus was sympathetic toward his Jewish captives and willing to help them restore their temple and city. Zoroaster's disciples were known as Magi. They were the teachers and priests exerting powerful influence on the states.

Darius Hystaspes was Cyrus's son-in-law and successor to this king. Darius and Xerxes (influenced by his wife Esther) marched upon the nations to destroy any form of idols or idolatrous temples. This explains the eventual conflict and overpowering of the Greek, Alexander the Great, becoming the third world ruling Empire.

This may be boring, but I feel it sets the stage for understanding the coming events in the Biblical timeline of events of History and in our future. Again, the Bible gives purpose and motive for most of the secular history we study. The Bible is telling us with history and personal encounters that we are born for a purpose and destiny.

The biblical information can give us answers for the reason we are born into this chaos and daily struggle for success and happiness.

The next dominating Empire on the world scene is Greece. God allowed the Greeks to influence the world with a higher education of culture and information. They were intellectually curious, and by this need to know they presented the world with philosophical intelligence, with a deeper understanding of life and awareness of our mental capabilities to learn and understand many things. Their presence and influence raised the quality of life in an ancient world to a more civilized standard of living.

Beginning with their innovative machines and swiftness, they conquered more of the known world than the earlier empires.

THE EMPIRE OF GREECE

Alexander the Great did more in twelve years to affect the future of the world than any other person. He combined his genius and learning with valor and superior military and cultural conduct. He entered Asia with a sword in one hand and the book of Homer in the other, as an armed leader of culture, art, and civilization. Schools of philosophy and academies of learning were left behind everywhere he set foot to conquer. He carried the soul of Greece and the Greek language to the largest part of humanity in existence in his time.

In twelve years, the Greek language and literature was set up in every city of the known world. The Mediterranean area of the world became Greek. Alexander granted the Jews many favors that were not allowed to other countries he conquered. It became necessary to translate the scriptures into the Greek language in many places, because Greek was the only language spoken.

Here we see God's providence working in the nations of the world. I will not spend more time on Alexander the Great. He is well known in history as the youngest and fastest conqueror of nations who ever lived. His sudden death left the Empire divided among his four generals. This event is prophesied in the eighth chapter of Daniel.

THE ROMAN EMPIRE

The Fourth and longest lasting empire was Rome. Its origin began to manifest in history many years before it becomes a world empire. It spawned from one of the four Generals who fell heir to part of the Grecian Empire of Alexander the Great.

Once again, Israel and the Jews were persecuted by the pagans, as men like Antiochus warred against all the nations, conquering, and setting up their iron will over their captors until their siege became the Empire that would influence the world for thousands of years to follow.

In a spiritual sense Roman influence is still within western cultural traditions. The next part of my journey in historic foundational information is what has helped me to understand the reason for the many diverse Christian religions and churches in existence today.

It is especially important background information for understanding the contradictions, confusion, and controversy that rise out of religious opinions and churches. The Roman Empire exerts more influence upon the world by force than the Greeks ever do with their learning and philosophy.

The prophet Daniel characterizes the Romans to be the masters of the world. Their love of conquest and military glory became the extension of their dominion over foreign nations, and the Roman influence is to this day a large part of most civilizations.

We live by Roman-named days of the week, months of the year, and many other lasting cultural characteristics and traditions from the Roman Empire and its many philosophies. Roman days start and end at midnight. From the beginning of time until Roman influence, God's day starts and ends from sunset to sunset. I have come to see this little change in man's belief causing a lot of contradictions in timelines and understanding events in the bible.

The Roman Empire is the fourth kingdom referred to in the book of Daniel. It is described to be the most dreadful and influential carnal power over mankind. This begins from its establishment, until mankind's empires and governments are completely destroyed by God. Its power and influence, civil and religious, is dominant in all of Western civilization to this very day.

The Eastern culture is still resistant to its influence on some degree. However, modern times of communication and technology have let some of it slowly creep into their cultures. The countries under the rule of dictators still resist the form of Roman democracy for their peoples.

Communistic and socialistic countries still exist in Eastern and Middle Eastern parts of the world. God gave Daniel the only overall view of the plan for the governments of mankind.

In the ninth chapter of Daniel, we find what biblical scholars call the Seventy Weeks Prophecy. It is a nutshell outline of events that are predicted to involve the Israelite Jews up to the 1st appearance of Christ and on through time until Christ comes the second time.

As most all prophecy, this prophecy is mysterious in its language. The mystery is because it is written in metaphors created with the use of animals and geographical phenomenon of those times.

Modern day prophets, which I believe there are none, would use many of modern inventions and terms. This does not mean it is impossible to interpret. There are many diverse and varied interpretations by biblical scholars. I have found that a little of each different interpretation holds some truth about the prophecy.

The significance of this particular prophecy confirms the timeline of the predicted Messiah, sets the stage for His message for all nations while He is here, and reveals His intentions for all nations when He returns sometime in the future. There are many details for the interpretation of this prophecy.

INSET:

There is one bit of information I believe is noteworthy before we study this prophecy. When prophecy is speaking to Israelites, Jews, or the term God's people, I believe it also is speaking to Christian believers. This is in the sense of what the Apostle Paul says about all people who believe in Christ. Paul refers to us as spiritual Israelites.

Romans 9:24-26 Even us, whom he hath called, not of the Jews only, but also of the Gentiles? (25) As he said also in Hosea, I will call them my people, which were not my people; and her beloved, which was not beloved. (26) And it shall come to pass, that in the place where it was said unto them, you are not my people; there shall they be called the children of the living God. (Spiritual Israelites)

This is not a new teaching introduced by the apostle Paul. He is actually quoting from the prophet Hosea.

Hosea 2:23 And I will sow her unto me in the earth; and I will have mercy upon her that had not obtained mercy; and I will say to them which were not my people, thou art my people; and they shall say, Thou art my God.

Christians often discount the words of the prophets because their writings are in the Old Testament. She whom God sows is the Church, of whom God speaks as her because she is the Mother of the faithful. He does not say in their own land (i.e., Judea), but the earth. The whole earth is to be the seed plot of the Church, where God will sow her to Himself, plant, show, cause her to increase, and multiply her mightily. At one and the same time those promises are fulfilled in Christ; the one through the other.

Israel is not multiplied by itself but through the bringing in of the Gentiles. Nor is Israel alone or chiefly brought into a new relationship with God. The same words promise the same mercy to both, Jew, and Gentile. There seems to be more affection in the brief answer, You are my God. This sums up the whole relationship of the creature to the Creator in one Hebrew word, Elohai, my God.

The prophet declares, as before, when God calls them His people, they by His grace will obey His call and surrender themselves to Him. In this context, the church is a spiritual organism and we Christians are Spiritual Israelites today.

John 4:23-24 But the hour cometh, and now is, when the true worshippers shall worship the Father in spirit and in truth: for the Father seeks such to worship him. (24) God is a Spirit: and they that worship him must worship him in spirit and in truth.

God is now looking for, by the ministry of his Son, and the gift of His Spirit, those who approach Him. This should be done with a deeply felt need and true affection, in your spirit, not in ritualistic ceremony; and expressed in truth, not in hypocritical or heartless profession.

This is another sign of the high truth taught by Jesus Christ while on the earth. I will take some time here to briefly explain the outline in the 9th chapter of Daniel. It illustrates the longevity of the Roman Empire's birth, death, and resurrection in history up to present day. Though it is a latent influence today, it will become a major influence in a religious manner before the second return of Christ.

THE SEVENTY WEEKS PROPHECY

aniel 9:24-27 Seventy weeks are decided upon thy people and upon thy holy city, to finish the transgression, and to make an end of sins, and to make reconciliation for iniquity, and to bring in everlasting righteousness, and to seal up the vision and prophecy, and to anoint the most Holy. (25) Know therefore and understand, that from the going forth of the commandment to restore and to build Jerusalem unto the Messiah the Prince shall be seven weeks, And threescore and two weeks: the street shall be built again, and the wall, even in troublous times. (26) And after threescore and two weeks shall Messiah be cut off, but not for himself: and the people of the prince that shall come shall destroy the city and the sanctuary; and the end thereof shall be with a flood, and unto the end of the war desolations are decided. (27) And he shall confirm the covenant with many for one week: And in the midst of the week, he shall cause the sacrifice and the oblation to cease, and for the overspreading of abominations he shall make it desolate, even until the consummation, and that decided shall be poured upon the desolate.

The 70 Weeks prophecy is the only timeline of events the Messiah revealed in the Old Testament. <u>It covers history from the rebuilding of the Jewish temple until Christ returns</u>. It is a snapshot of the redemption and saving of God's people up to the return of Christ until the beginning of the seventh Millennium of Mankind's existence. This and all references to salvation are to be viewed from a spiritual perspective. These are priestly matters, with hidden values and meanings that are understood by a spiritual revelation. It is the priests of God, not the leaders of nations, whom God uses to express His will.

This prophetic time period is calculated by a formula principle from the Bible. The formula reveals the historic record of events from a designated clue in the prophecy. There is nothing mysterious about symbolism of certain numbers in scripture.

It is common knowledge among Bible scholars that God uses specific numbers as a signature of His will. Seventy Weeks is a prophetic symbolism equal to 490 years of time. This is calculated by the formula of one day equals one year. Seven days times seventy weeks are 490 years.

Numbers 14:34 After the number of the days in which ye searched the land, even forty days, each day for a year, shall ye bear your iniquities, even forty years, and ye shall know my breach of promise.

This would be a good time to cover what I learned about numerical significance in the order of God's plans. I will introduce some of the numerical values associated with God's signature. This is a numerical code that makes sense with God's will.

INSET: BIBLICAL NUMERIC CONNECTIONS AND SIGNIFICANCE

Mathematics play a part in all things of the physical and heavenly environment that surrounds us. Musical rhythms are shown by a numerator and denominator, appointing beats per measure of noted symbols. The rotation of the earth creates the light and dark periods of a day from your fixed position on the earth. This becomes the numerical value of a day.

Jesus uses the numerical value of 3 days and 3 nights as a sign for His divine resurrection as the true Son of God.

John 11:9-10 Jesus answered, Are there not twelve hours in the day? If any man walks in the day, he stumbles not, because he sees the light of this world. (10) But if a man walks in the night, he stumbles, because there is no light in him.

[12 hours in daytime + 12 hours in nighttime = 24-hour day. Seven days of creation set the standard for a week.]

Combined with the position of the appearing moon each night, days are calculated into months according to the lunar cycle. The earth's elliptical orbit around the sun combines the days, weeks, and months into years or solar cycles. The Bible uses many numeric repetitions as markers to show specific confirmation of order and design. These numbers show times and signs for calculating things of God for man to mark time and seasons.

God also uses numerical values to set precedence for certain events of prophecy. Following is a list of a few of the significant numbers of repetitious appearance.

The Number ONE: Obvious in things of unity and oneness. One God, Spirit, Lord, body, faith, baptism, and most important; our oneness in the will of God. No significance given to first day of week as anything more than a day.

The Number Three: Usually found in things of validation or completeness. Father, Son, and Holy Spirit at God's Throne in the third heaven, appointing one of three environments called heaven. Only sign Jesus gives for validation as the Messiah, Three days, and nights in the grave as Jonah is the same in the belly of the great fish. Jesus prays three times in Gethsemane, Crucified at three o'clock in the afternoon. Three crosses on Golgotha.

The Number Six: The number of man and humanity. Man is created on the sixth day, six-thousand years of man's government on earth, and the Man of sin or false prophet is number 666.

The Number Seven is the paramount number for God's Word and Plan for humanity. It is the number for completeness and perfection of the things of God. To name a few: seven days of creation, week, feasts of God, annual Holy Days, weeks of harvest, churches, angels to churches, divisions of the Bible, spirits, thunders, seals, trumpets, plagues, bowls of wrath. The Seventh Day weekly Sabbath. Seventy-Weeks Prophecy, a prophecy with seven events. 70 th prophetic week in two periods of time of 3.5 years each. 3.5 x 2=7 years. Day for a year 70th week. The Gospel Witness.

1. 3.5-year Ministry of Christ pre crucifixion.
2. 3.5-year Ministry of Two Witnesses before Second Return of Christ.

The Number Ten: The number of responsibility and law. The Ten Commandments, the tithe or tenth of increase back to God.

The Number Twelve: Associated with appointment, divine anointing, and completeness in foundational government. The twelve tribes of Israel, twelve princes of Ishmael, twelve judges, age of accountability, twelve apostles, twelve gates of pearl, twelve foundations of different precious stones bearing the walls of the Holy City.

The Number Forty: Symbolic of trials and testing. Christ's temptation period from Satan, forty days and nights, Jesus appears to the disciples forty days following resurrection, Forty years from crucifixion to destruction of Jerusalem. The life of Moses can be characterized in Forties, Forty years in Egypt, Forty in the dessert, Forty years in the wilderness. Moses was Forty days on Mount Sinai with God. Jewish punishment, 40 designated stripes, thirty-nine administered.

The Number Fifty: Redemption and release, Old Testament jubilee = 50 years with the choice of release from slavery or continue a lifetime service commitment. Pentecost = redemption 50 th day of First Fruits harvest season. There are many other numbers of significance not listed here, but I think we get the picture. God is the Master Creator of everything, and mathematics is part of the identity of God's mighty works. Every scientific discovery is a process of numerical values and formulas of numbers to help us arrive at discovery.

The words of the Bible do not originate in the minds of the human authors. The words come from God's Spirit through the human authors. These numbers are significant in revealing spiritual information of the bible.

2Timothy 3:16 All Scripture is given by inspiration of God, and is profitable for doctrine, for reproof, for correction, for instruction in righteousness:

Without impairing the intelligence, individuality, or personal feelings of the human authors, God, through the power of the Holy Spirit, directs the writing of the Bible as a correct record of His comprehensive and infallible revelation to humanity. The Bible is an educating power with no equal. To the extent, the Bible is studied, and its teaching received, it creates strength of, noble ambition, keenness in belief, and sound judgment. The one day is equal to one year formula confirms a time-line of events related to the prophesies from God.

There are aspects to the 70 Weeks Prophecy which outline the plan of God for mankind. These are found in the last 4 verses of the 9 th chapter of Daniel. 70 weeks are decided—a time limit of the events concerning

God's people: A specific time period is decided upon the chosen people and their city.

1. Finish the transgression: Jesus raises the law to spiritual level to clean up the moral and religious corruption of the Jews.

2. Make and end of sins: Jesus supplies the means to bring a stop to sin by His sacrifice.

3. Make reconciliation for iniquity: His sacrifice creates the expiation for the penalty of sin and immoral conduct upon repentance.

4. Bring in everlasting righteousness: Reference to the end time Kingdom of God to be set up upon the earth for a thousand years.

5. Seal up the vision and prophecy: Fulfill these events to cause the prophecy to be valid and complete its predictions.

6. Anoint the Most Holy: Here is a visionary description of the throne room where the Father is sitting. It tells of the Son of man, Jesus Christ, coming to the Ancient of Days, the Father. The Father then turns over to Jesus the Kingdom of God on earth for a thousand years. The Millennium.

The passage in Daniel also compares to the Revelation of the Worthy Lamb of God to Judge and rule the kingdom. Verse 25 begins the timeline of the events that will happen to fulfill the prophecy.

From the command to restore and rebuild Jerusalem until the time the Messiah appears upon the earth is a total of 69 weeks or 483 years.

The 7 weeks is referring to the 49 years of restoring the temple, city, and walls surrounding the city.

Troublous times is a reference to when Nehemiah had to arm his workers to fight while building the walls.

Verse 26 outlines the events leading up to the Messiah and events soon after His ascension to heaven. After 62 weeks signifies the time of the crucifixion of Jesus Christ the Messiah.

The 62 weeks must be added to the 7 weeks of verse 25. This equals the 69 weeks of the 70 weeks determined. Once in the middle of the weekly cycle Jesus is cut-off by crucifixion.

That would be a Wednesday, not the traditional Good Friday ordered by the Catholic Church to be recognized as the day of crucifixion.

The Catholics do not recognize the Annual Sabbath of the 1st day of Unleavened Bread is not the weekly 7th day Sabbath. The first 3.5 years into the 70th prophetic week Jesus is cut off not for Himself, signifying that Christ is sacrificed for all of humanity's sins.

Duality, middle of the literal weekly cycle and the middle of the Prophetic 70th week. The remaining 3.5 years of the 70th week will be fulfilled by the two witnesses of Revelation the

11th chapter. They will perform the witness of the true Christ, during the Great Tribulation, prior to His return to earth!

The first sentence of verse 26 is the end of Messiah's first advent when He is sacrificed for all the sins of mankind, the ending of the sacrificial system added because of Israel's sins.

Jeremiah 31:31-32 Behold, the days come, says the LORD, that I will make a new covenant with the house of Israel, and with the house of Judah: (32) Not according to the covenant that I made with their fathers in the day that I took them by the hand to bring them out of the land of Egypt; which my covenant they brake, although I was an husband unto them, says the LORD:

The last part of verse 26 is referring to the people of the prince as an insert to the end-time overall framework referring to the destruction of the temple and sanctuary of the Jews in 70 A.D. by Titus and the Romans which Jesus predicted to His disciples before His crucifixion. Flood showing the Roman army decimates the Jewish way of life and leaves them in astonished destruction and scattered throughout the Gentile nations.

Just like the flooding current of a river of water cutting into the nations scattering and destroying them. Verse 27 outlines the ministry of the Messiah both former and latter times of Christ's appearance upon earth. Christ confirms His saving power during the Prophetic 70th Week, which is a total of 7 years. The first 3.5 years during Christ's first appearance. The last 3.5 years by the Two Witnesses at the end time before Christ's second return.

The key-word is consummation; which in the Greek language is, kâlâh, pronounced kaw-law' a completion; adverbially completely; also, destruction: - altogether, (be, utterly) consume (- d), consummation (-ption), was decided, (full, utter) end, riddance. This completion and riddance of man's governments does not happen until Christ's second return.

Christ causes the sacrifices and oblations to cease as He becomes the ultimate sacrifice for humanity in 30 A.D. The first of the 70th Prophetic week begins at the end of His 3.5-year ministry ending in 30 A.D. on the Cross. Because it is a prophetic scenario, the last 3.5 years reconciling ministry will be fulfilled by His Two Witnesses near the second return of Jesus Christ sometime in the 21st century. In the interim years between, Jesus refers to Jerusalem being trodden down by the Gentiles. This is reference from Babylonian domination (604 B. C.) and foreign interferences upon Jerusalem, known Times of the Gentiles, until Christ's second return.

Luke 21:24 And they shall fall by the edge of the sword and shall be led away captive into all nations: and Jerusalem shall be trodden down of the Gentiles, until the times of the Gentiles be fulfilled.

This is how ever long God decides to allow the governments of mankind to continue until He commissions the Two Witnesses who will speak for Christ.

Revelation 11:3 And I will give power unto my two witnesses, and they shall prophesy a thousand two hundred and threescore days, clothed in sackcloth. God will then send Jesus back to earth to bring the confusion and corruption of man's governments and wars to a conclusion.

Revelation 19:11-13 And I saw heaven opened and behold a white horse; and he that sat upon him was called Faithful and True, and in righteousness he doth judge and make war. (12) His eyes were as a flame of fire, and on his head were many crowns; and he had a name written, that no man knew, but he himself. (13) And he was clothed with a vesture dipped in blood: and his name is called The Word of God.

For the abominations of the wicked Christ will completely destroy the wicked and the system of religion that fosters such deceit and wickedness.

Revelation 19:15-16 and out of his mouth goes a sharp sword, that with it he should smite the nations: and he shall rule them with a rod of iron: and he treads the winepress of the fierceness and wrath of Almighty God. (16) And he hath on his vesture and on his thigh a name written, KING OF KINGS, AND LORD OF LORDS.

In a sense, this 70-weeks prophecy mirrors the overall outline of the Gentile kingdoms portrayed in the Image of Nebuchadnezzar in the 2ⁿᵈ chapter of Daniel.

Daniel 2:44-45 And in the days of these kings shall the God of heaven set up a kingdom, which shall never be destroyed: and the kingdom shall not be left to other people, but it shall break in pieces and consume all these kingdoms, and it shall stand for ever. (45) Forasmuch as thou saw that the stone was cut out of the mountain without hands, and that it breaks in pieces the iron, the brass, the clay, the silver, and the gold; the great God hath made known to the king what shall come to pass hereafter: and the dream is certain, and the interpretation thereof sure.

I realize this is quite a bit of detail, but it truly is only the highlights of the information. There is an intense amount of math and calculation, along with many companion scriptural references that confirm the prophetic information. It is an important part of my personal study to help me get somewhat of a grip on the overall plan God has for mankind.

It is what has been in my mind since I first understood it as a teenager at the dining room table of our home in 1964 during family bible study. These two scriptures, Daniel 2:44 and Revelation 19:11, have been what I hope to live to see or be a part of if I live or die before the time comes! Moving on:

Daniel 12:8-13 And I heard, but I understood not: then said I, O my Lord, what shall be the end of these things? (9) And he said, go thy way, Daniel: for the words are closed up and sealed till the time of the end. (10) Many shall be purified, and made white, and tried; but the wicked shall do wickedly: And none of the wicked shall understand; but the wise shall understand. (11) And from the time that the daily sacrifice shall be taken away, and the abomination that makes desolate set up, there shall be a thousand two hundred and ninety days. (12) Blessed is he that waits, and cometh to the thousand three hundred and five and thirty days. (13) But go thou thy way till the end be: for thou shalt rest and stand in thy lot at the end of the days.

These last few verses from Daniel's writings tell us to look at the things Jesus says in Matthew: 24 and what He reveals to the apostle John;

John writes them in the last book of the bible, The Revelations. This is an important piece of the puzzle that helps me to understand and achieve a peace of mind about how things will eventually be completed for me. Even if I die before these events happen, I will be with Jesus at the proper time. (More about this later in my story.)

Daniel is incredibly special to God. He lives to be in his 80s and is promised to stand with God someday in the future. It is no small thing that God sent one of the only two archangels to speak with Daniel concerning this overview of God's plan of events for mankind.

Daniel 9:21-23 Yea, whiles I was speaking in prayer, even the angel Gabriel, whom I had seen in the vision at the beginning, being caused to fly swiftly, touched me about the time of the evening oblation. (22) And he informed me, and talked with me, and said, O Daniel, I am now come forth to give thee skill and understanding. (23) At the beginning of thy supplications the commandment came forth, and I am come to shew thee; for thou art beloved: therefore, understand the matter, and consider the vision.

This is not to say the other Old Testament prophets are any less in the importance of their messages from God. They all hold pieces of the puzzle that makes up the plan for mankind's destiny. Daniel is given prophetic information by God relating to the future, but Daniel is not given the details of the end times. They are sealed until Jesus reveals them to John the apostle in 100 A. D.

Daniel 12:8-9 And I heard, but I understood not: then said I, O my Lord, what shall be the end of these things? (9) And he said, go thy way, Daniel: for the words are closed up and sealed till the time of the end.

Daniel is instructed to go on his way and not fret about the end time events. He is told he will stand with the saints at the end time days.

INSET

Before I move on, I wish to point out that it is during the last days of Daniel's life that the Book of Esther is written. Her saving of the complete destruction of the Jews is a great story and by no accident does she become the wife of Xerces (Ahasuerus, Hebrew name). Also, the books of Ezra and Nehemiah are written during this time of favor from the Medes and Persians towards the Jews after the conquering of Babylon.

MALACHI

*M*alachi, last of the Old Testament prophets from writings of the Old Testament. Malachi helps me to understand the things that happen with the coming of the Messiah and why the Jews respond to Him in the manner they do. It gives a hint of what God is looking for today in people who choose to believe in Him and His plan for mankind.

There is a 400-year silence in history from inspired people about the Invisible God. There are some historical writings from these silent years; however, that are not included in canonized scriptures. Why? I can only say, when I read the Apocryphal Books, I find them to be less inspirational and more academic writings of men, with political thoughts driving them.

They appear to me as a collection of information documenting the struggles of the Jewish nation under the Roman domination of the Cesar's whims and the writer's agenda. Malachi's writings are a stern warning against priests and leaders of the Jewish nation. A formal accusation to return to the patriarchal Fathers' worship of the Invisible God.

His writings encourage me as I read them. This is because of the hope they present for anyone who will esteem the Invisible God as the righteous source of true living. They also predict the conditions of the world when Christ returns in the future. It is what the spiritual church understands.

Malachi 3:16-18 then they that feared the LORD spoke often one to another: and the LORD hearkened, and heard it, and a book of remembrance was written before Him for those that fear the LORD, and that think upon his name. (17) And they shall be mine, says the LORD of hosts, in that day when I make up my jewels; and I will spare them, as a man spares his own son that serves him. (18) Then shall ye return, and discern between the righteous and the wicked, between him that serves God and him that serves him not.

It may not be clear to you just yet, and it wasn't to me until I finished a thorough study of the New Testament information. Verse 18 is a clue to one of the two destinies available for us as God's created humans. The book of remembrance will be addressed later in this book.

Malachi writes about the last half of the Fifth Century B.C. His name means My Messenger, an abbreviated translation of Messenger of the Lord. Malachi is a John the Baptist of the Old Testament, warning the Jews to get ready for the coming savior.

As the final words of the Old Testament, it is a comparison to a type of Elijah we will see in John the Baptist. This is information that should help the Jews recognize the coming Messiah.

Malachi 3:1 Behold, I will send my messenger, and he shall prepare the way before me: and the Lord, whom ye seek, shall suddenly come to his temple, even the messenger of the covenant, whom ye delight in: behold, he shall come, says the LORD of hosts.

The chosen people of the Exodus, the Israelites, are not prepared for Christ's first Coming. The messenger is the same whom Isaiah has foretold, and Malachi quotes from the prophet Isaiah.

Isaiah 40:3 "The voice of one crying in the wilderness, Prepare ye the way of the Lord, make straight in the desert a highway for our God.

Luke_1:76. "Thou, child," is the prophecy on John the Baptizer's birth, "shalt be called the prophet of the Highest, for thou shalt go before the face of the Lord to prepare His way, to give knowledge of salvation unto His people, for the remission of their sins."

Repentance is to be the conditional attitude for preparing for citizenship in the kingdom of Christ the Messiah, for whom they look so impatiently.

Now, Roman domination of the world is well set up. Even with the murder of the Roman Emperor, the empire keeps control of its conquered nations, including Judea. The Jews are about to be scattered among the nations as foretold by the prophets of old. The tribe of Judah (Jews) and Benjamin are under the rule of Rome in Palestine.

The second captivity of the Jews occurred in 164 B. C. This was not a dis-locating captivity. Unlike the Babylonians, by the time the Roman Empire ruled the world, Greek and Roman thinking was less restrictive in the conquering of nations. The Romans allowed their conquered nations to rule themselves. This is allowed under Roman oversight, policed by

Roman soldiers. It is a progressive attitude for controlling their enemies after they are subdued by iron clad force.

The Seleucia General, Antiochus, captured the Jewish temple and city in 164 B.C. He then humiliated the Jewish priests by violating their most sacred religious rights. A noble attempt was marshaled by the Jewish Maccabees to stop him, but they were defeated.

In 47 B.C. 18 years after the Empire was official, Julius Caesar appointed Antipater the overseer of Judea. Antipater appointed his son, Herod, to be governor of Galilee. After the murder of Julius Caesar, Herod fled to Rome and is then appointed king of the Jewish nation. This was about 40 B.C. Herod then married into a Jewish family for the appearance of the prophesied messenger and eventual birth of the Messiah.

The Romans allowed the Jews to keep their own form of religion, government, and small army to keep the peace among themselves. This was overseen by at least 100 Roman soldiers stationed in Jerusalem at all times. This Roman army was commanded by a Centurion under a Procurator who is the ruler over any Jewish king and governor.

Religiously speaking, the Jews by this time were void of the sin of Idolatry. Their captivity and desecration of Temple sacraments had turned them back to the ways of the patriarchal Fathers. It is important to point out at this juncture in the timeline history of the Jewish Priests.

After many times of destruction and captivity, the priests reverted to austere reforms of rituals to control and keep their people pure from idolatrous behavior. It is during this time period we can see the first formal church services of Jewish history! The Jews begin the ritual of congregating weekly in the synagogues throughout Judea. This is their solution to keeping the people in constant remembrance of their prescribed way of life. They read from their revised version of the original Pentateuch writings of Moses, calling their version the Torah.

The <u>Torah is their carnal interpretation</u> for application of the laws of Moses. They added over 600 new ritual requirements for worship. This is when the original intent of <u>the laws became radical legalism of the Jewish faith</u>. The radical legalism is a product of religious zealots in the priesthood, applying their interpretation of laws from Moses for the people. It is more political in nature.

Two major parties appeared, the Pharisees and the Sadducees, not unlike our Republican/Democratic parties of today. Remember, there is no separation of religion and state government in the Jewish nation of the historical times. Malachi's warnings are directed at these priests who teach one form of morality and see another themselves—the same issue that Jesus is confronted with while living among them.

Malachi 4:5-6 Behold, I will send you Elijah the prophet before the coming of the great and dreadful day of the LORD: (6) and he shall turn the heart of the fathers to the children, and the heart of the children to their fathers, lest I come and smite the earth with a curse.

The writings of the Old Testament come to an end with a statement of warning to all of mankind. The formal accusation is for people to return to the Ten Commandments for righteous living, not the religious order of the Pharisees.

THE NEW TESTAMENT

The New Testament begins with a brief genealogy concerning Jesus Christ being born of Mary's lineage (Matthew 1:17). So, all the generations from Abraham to David are fourteen generations; and from David until the carrying away into Babylon are fourteen generations; and from the carrying away into Babylon unto Christ are fourteen generations. Here are some interesting things about God's numbers: 14 generations between the main 3 characters. 2 x 7 = 14 The Number Seven is the paramount number for God's Word and Plan for humanity. It is the number for completeness and perfection of the things of God. 3 generations from Abraham to Christ. The Number Three—Usually found in things of validation or completeness. 3 x 14 = 42. The complete years of generations is also 42 ÷ 7 = 6. The Number Six — The number of man and humanity. Man was created on the 6 th day.

The New Testament writings plainly show us that God used devout, righteous, converted men to pen the most important aspects of the witness and testimony of the saving power and faith in Jesus Christ. They document the Way of Life for the Christian Virtues that reflect the presence of Jesus Christ in us before the world.

Six of these men are apostles chosen by Jesus himself. Three are eyewitnesses of Jesus Christ's ministry: Matthew, Peter, and John. Two are brothers of Jesus, James, and Jude.

Paul is personally taught by Jesus for three years through visions. The last two are Mark and Luke.

Luke wrote the Acts of the churches. These men needed no further research, for their writings were true and their lives were given willingly to the Gospel of Jesus Christ and the Spirit of His Prophesies. Their dedication to the Gospel of Jesus Christ ceased only because of their death.

The New Testament is a work in progress during the life of Christ and for at least 70 years after the crucifixion. The Gospels were written and canonized by their authors. The Acts of the Apostles and Epistles or letters of Paul are set in order by Paul, Mark, and Luke. Last of all, the completely New Testament is finished by John, Peter, and James. These three are the close confidantes of Jesus and are entrusted with the preservation of the Gospel.

The New Testament can be characterized as follows: The first four books are the witness account of four different authors. These men testify about the history, works, and words Jesus Christ spoke and taught to the disciples and masses of people while He ministered. They include the confrontation with the evolved religion of the classis of Jews— Priests, Pharisees, Sadducees, and Essenes who perverted the original religion of the Levitical Priesthood under Moses and Aaron.

The Acts of apostles and the administrative order of the church Jesus built through the Holy Spirit filled individuals 50 days after His ascension or the Day of Pentecost. Most of the spreading of this New Covenant religion set up by Christ was carried out by the Apostles, and one Apostle called from among the Jewish Sect of Pharisees personally by Christ after His ascension:

Paul, or Saul of Tarsus. Letters from Paul the Apostle to the Gentile world reveal the finer points and details of the aspects of the new Faith for Christian administrations and living.

A combination of personal books and letters written by specific individuals take their knowledge from their direct experience with Christ. These individuals include James, Peter, John, and Paul's letter specifically sent to the Hebrews. The Revelation of Jesus Christ to John the Apostle concerning the overall future just ahead of him and to the end of God's revealed plan for the overall judgment and redemption of mankind.

THE HUMANITY OF JESUS

At this point in my story, I will express my personal opinion on a very touchy subject about the humanity of Jesus Christ. I will address this now because it is an issue just ahead in this Biblical timeline shortly after His coming and leaving. This will not be an easy read for some people.

(Remember, <u>I report, you decide for yourself</u>; this is my study of world history, science, and the bible to figure out why I was born.) I feel it is important for a deeper understanding and appreciation of God and His plan for the complete transformation of man through the process of salvation.

The Ancient Babylonians Created the Doctrine of the Trinity. Most everyone has heard of the Trinity concept of the Godhead Deity—the 3 in 1 doctrine. Though the specific word, Trinity, is not a part of Holy Writ, the conceptual thought is Father, Son, and Holy Spirit. This teaching and interpretation of Deity has roots from Babylon Mystery Religion. In the unity of that one Only God of the Babylonians, there were three persons, and to symbolize that doctrine of the Trinity, they employed the equilateral triangle; signifying that all three were equal in power.

The Egyptians also used the triangle as the symbol of their tri-form divinity. The history of the Triune Divinity is found in all Babylonian, Egyptian, Roman, Chinese, and Indian temples, and artifacts. The Triune God is depicted with three heads on one body.

In India, this image is Dko Deva Trimurtti—one God, three forms!

In Japan, the Buddhists worship their great image Buddha with Three Heads in the very same form, under the Divine Title, San Pao Fuh.

Isaiah 40:18, 25 to whom then will ye liken God? Or what likeness will ye compare unto him? (25) To whom then will ye liken me, or shall I be equal? Says the Holy One.

The next concept is based on the Hebrew word for God, Elohim. Coupled with a misinterpretation of Psalms 110, it produces concept closer to the truth than the difficulties with the Trinity and the Holy Spirit taught as being a third person in the Godhead.

We must consider that the Psalms are prophetic in nature, and what David expressed about Jehovah and Adonai is in the prophetic context that Jesus Christ is the Lord and Master of mankind and would become the <u>Spiritual form of Melchizedek the High Priest for mankind forever</u>.

Because Jesus was resurrected and born into the God Family, He has neither beginning nor ending of days like humans. Many do not understand the term Melchizedek. It is a Hebrew word combined from two other Hebrew words, melek and tsedeq. First means King or Royalty; the second means righteous or right, naturally moral, or legal. Equity or prosperity—that which is altogether just. Justly.

Elohim is the plural form of the English word God. It can and is all inclusive of all the created and existing Spirit Beings in the God Family.

Some have suggested that the Word found in John: 1 is a "being" that existed beside God Jehovah until It decided to give up Its powers and become a human being. This is based on

John 1:14: The Word became flesh and dwelt among us, and we beheld Him as the only begotten son of God.

But this is only speculation, for it does not say the Word or Logos was a separate intently from God Almighty Jehovah at the beginning of time as we know it. Another support scripture for only two Deities in the very beginning of our time is what Jesus said the night before His crucifixion.

John 17:5: Glorify me with yourself with the glory which I had with you before the world was.

The Greek word here is a baffling wind or power. Christ knew He was a begotten human being from God Almighty and would become the Almighty's <u>FIRST AND ONLY BORN SON</u> into the Pre-existing family of God. Jesus was begotten by God Almighty by the power of God Almighty's word speaking the Holy Spirit power essence and placed into the physical womb of the human host Mary.

At the River Jordan, when the Holy Spirit fell upon Jesus after baptism by John the Baptist, God confirmed Jesus as His <u>BEGOTTEN SON</u> with the voice of an angel from heaven. Jesus knew in His heart that if He fulfilled His destiny as the Pioneer of the salvation process for human beings to become born into spirit children of God, He would have eternal existence from His (now Holy Father) progenitor God Almighty.

The third opinion is from my own study and prayer about the Godhead Deity. I could never justify either of the first two concepts with logic. It says plainly that the Archangel Gabriel told Mary she would become pregnant <u>by the overshadowing of the Holy Spirit</u>. It is difficult to get clinical when talking about Spirit essence, for the Bible and Jesus says it is like the wind. You cannot see it, but you can see its effect.

Now, if the concept of Trinity were a true account of the existence of the Godhead Deity, then the Holy Spirit would be the Father of Jesus and not God Almighty, logically, and clinically speaking.

If the second concept, Two Beings having Holy Spirit power is true, <u>when did the second being decide</u> to give up Spirit form and essence be reduced to the size of an atom and be implanted into Mary's womb? Did God almighty have to talk the second being John calls the Word, or was it a voluntary mission? Either way it is still speculation.

Now, consider what I have studied and thought about for over two years now. First, look at creation scenario itself.

Genesis 1:1 In the beginning God created the heaven and the earth. I have already proven that this happened millions of years before mankind was even a consideration for creating.

Genesis 1:2 And the earth was (became) without form, and void; and darkness was upon the face of the deep. And the Spirit of God moved upon the face of the waters. [Was a mistranslation of the Hebrew word haw yaw meaning "became."] The rest of the chapter uses the words said, called, blessed, let, and commanded. <u>All of these are voice inflected or verbal utterances.</u>

Now John describes in John 1:1 that in the beginning was the Word. Greek for this is Logos, in the Strong's concordance meaning something said, including thought, or a Divine expression. This word is taken from the Greek word Lego, meaning lay forth in words, in systematic discourse after an individual expression or speech respectively, breaking silence.

So, God speaks things into creation. The actual work is performed by the angels who are God's messengers and created beings or workers to fulfill His purpose. God's throne is actually propelled by Angels called Seraphim (Ezekiel 1:1–27). So, in Genesis 1:26, when God says, "Let us make man in our image," he is speaking with the angels who can to this day appear as men walking the earth.

The Old Testament prophets and even Mary describe the angels as a manly form of shimmering and shining light. The angels are the Spiritual extension of God's will when spoken by God. Next, John 1:1. Think of this scripture in this context for a moment.

John 1:1-4 In the beginning was the Word, (God Almighty is the beginning and end of all we know and God Speaks His Word) *and the Word was with God,* (The Word is the word of God Almighty as spoken by Him and comes from Him, therefore it is with Him) *and the Word was God.* (The Word was and is God because it comes from God Almighty as He expresses Himself in Voice)

(2) *The same was in the beginning with God.* (God's Word is always with Him because it comes from Him as He speaks) (3) *All things were made by Him; and without Him was not anything made that was made.* (Yes, Genesis relates God Almighty creates light, plants, animals, mankind, etc. by speaking it from His thoughts and some of it is performed by His Angelic creation.) (4) *In him was life;* (Genesis again, God makes man from the dust of the earth and breathes life into him from Himself!) *and the life was the light of men.* [The life breath of God Almighty is our light or enlightenment to purpose and place in God's creation!]

John 1:14 And the Word was made flesh, and dwelt among us, [Yes, God Almighty spoke His Word and the Power of His Holy Spirit Life impregnated Mary the human host of the FIRST BEGOTTEN SON OF GOD ALMIGHTY.] *And we beheld his glory, the glory as of the only begotten of the Father, full of grace and truth.* <u>Jesus Christ is the WORD.</u> For <u>God, Almighty created Jesus by the Word of His Power</u> just as He spoke and created light, plants, animals, and mankind.

Now, before you burn me at the stake, think about other clues Jesus gives us to support this concept of why <u>Jesus has the pre-eminence over all of mankind and judgment is given to Him as King of King and Lord of Lords.</u>

1 John 4:1-3 Beloved, believe not every spirit, but try the spirits whether they are of God: because many false prophets are gone out into the world. (2) Hereby know ye the Spirit of God: Every spirit that confesses that Jesus Christ is come in the flesh is of God: (3) And every spirit that confesses not that <u>Jesus Christ is come in the flesh</u> is not of God: and this is that spirit of antichrist, whereof ye have heard that it should come; and even now already is it in the world.

Later in this story I will show you about false teachings and scripture tampering, and what some people would have you believe about Jesus as a person begotten by the power of the Holy Spirit in the Host Human Being, Mary. Origen, one of the theologians of history (185-254 A.D.), taught that the Logos or <u>WORD is ktisma, which means Jesus Christ is a created being who does not have eternal existence as God as a created being</u>. In other words, a literal human being like we are! We are created through the process God created to beget human life.

How difficult is it for God to impregnate the human host Mary by speaking the word just as he spoke into creation the things of the earth and recreated the surface of the earth in Genesis 1?

The last sentence in the scripture above says that the Apostle John and others are already aware of conspiracies to undermine the life and gospel of Jesus Christ soon after His ascension to heaven.

Think about this: If Jesus Christ was not a physical human being transformed by God the Father to become His Spiritual Son, we have no legitimate savior.

Hebrews 2:16-18 for verily <u>he took not on him the nature of angels; but he took on him the seed of Abraham</u>. (17) Wherefore in all things it behooves him to be made like unto his brethren, that he might be a merciful and faithful high priest in things about God, to make reconciliation for the sins of the people. (18) For in that he himself hath suffered being tempted, he is able to succor them that are tempted.

Hebrews 5:7 who <u>in the days of his flesh,</u> when he had offered up prayers and supplications with strong crying and tears unto him that was able to save him from death and was heard in that he feared.

This next scripture is what the writer of Hebrews is referring too:

Matthew 26:38-42 then said he unto them, my soul is exceeding sorrowful, even unto death: tarry ye here, and watch with me. (39) And he went a little further, and fell on his face, and prayed, saying, O my Father, if it be possible, let this cup pass from me: nevertheless, not as I will, but as thou wilt. (40) And he cometh unto the disciples, and finds them asleep, and said unto Peter, What, could ye not watch with me one hour? (41) Watch and pray, that ye enter not into temptation: the spirit indeed is willing, but the flesh is weak. (42) He went away again the second time, and prayed, saying, O my Father, if this cup may not pass away from me, except I drink it, thy will be done.

I see Jesus agonizing over His impending death for the sins of the world. His fleshly body and organic brain cells which medical science proves is the soul of a person doesn't want to die. Jesus knew He was about to die as a human being. But His human spirit—sustained by blood, oxygen, and brain cells, transformed by the Holy Spirit which was begotten in Him from God at the baptism by John—said, "Not my will [his human spirit], but your will, Father God." [God's Spirit will.]

Jesus trusted God completely to save Him and place His Spirit into a Spiritual Body. More about the clinical aspects of human spirit and holy Spirit later as I discuss the Alpha, Beta, Delta, and Theta waves the work inside and outside our bodies.

For Jesus to be the sacrifice for the sins of all flesh and be the pioneer of the process of salvation for human beings, His physical body had to die for His Spirit to be housed in a Spiritual body as a literal born child of God. He had to be made of flesh and blood like unto us. Not only this fact, but it is often overlooked that <u>Jesus made His decision to give His life for us by His own free will</u>. *John 10:17-18 therefore doth my Father love me, because I lay down my life, that I might take it again. (18) No man taketh it from me, but I lay it down of myself. I have power to lay it down, and I have power to take it again. This commandment have I received of my Father.*

God told the human being, Jesus, that it would be His choice to complete the process or to fail the mission. This was heavy information and the ultimate burden for a human being to carry on his physical brain cells. No wonder the bible describes him with sweat drops of blood as he agonized the mission while praying in the garden.

This is why Jesus only has the preeminence of being the <u>Firstborn Son of God</u>. The Jews were incredibly careful to ensure there was no attempt at fraud in the claim of a person born of a woman to become the Messiah. Remember, the Jews were in charge of the oracles concerning God. They kept a meticulous accounting of every event concerning the priests and order of worship in their religious government over their people. Likewise, the Romans were very meticulous record keepers of their leaders and officials in charge of all the governing activities of the Roman Empire. This supplies a reliable source of information and timeline for events between the Jews and Romans.

The Gospel accounts of these times can be verified by a comparison of these Civil and academic records with the writings of Matthew, Mark, Luke, and John. I do not wish to bore you with the details of information dealing with the approximate time the Christ Child was born.

The birth of Jesus has always been dated as sometime between 6-4 B.C.; there is proof that 5 B.C. is the year of His birth. His birth occurred in the year between the suggested span of years. The birth of Jesus Christ is part of the foundational cornerstone of true Christianity. An abundance of scriptural and historical information proves Jesus was not born on December 25 The correct season for the date of the birth of the savior is not essential to personal salvation.

However, proving the logical time of in conjunction with the many prophesies of the Messiah's predicted birth can supply the believer deep insight into the truth and accuracy of the Bible. It confirms the meaning of the life, mission on earth, and future events, of Jesus the Christ are from Divine Intervention.

It requires an Indiana Jones–type of zealous ambition to prove things from the Bible. While discovery takes place, the evidence must be factual truth defining the treasure's worth and confirms the deep things of God. Evidence can be explored to produce the logical and probable time of Christ's birth.

John 1:1-3 In the beginning was the Word, and the Word was with God, and the Word was God. (2) The same was in the beginning with God. (3) All things were made by him; and without him was not anything made that was made.

John 1:14 And the Word was made flesh, and dwelt among us, (and we beheld his glory, the glory as of the only begotten of the Father,) full of grace and truth.

God the creator speaks into creation the physical things we can see and touch, and God said let there be light; and God said let there be a child in the womb of Mary. Through the power of the invisible God's Holy Spirit power, He created all we can see.

What an impressive revelation. How fitting for the Invisible God to eventually create by the power of His Word a physical human being to come and sacrifice His physical existence for His most precious creation, mankind.

The Biblical narrative reads in highpoints as a chronology of events preceding and after the births of both John the Baptist and Jesus the Christ. I will not bore you with the many details and various aspects that narrow down the date of His birth to September of 5 B.C. There is so much calculating and comparing of records both Roman and Jewish to be expressed.

His birth time can be proved from bible narrative, astronomy, and Roman records. It is not my intent to debate this issue of the birth of the Savior and the way He was begotten. I simply wish to tell you there is factual information from the personal records of the Civil Roman archives, the Jewish Talmud, and a biblical timeline producing the logical season and year the Savior is born. Just this past year, 2015, we saw two complete eclipses of the moon, one in the spring and one in the fall. The same astrological event happened the year John the Baptist and Jesus were born.

This is found in the writings of Josephus the Jewish historian. These total eclipses of the moon occur only about every 1,900 or so years. Interesting, don't you think? We are all familiar with the Christmas version of the birth, passed down through the European culture and carried over to America. It is a sweet story but is not the factual timeline of the birth of the Messiah extrapolated from true history.

BIRTH OF THE MESSIAH

The night of the birth of the Messiah is a fact of eyewitnesses and history. The following is a paraphrase of actual records from the Jewish Civil Talmud.

The shepherds watching their flocks that night, are bedded down around small fires. Some are tending the sheep and others are asleep. Those sleeping are awakened by the others asking questions. What is going on? How come it so light and this is only the 3rd watch of the night? (3rd watch would be around 9 P.M.)

Suddenly the air seems filled with human voices saying, "Glory! Glory! Glory to the Highest God!" "Happy are you Bethlehem, for tonight God is fulfilling His promise to the Fathers; and the King is born that shall rule in righteousness!"

These strains of sound rise up into the heavens, then sinking down in mellow strains along the foothills of the nearby mountains as they die away in a soft melodious sounds up into the heavens. These strange, yet moving voices, repeat again,

several times. In conjunction with these voices, the light seems to burst out in the sky and descend in softer rays lighting the hills and valley, making everything visible as the light of day, clear as the light of the brightest moon! At first, the shepherds are very afraid, then they feel a calmness in their spirit. This calmness becomes an emotional feeling of needing to give thanks more than anything else. As the city is affected by these events, the people awake and come out of their homes.

Some are exclaiming, "the world is on fire!" Some cry out, "the gods are coming down to destroy us!" Others shout, "A star has fallen!" Melker, a Jewish priest comes out of his parish shouting and clapping his hands frantic with joy.

The people gather around him, and he tells them it is the sign that God is coming to fulfill the promises made to their Father Abraham! Melker reminds the people that fourteen hundred years ago, God had appeared to Abraham, promising if the people of Abraham, Isaac, and Jacob would be faithful and obedient, He will send them a Savior to redeem them from their sins!

After Melker speaks the people with a loud voice, he and all the old Jews go to the local synagogue and remain there praising God and giving thanks! Melker lived for a while in India, and his father is priest at Antioch. This is where Melker studies the Jewish faith and the sacred scrolls most all his life. He tells how he remembers the Old Testament scrolls predicting this time will come and the Jews will be saved from their sins and Roman oppression.

Melker is a man of great learning and is well respected among the people. He says that these physical sounds and lights are declared in the prophecies for announcing the birth of the Messiah! In the past, some virgins have pretended to be with child by the Holy Spirit. However, at the time of their delivery there is no light from the heavens, no angels talking in the clouds and declaring their child is the Messiah! These events and rhetoric are a brief summary taken from an ancient letter written by Melker, the Priest of the synagogue in Bethlehem. He sent this letter to the Higher Sanhedrin of the Jews at Jerusalem.

I am telling you this because I want you to remember this is an eyewitness account from the city of Bethlehem to the High Priests of Jerusalem. Think of this Melker, priest of Bethlehem, as a governor of a state in America, sending a report to the congress at Washington DC.

Following is what Melker says as he ends his report. "Noble Masters of the Sanhedrin, I am not alone. I am not the only witness of these things. The principle people of Bethlehem see them and hear them as I do." Melker goes on to say, "What is occurring here in Bethlehem will settle the question of the day when our redemption will be drawing near. This redemption is promised to the patriarchal fathers of the "covenant people"! It is part of our religion in prophecy presented by the Old Testament prophets! I believe in this event of the last few days; these prophecies are being fulfilled! By the two events; Birth of John the Baptist and Birth of Jesus! Let the spirit of prophecy bear us on with the prophet to the future times far beyond the kingdoms of men. It is the spirit of the invisible God that sets the tongue of the prophet on fire! Those prophets see clearly, long before the event, the gathering light; the travailing of the virgin, the helpless infant in the manger; they hear the mighty chanting of the heavenly host; they predict the ultimate sacrifice for mankind!" "The whole body of prophecy is telling us that the kingdoms of men of this world become subject to the kingdom of the Savior of all mankind! How can men who live in different ages of the world, men that do not consult with each other, have no personal interest in the subject, men who jeopardize and some lose their lives over such utterances of these prophecies? How can they point out the place, the time, and the names of the parties so plain and clear? This information is revealed to them by the invisible God we serve! There is no other explanation but divine providence to reveal and predict the time of such an event!"

Melker spoke and wrote of what he saw with conviction and a foundational knowledge of the scriptures available during his time. His conviction says, <u>I was there, I saw it, it happened</u>.

The expectation of a remarkable personage is universally prevalent among the Jews at the time of the birth of Jesus Christ. The coming Messiah was perceived to be a prophet like unto Moses, but even greater. The birth of a Messiah had been predicted centuries before the actual event. There is a lengthy list of scriptures that reach back as far as the writing of Moses that eluded to a coming Messiah.

Genesis 49:10 The scepter shall not leave from Judah, nor a lawgiver from between his feet, until Shiloh come; and unto Him shall the gathering of the people be.

The reference is to a progeny that would someday come from the linage of Judah that would remove the ruling authority from the Jews and allow all people to come to the authority of God through Jesus Christ.

Deuteronomy 18:15 The LORD thy God will raise up unto thee a Prophet from the midst of thee, of thy brethren, like unto me; unto him ye shall hearken.

Deuteronomy 18:18-19 I will raise them up a Prophet from among their brethren, like unto thee, and will put my words in his mouth; and he shall speak unto them all that I shall command him. (19) And it shall happen, that whosoever will not hearken unto my words which he shall speak in my name, I will need it of him.

These are references from Moses to a coming Messiah who would also, like Moses, set up God's law among the people. In fact, Jesus raised the law to a spiritual status, ignoring the over six hundred added laws the Pharisees added during the 400 years of silence.

John 5:45-47 do not think that I will accuse you to the Father: there is one that accuses you, even Moses, in whom ye trust. (46) For had ye believed Moses, ye would have believed me: for he wrote of me. (47) But if ye believe not his writings, how shall ye believe my words?

This is a direct reference to the scriptures in Genesis and Deuteronomy from Jesus. One of the most quoted references is found in Isaiah. It is often read at Christmas time, announcing the coming birth of the Messiah. It also includes a reference to what I said about the throne of David lasting forever, in what I learned from Daniel's interpretation of Nebuchadnezzar's dream concerning kingdoms that would be set up. (That throne is currently occupied by the British Monarchy.)

Isaiah 9:6-7 For unto us a child is born, unto us a son is given: and the government shall be upon his shoulder: and his name shall be called Wonderful, Counsellor, The mighty God, The everlasting Father, The Prince of Peace. (7) Of the increase of his government and peace there shall be no end, upon the throne of David, and upon his kingdom, to order it, and to set up it with judgment and with justice from henceforth even forever. The zeal of the LORD of hosts will perform this.

This is a key prophecy for the eventual coming of Jesus Christ to earth in our future. There are many other prophesies and information that foretell the coming Messiah. Some are detailed even to the aspect of His suffering death and no broken bones in the process. I will leave those for you to explore.

INSERT

In the timeline of events covered we are now at about 26AD as the ministry of John the Baptist is announcing the coming of the Messiah to the Jews. The dates I have verified are not the same dates reflected by most biblical timelines. This is because of John the Baptist and Jesus being born in the fall of 5BC rather than most published dates for the birth of the Messiah.

JOHN THE BAPTIST

John the Baptist began the war against the Jewish hypocritical religious piety. He did it as a man of no reputation in the power and attitude of the ancient prophet Elijah. This is by design, I believe, because the Jewish priests were privy to the Old Testament writings and knew about Elijah's providential blessing and power from God. Malachi referred to Elijah as his official position of spiritual integrity standing for and prosecuting the will of God, and not Elijah the man. In this sense, John the Baptist is Elijah in spirit, but not the literal Elijah resurrected.

Luke 1:16,17 And many of the children of Israel shall he turn to the Lord their God. (17) And he shall go before him in the spirit and power of Elias, to turn the hearts of the fathers to the children, and the disobedient to the wisdom of the just; to make ready a people prepared for the Lord.

Elijah is used in this prophecy because of his dedication and boldness for the Invisible God. His life brings intensity and boldness to the era of John the Baptist. It is clear that a succession of prophets is raised up by God, both in faithful Judah and in idolatrous Israel, to see about God before the people of both countries. This is to leave them without excuse if they forsook His worship.

This is during a time when a grosser and more deadly idolatry than had been practiced before was introduced into Israel by the authority of Ahab, and the total apostasy of the ten tribes was so imminent. This prophet of unusual vigor and force of character was endowed with miraculous powers of an extraordinary kind. He was successively raised up, so the wickedness of the kings was boldly met and combated. This was done in hopes of having a remnant of faithful men preserved in the land.

John the Baptist like Elijah did not stutter or mince words about sin! Comparison of their approach to evil is interesting.

1Kings 18:21-22 And Elijah came unto all the people, and said, how long halt ye between two opinions? if the LORD be God, follow him: but if Baal, then follow him. And the people answered him not a word. (22) Then said Elijah unto the people, I, even I only, remain a prophet of the LORD; but Baal's prophets are four hundred and fifty men.

Matthew 3:7 But when he saw many of the Pharisees and Sadducees come to his baptism, he said unto them, O generation of vipers, who hath warned you to flee from the wrath to come?

John the Baptist knew his reason for being born. He never assumed the full mission of the prophecy of Malachi. Though he wore the cloak of Elijah spiritually, he knew his mission was solely to show and announce the One who would fulfill the prophecy concerning the Messiah.

This is why the Jewish priests asked John if he was the Elijah. We can know this by John's answer when he is asked, "Are you Elijah?"

John 1:19-21 And this is the record of John, when the Jews sent priests and Levites from Jerusalem to ask him, Who art thou? (20) And he confessed, and denied not; but confessed, I am not the Christ. (21) And they asked him, What then? Art thou Elias? And he said, I am not. Art thou that prophet? And he answered, No.

Think of it this way. As Moses stood for the Law, Elijah stood for the Prophets. There was no prophet predicting an intervention in the affairs of mankind after Malachi. It was 400 years of silence, before John the Baptist came onto the scene.

It is no accident that John the Baptist was a miracle baby, much like Isaac was to Sarah. Elizabeth, his mother, was barren and visited by an angel, who told her she would bear a child. John was born 6 months before the birth of the Messiah.

The history of human advancement in progressive knowledge is marked by periods of rest, and then progress. I think God withholds prophets for a time to see if mankind might look for after Christ with a greater desire when He begins His ministry. God appears in human form to set mankind an example of how to treat one another. The office of Christ's forerunner (John the Baptist) is to bring them to repentance for unruly behavior and return to the original law (the Ten Commandments). It is part of the process to make ready a people prepared for the Lord at His coming.

However, history reveals the Jews did not recognize the Messiah when He began His ministry of progressive changes. They rejected Jesus telling them how all of mankind would be redeemed back to God through the salvation process He would pioneer.

Malachi told them to remember the law, because in the four hundred years ahead they were likely to forget it, during the absence of the Prophets of God.

Malachi 4:4 Remember ye the Law of Moses my servant, which I commanded unto him in Horeb for all Israel, with the statutes and judgments.

As I said before, during these four hundred years of silence the Jews changed the laws of God into a burden and legalistic ritual, corrupting the office of Moses. They set themselves up as the intercessors between God and mankind with their carnally and profit-driven system of worship.

As our story progresses, you will see that over 20 centuries have passed since the brief 3.5 years of the ministry of the greatest prophet, Jesus. He is the last prophet encouraging mankind to choose God's plan and way of life.

These past 20 centuries of prophetic silence have been overseen by the Invisible Holy Spirit of God. The spiritual comforter, Jesus, promises to indwell people who choose to believe in Him. Jesus comes to restore the corrupted intent of the law and raise it to a Spiritual level for mankind.

Moses and Elias were the human revelators for the knowledge of a coming Messiah from the Invisible God. Christ's birth, ministry, and death became everything the Old Testament writings were about.

The Old Testament was about Physical Salvation for mankind. Christ was about to change that process to Spiritual Salvation through Him as He became the FIRSTBORN SON OF GOD. Jesus was the first human to be transformed into a Spirit Being.

Colossians 1:12-19 Giving thanks unto the Father, which hath made us meet to be partakers of the inheritance of the saints in light: (13) Who hath delivered us from the power of darkness, and hath translated us into the kingdom of his dear Son: (14) In whom we have redemption through His blood, even the forgiveness of sins: (15) Who is the image of the invisible God, the firstborn of every creature: (16) For by Him were all things created, that are in heaven, and that are in earth, visible and invisible, whether they be thrones, or dominions, or principalities, or powers: all things were created by

Him, and for Him: (17) And He is before all things, and by Him all things consist. (18) And He is the head of the body, the church: who is the beginning, the firstborn from the dead; that in all things He might have the preeminence. (19) For it pleased the Father that in him should all fullness dwells.

I will elaborate on this process and Christ's preeminence later in my story. The turning of the heart of the father to the children was Malachi's hope for the restoration of religion, until all should be of one heart in the obedience to God. This expression from his writing seems to imply the preaching from Elijah is to affect the Jews as the children of the Patriarchal Fathers. This was done to lead them back to the faith and love which their fathers, the patriarchs, practiced.

Jesus referred to this theme:

John 8:56 Your father Abraham rejoiced to see My day: and he saw it and was glad. (57) Then said the Jews unto him, Thou art not yet fifty years old, and hast thou seen Abraham? (58) Jesus said unto them, Verily, verily, I say unto you, Before Abraham was, **I Am**. *(59) They then took up stones to cast at him: but Jesus hid Himself, and went out of the temple, going through the midst of them, and so passed by.*

The Law and Prophets all point to the coming of Jesus, the savior of mankind. Malachi's was the last word on the subject before the 400 years of silence. It was during the years of Roman domination spreading over the world when God chose to deal with mankind in a one-on-one situation once again. God did this by coming to mankind in man's created form.

This is the fulfillment of many prophecies from times past, showing a human Messiah for mankind. There is a lot of interesting information concerning the appearance of God as a human being upon the earth to consider and expose.

THE OLD COVENANT
CHANGE FOR MANKIND

The coming of Christ is the opening of God's message and way of life for all of mankind. (Genesis 49:10, removing the authority from the Jewish priests.) Jesus was about to make spiritual salvation a possibility for all mankind.

Think about the concept of the invisible Creator God, allowing His Spirit Essence and power to impregnate Mary, the physical human host, and then freely give up His new existence to pioneer the way for all human beings to accept the Holy Spirit into their Human Spirit and eventually be born again as Spiritual children of God in every sense of a complete Spiritual Being. What an awesome design and destiny.

The coming of a Messiah to deliver the Jews from the Romans and restore the nation of Israel to a national power is what the Jews were looking for; it had been part of the Jewish religion for centuries. (The orthodox Jews are still looking.)

The priests were well versed in the prophetic predictions for a coming Messiah. The anticipation of this event is the driving force behind the strict policing of any attempt of a fraudulent birth of this human baby to become the Messiah.

The Sanhedrim sent Gamaliel, one of their priests, to interview Joseph and Mary as soon as word came from Melker of the birth, followed by heavenly signs and wonders. Following is a paraphrase of the interrogation from the Jewish Talmud, 27B.

Gamaliel finds Joseph and Mary at Mecca, in the land of Ammon or Moab. (This is the modern-day land of Jordan.)

He does not find Jesus with them. Gamaliel travels to a place he is told he can find Jesus and is told Jesus is somewhere else. He follows Jesus from place to place, until he despairs of ever finding Him! He wonders if Jesus knows he is looking for Him and is eluding him!

Gamaliel says Joseph, Mary's husband, is a wood-workman, very tall and ugly. His hair looks as though it might have been dark auburn. His eyes are grey and vicious.

Joseph is anything but prepossessing in his appearance. The depth of his mind seems to express no more than yes and no answers. He seems very disagreeable to his own family. (Pharisees like Gamaliel are very judgmental people)

When Gamaliel asks about the encounter with the angel, Joseph says it is more like a dream than a vision. He says he cannot tell if he is asleep or awake. He relates that after agreeing to marriage, something makes him feel Mary is with child. He actually decides to have nothing more to do with her.

A few days later, while working under the shed, a "man" in snowy white clothing appears beside him and tells him to not doubt the virtue of Mary. He goes on to say that the child she is carrying is by the Holy Spirit. He also says that Mary is holy before the Lord. The "man" then tells Joseph that Elizabeth, Mary's cousin, will have a child in her old age that will be telling the people of the coming of Mary's child to be the Messiah.

After this, Joseph says the "man" disappears like the melting of light. Mary tells Gamaliel the same angel appears to her and says the same things. She says after she tells Joseph, he agrees to marry her. They believe what the angel or man says must be the truth.

It is important to understand the mind-set of the Jewish priests and teachers during the time when Jesus begins His ministry. The Jews' expectations for this Messiah are based on the Old Testament Psalms, specifically chapter two.

Psalms 2:1-12 Why do the heathen rage, and the people imagine a vain thing? (2) The kings of the earth set themselves, and the rulers take counsel together, against the LORD, and against his anointed, saying, (3) Let us break their bands asunder, and cast away their cords from us. (4) He that sits in the heavens shall laugh: The Lord shall have them in derision. (5) Then shall he speak unto them in his wrath and vex them in his sore displeasure. (6) Yet have I set my king upon my holy hill of Zion. (7) I will declare the decree: the LORD hath said unto me, you are my Son; this day have I begotten thee. (8) Ask of me, and I shall give thee the heathen for thine inheritance, and the uttermost parts of the earth for thy possession. (9) Thou shalt break them with a rod of iron; thou shalt dash them in pieces like a potter's vessel. (10) Be wise now therefore, O ye kings be instructed, ye judges of the earth. (11) Serve the LORD with fear and rejoice with trembling. (12) Kiss the Son, lest he be angry, and ye perish from the way, when his wrath is kindled but a little. Blessed are all they that put their trust in him.

Kiss the Son lest He be angry is a way of saying we need to embrace the believing in Jesus as the Son of God and accept Him into our lives as our savior. When the Jews are characterizing heathens, they are referring to all nations other than themselves!

The word heathen in the Hebrew Language— gôyim—properly means nations without respect, so far as the word is concerned to the character of the nations. It is applied by the Hebrews to the surrounding nations or to all other people than their own; and as those nations are in fact pagans, or idolaters, the word comes with this signification.

It is part of the prejudice expressed by the leadership of the Jews. They are a proud and stubborn people. This is carnal response to the fact that God happened to choose them. It became clear that the Jews disregarded the Spiritual aspect of the Messiah's purpose for coming to the world. They are stubborn about staying in the system of physical salvation through works rather than faith in what Jesus taught.

I can see why the Jews take this approach as I consider the whole of Psalms 2. They were living under the Roman boot heel and wanted their independence and national status restored.

They were looking for the Messiah to deliver them in every way from the physical political oppression of the Romans. They could not perceive the spiritual and future advents that were to someday be fulfilled by the Messiah for the saving of all mankind.

They had no clue that the appearance of the Messiah was one of two scheduled advents. This made it exceedingly difficult for them to accept Jesus as the Messiah as Jesus revealed His purpose for coming to the world. They are steeped in traditions and centuries of religious beliefs, and something different is extremely hard to consider.

This is true of all people who lack a certain amount of goal when approached with information that is different. Actually, the information is delayed until the second return of Jesus. Patience is a spiritual virtue. In our world of fast cars, internet, and food, it is not a popular virtue.

The Jews completely missed the point of God's first visitation to mankind as the first-begotten and then born into spirit being son of the Invisible God. I do not wish to debate the fact that the Son of God was not the Son of God before He was born as a child from the human host, Mary.

I simply say consider the following scriptures and decide for yourself. Let the Bible report and you decide.

John 1:1-3 In the beginning was the Word, and the Word was with God, and the Word was God. (2) The same was in the beginning with God. (3) All things were made by Him; and without Him was not anything made that was made.

John 1:14-17 And the Word was made flesh, and dwelt among us, (and we beheld His glory, the glory as of the only begotten of the Father,) full of grace and truth. (15) John bare witness of Him, and cried, saying, this was He of whom I spoke, He that cometh after me is preferred before me: for He was before me. (16) And of His fullness have all we received, and grace for grace. (17) For the law was given by Moses, but grace and truth came by Jesus Christ.

I also cite the letter from the Apostle Paul to the Colossians. When you read this, remember, the main topic is about God the Father. Paul is thankful to the Father for giving us Jesus.

Colossians 1:12-18 Giving thanks unto the Father, which hath made us meet to be partakers of the inheritance of the saints in light:(13) Who hath delivered us from the power of darkness, and hath translated us into the kingdom of His dear Son: (14) In whom we have redemption through His blood, even the forgiveness of sins: (15) Who is the image of the invisible God, the firstborn of every creature: (16) For by Him (this is speaking of the Father God) were all things created, that are in heaven, and that are in earth, visible and invisible, whether they be thrones, or dominions, or principalities, or powers: all things were created by Him (God the Father), and for Him: (17) And He is before all things, and by Him all things consist. (18) And He (Jesus) is the head of the body, the church: Who is the beginning, the firstborn from the dead; that in all things he might have the preeminence.

I can see why the Jews reject Jesus. They see Him as their deliverer from the Romans. They do not realize He comes to deliver them from their own Priests and raise the process of salvation to a Spiritual level. The Priests suddenly realized Jesus was there to replace their official position as mediators between God and mankind for the forgiveness of sin. This did not set well with them. Their attitude was not unlike the pagans when the apostle Paul condemned idol worship which threatens the craft of making and selling idols.

Acts 19:23-28 And the same time there arose no small stir about that way. (24) For a certain man named Demetrius, a silversmith, which made silver shrines for Diana, brought no small gain unto the craftsmen; (25) Whom he called together with the workmen of like occupation, and said, Sirs, ye know that by this craft we have our wealth. (26) Moreover ye see and hear, that not alone at Ephesus, but almost throughout all Asia, this Paul hath persuaded and turned away much people, saying that they be no gods, which are made with hands: (27) So that not only this our craft is in danger to be set at naught; but also that the temple of the great goddess Diana should be despised, and her magnificence should be destroyed, whom all Asia and the world worships. (28) And when they heard these sayings, they were full of wrath, and cried out, saying, Great is Diana of the Ephesians.

I now understand the Jews' interpretation of the Old Testament law and prophets does not include an understanding of the changes in priesthood and worship toward God.

John 1:4-11 In Him was life; and the life was the light of men. (5) And the light shines in darkness; and the darkness understood it not. (6) There was a man sent from God, whose name was John. [John the Baptist] (7) The same came for a witness, to bear witness of the Light, that all men through him might believe. (8) He was not that Light but was sent to bear witness of that Light. (9) That was the true Light, which lights every man that cometh into the world. (10) He was in the world, and the world was made by him, and the world knew him not. (11) He came unto his own, [the Jews] and his own received him not.

As I compare the bible narratives with Josephus's academic history of the Jews, I plainly see why they are refusing to accept Jesus as the Messiah. Just think about what is read to the Jews every Sabbath day, every week. Daniel 2 and 7 are read each Sabbath. The Old Testament prophecies are a sign of why the Jews expect freedom and the restoration of their kingdom from this Messiah. Daniel foretold the rising of four world monarchies: the Babylonian, the Persian, the Grecian, and the Roman, the last of which was characterized as the most terrible kingdom of Iron.

The Jews lived for this Messiah to become a reality and deliver them from the Romans. They were not aware of the period God is working with!

Daniel 2:44 And in the days of these kings shall the God of heaven set up a kingdom, which shall never be destroyed: and the kingdom shall not be left to other people, but it shall break in pieces and consume all these kingdoms, and it shall stand for ever.

Daniel 7:13-14 I saw in the night visions, and behold, one like the Son of man came with the clouds of heaven, and came to the Ancient of days, and they brought him near before him. (14) And there was given him dominion, and glory, and a kingdom, that all people, nations, and languages, should serve him: his dominion is an everlasting dominion, which shall not pass away, and his kingdom that which shall not be destroyed.

This is why the Jews believe a true Messiah cannot die. But Jesus says He must die and be lifted to draw all people unto Him. Jesus is on a different mission this time. (He will be back to fulfill Daniel's prophecy in this 21st century.) The Jews heard Him say this and were disappointed in this Jesus of Nazareth. They began to doubt He was the predicted Messiah. They rejected Him because they were not thinking spiritually about the gift of salvation for all of mankind through Jesus.

The Jews' expectations were known at this time by surrounding nations. The concept of the Jews marshaling universal dominion is no small political disturbance among the other nations. One reason the Jews were so restive under the Roman dominion is the expectation of this Messiah's delivering them and setting up His kingdom. The Romans were consistently looking for anyone who might try to overthrow their dominion.

Jesus preached and taught with reasonable caution because of the watchful eyes of the Roman authorities. He withdrew as soon as a large crowd gathered around to listen to Him. Jesus did not want a hint of sedition or disturbance to interrupt His mission from God to complete His divine purpose while on earth. When Jesus felt like the authorities might take Him away by force, He went into the mountains to be alone for a while. The conditions Jesus faced in His ministry were common problems for His cousin, John the Baptist. Telling religious people to change something is not the way to win friends and influence enemies.

Matthew 3:1-7 In those days came John the Baptist, preaching in the wilderness of Judaea, (2) And saying, Repent ye: for the kingdom of heaven is at hand. (3) For this is he that was spoken of by the prophet Esaias, saying, the voice of one crying in the wilderness, Prepare ye the way of the Lord, make his paths straight. (4) And the same John had his raiment of camel's hair, and a leathern girdle about his loins; and his meat was locusts and wild honey. (5) Then went out to him Jerusalem, and all Judaea, and all the region round about Jordan, (6) And were baptized of him in Jordan, confessing their sins. (7) But when he saw many of the Pharisees and Sadducees come to his baptism, he said unto them, O generation of vipers, who hath warned you to flee from the wrath to come?

John was very blunt with his message to the Jewish leadership. John the Baptist spoke with the authority and boldness of Elijah the prophet. He did not hesitate to acknowledge the hypocrisy of the Pharisees and Sadducees, chiding them with harsh words while reminding them of the coming judgment of God. He did not sugarcoat or compromise the task he was born to perform. He was remarkably effective in announcing and acknowledging the man Jesus as the one sent from God.

John fell victim to the Jews and their outrage against his opposition to their traditions of worship. He preached repentance and baptized people in the Jordan River, not the traditional baths of the temple. His message was straightforward about the coming savior and the forgiveness for sin after repentance. John knew his purpose for being born as the forerunning messenger for the coming Messiah. When he met Jesus at the river one day, he was reluctant to perform the baptism.

Jesus was baptized, and at once there was confirmation from heaven as the voice of an angel proclaimed Jesus as the Son of God. The Holy Spirit fell upon Jesus.

Matthew 3:16 And Jesus, when he was baptized, went up straightway out of the water: and, lo, the heavens were opened unto him, and he saw the Spirit of God descending like a dove, and lighting upon him: [Gospel description of what the angel confirms by voice.]

Mark 1:10 And straightway coming up out of the water, he saw the heavens opened, and the Spirit like a dove descending upon him: (Notice it is not a person descending)

Luke3:22 And the Holy Spirit descended in a bodily shape like a dove upon him, and a voice came from heaven, which said, Thou art my beloved Son; in thee I am well pleased.

John1:32 And John bare record, saying, I saw the Spirit descending from heaven like a dove, and it abode upon him.

More about this later. Shortly thereafter Jesus began His ministry of reconciliation for the remission of sin under the New Covenant terms. John was eventually beheaded by Herod Antipater's son, Herod Antipas. He claimed that he committed this act of violence against John because the Jews wanted John silenced.

His daughter played into the conspiracy by enticing Antipas to give her any wish she wanted. Antipas agreed and she asked for the head of John the Baptist. This sealed the fate of John the Baptist. Jesus remarked how great this man was in the calling God had put upon him. Jesus continued His ministry for three- and one-half years before He was crucified.

The last week before His death, Jesus set the stage for His disciples to continue what He began. It was a busy week of events for Jesus. He made a triumphant entry into Jerusalem, and before the week was over He was put to death by those who rejected His purpose for coming. Within the first one hundred years after the crucifixion of Jesus and the murder of the Apostles, men of power and authority mutilated the teachings of Jesus and the writings of the Apostles.

The things Jesus taught, and the changes taught in the relationship between God and mankind have been contentions of many religious zealots from the time Jesus returned to heaven up to present day.

The story now becomes a journey of deceit and power struggles to control people of faith in Jesus. Most of it begins with the murder of the Apostles of Jesus Christ.

Within 30 years of what Jesus told the disciples would happen to Jerusalem and the temple, the events He predicted become a harsh reality in 70AD.In the timeline of the bible, we have come from the beginning of mankind to about 30AD. From this time send the events of the bible concerning the timeline after 30AD turn to the developing of the church Jesus starts.

THE APOSTLES

*J*esus chose these men to take His New Covenant message to the rest of the world. All of them, with the exception of John, were eventually murdered by the Jews as they conspired to overthrow the new way of life taught by Jesus.

The church Jesus built begins on the day of Pentecost in 30 A.D. Jesus laid the foundational administrative aspects at the Last Supper on the night before His crucifixion.

John 13:12-20 So after he had washed their feet, and had taken his garments, and was set down again, he said unto them, know you what I have done to you? (13) Ye call me Master and Lord: and ye say well; for so I am. (14) If I then, your Lord and Master, have washed your feet; ye also ought to wash one another's feet. (15) For I have given you an example, that ye should do as I have done to you. (16) Verily, verily, I say unto you, the servant is not greater than his lord; neither he that is sent greater than he that sent him. (17) If ye know these things, happy are ye if ye do them. (18) I speak not of you all: I know whom I have chosen but that the scripture may be fulfilled, He that eats bread with me hath lifted up his heel against me. (19) Now I tell you before it come, that, when it is come to pass, ye may believe that I am he. (20) Verily, verily, I say unto you, He that receives whomsoever I send receives me; and he that receives me receives him that sent me.

The washing of their feet was a symbolic washing to drive home the principle that they were to be servants of the people of the church, not overbearing dictators. Foot washing was a custom during those times and was performed by the hired servants of the home. The dusty roads left the feet very dirty and dry when one entered the home.

Jesus often taught by parables, analogies, and examples from the customs of those times.

INSERT

One of the analogies Jesus used was the concept of sheep and shepherds.

John 10:7 Then said Jesus unto them again, Verily, verily, I say unto you, I am the door of the sheep.

John 10:9 I am the door: by me if any man enter, he shall be saved, and shall go in and out, and find pasture.

He was illustrating in terms they would easily understand. In those days, the sheep were corralled, and the shepherd lay at the opening of the corral at the point of entry to guard the sheep from wolves. The sheep had to go through the shepherd to enter the fold. There was no gate; <u>the Shepherd was the door or gate</u>. This scripture was later twisted from its intent by men of power to fabricate a premise for their authority.

Matthew 16:18 And I say also unto thee, That thou art Peter, and upon this Rock (Jesus)I will build my church; and the gates of hell shall not prevail against it.

There is the Greek consideration upon the words, thou art Peter [Greek, petros—a little rock], and upon this rock [Greek, Petra], I will build my church. He did not promise to build His church upon Peter, but upon Himself, as Peter was careful to tell us (1Peter 2:4-9). The Church of Rome claimed its church was built upon Peter as its first Apostle and founder. This is not what Jesus told His disciples. On the night before His arrest, Jesus told His disciples how the government of His church would be set up.

He also introduced the new Sacraments for sustaining church membership.

Matthew 26:26-28 And as they were eating, Jesus took bread, and blessed it, and brake it, and gave it to the disciples, and said, Take, eat; this is my body. (27) And he took the cup, and gave thanks, and gave it to them, saying, Drink ye all of it; (28) For this is my blood of the new testament, which is shed for many for the remission of sins.

Luke 22:24-26 And there was also a strife among them, which of them should be accounted the greatest. (25) And he said unto them, The kings of the Gentiles exercise lordship over them; and they that exercise authority upon them are called benefactors. (26) But ye shall not be so: but he that is greatest among you, let him be as the younger; and he that is chief, as he that doth serve.

These scriptures were the basic principles for recognizing the church Jesus was creating. But, as we shall see, this is not what men of position and power who showed up a few years later claimed for the church.

Acts 1:7-8 And he said unto them, it is not for you to know the times or the seasons, which the Father hath put in his own power. (8) But ye shall receive power, after that the Holy Ghost is come upon you: and ye shall be sees unto me both in Jerusalem, and in all Judaea, and in Samaria, and unto the uttermost part of the earth.

Jesus promised to send the Holy Spirit power from God and Himself to help the apostles perform their work in the church. Their commission was to go to all the world as witnesses of the salvation of God for mankind through Jesus Christ.

The Day of Pentecost was the beginning of the Church of God taking the gospel message of Jesus Christ to all the world. This became a problem for the established Jewish religious leadership and the Roman Empire. Eventually, paganism and Christianity were combined to quell the discontent and compromise the truth Jesus taught.

Matthew 28:18-20 And Jesus came and spoke unto them, saying, all power is given unto me in heaven and in earth. (19) Go you therefore, and teach all nations, baptizing them in the name of the Father, and of the Son, and of the Holy Ghost: (20) teaching them to see all things whatsoever I have commanded you: and, lo, I am with you always, even unto the end of the world. Amen.

Jesus was extremely specific as to what they were to teach the new converts. This was another life-changing event for mankind. Jesus was the first to receive the Holy Spirit into His mind and personality. He promised the apostles that they too would get this power after He completed His mission on earth.

Acts 2:1-5 And when the day of Pentecost was fully come, they were all with one accord in one place. (2) And suddenly there came a sound from heaven as of a rushing mighty wind, and it filled all the house where they were sitting. (3) And there appeared unto them cloven tongues like as of fire, (symbolic of the Spirit of the Father and Jesus) and it sat upon each of them. (4) And they were all filled with the Holy Ghost, and began to speak with other tongues, (this is referring to other languages they had never learned to speak) as the Spirit gave them utterance. (5) And there were dwelling at Jerusalem Jews, and devout men, out of every nation under heaven. (There were no less than 17 different nationalities attending)

Acts 2:6 Now when this was noised abroad, the multitude came together, and were confounded, because that every man heard them speak in his own language. (this is key information; the miracle is in the hearing)

The first seven chapters is information about the beginning of the church Jesus started with the apostles. The Jews were very unhappy about this new covenant religion. The pagans were unhappy also because this new religion did not abide idolatry and graven images along with promiscuous moral behavior.

The new believers were persecuted radically by these two groups. Yet the apostles were not deterred by the beatings, imprisonment, and false accusations prosecuted by the Jews and Romans.

God makes an interesting example of the power of His Spirit when men receive it. I am speaking of the conversion of Saul of Tarsus. Named Paul, he was a devout Jewish Pharisee famous for prosecution of these new believers. God struck Paul down on the road to Damascus one day, and Paul became a powerful tool for God to get His unbiased salvation for all men proclaimed to the Gentile nations of the world.

The letters and actions of Paul is a better part of the New Testament that sets the standard for understanding the plan of God for all of mankind and the details for overcoming personal difficulties in the new belief. The fourteen letters of Paul to the churches give us some idea of the latitude God's grace supports believers who are seriously converted and dedicated to the new way of life.

Along with the Gospels and writings of James, Peter, and John, a moral standard of worship and conduct toward fellow man and God is the complete conceptual morality that is expected of the Christian both in personal and corporate living. The writings and work of these apostles cover a period from 30 A. D. to 100 A. D. with the last apostle staying alive, being John.

I will not go into the details of the murders of these great men of God for they are well documented. Again, my purpose is to supply the information that helped me to get an understanding of what my destiny is intended to be and why I was born.

I will cover the works of the apostles because it is important for my understanding why I and every human being is born.

MATTHEW, MARK, LUKE, AND JOHN

The diversity of these four men in their account of the life of Jesus is interesting. Each writer wrote to a specific group of people. Matthew was presented to the Semitic people. It was clearly the Gospel for the Jews, written in language and approach that was palatable to their understanding.

Mark projected the information for the people of servitude or servant class of that time in history. It appealed to the practical mindset.

Luke accommodated the Greek thinkers. Luke supplied a great history of the early churches and the works of the apostles as they began to organize and administer the new doctrines of the church. He wrote about the first Ministerial Counsel decision, which also show James as the head of the church in Jerusalem—not Peter.

Acts 15:19 Wherefore my sentence is, that we trouble not them, which from among the Gentiles are turned to God:

There is an authority here that does not appear in the speech of Peter, and this authority was felt and bowed to by all the council and the decree proposed by St. James adopted.

Luke presented a great accounting of the missionary works of Paul, an apostle called directly by Jesus from heaven. John supplied the most detail concerning the feelings of Jesus and illustrated Christ's enormous love for people of all nations. John's love for Christ was the most clear, as even Michelangelo's depiction of the Last Supper shows John right next to Jesus at the table. He was the one apostle that did not suffer murder at the hands of the Jews.

While exiled by Domitian on the Isle of Patmos, Jesus made the final Revelation unsealing information that was sealed since the time of Daniel.

(This information will be addressed later in the book as the timeline reaches our day.)

The Gospels have different information, yet together they tell the complete good news that Jesus teaches them to present to the world through the creation of His churches. They are a guide to the attitudes that support the good values of living life and also include quite a lot of prophetic information for the immediate future then and the future events in the days ahead in our time.

THE APOSTLE PAUL

*P*aul was the champion of grace and mercy extended to the gentiles. God chose a man who was highly educated in the Jewish faith and their traditions. I see Paul for the first time at the feet of the first martyr, Steven.

Paul was a zealot for the persecution of the new believers who accepted the faith of the teachings of Jesus. Paul was relentless in finding and bringing many new coverts to their death at the hands of the Jews. He was on his way to Damascus in pursuit of the new Christians to imprison and prosecute when Christ struck him blind.

Luke dedicates the majority of his writing about the first century church to the work of Paul. The book of Acts written by Luke is the history of the church started by Christ and organized by the apostles. Luke was Paul's best friend, and his documentation of the progress of the first century church is the basis for the early church authority and operation before it was corrupted after 100 A.D.

Once Paul was converted, he became one of the most powerful witnesses to the cause of Christ. Paul implemented what Jesus taught in theory. Paul broke down centuries of prejudice between the Jews and Gentiles. He challenged the prejudice of Peter toward the Gentiles and exposed Peter's hierocracy in service of the church.

Galatians 2:11-14 But when Peter was come to Antioch, I withstood him to the face, because he was to be blamed. (12) For before that certain came from James, he did eat with the Gentiles: but when they were come, he withdrew and separated himself, fearing them which were of the circumcision. (13) And the other Jews dissembled likewise with him; insomuch that Barnabas also was carried away with their dissimulation. (14) But when I saw that they walked not uprightly according to the truth of the gospel, I said unto Peter before them all, If thou, being a Jew, lives after the manner of Gentiles, and not as do the Jews, why compel thou the Gentiles to live as do the Jews?

As Paul built churches throughout Asia, he wrote letters to them that became detailed lessons for the church to be educated in the true principles of Christ. As problems were addressed in each church,

I see a development of doctrine that became the standard for behavior in the churches. There were two sets of problems to be worked through in showing the New Covenant relationship between God and mankind. The converted Jews had to step away from Pharisee traditions of religion, and the Gentiles had to step away from hedonistic pagan rituals.

Paul was very deep, spiritually speaking, and even Peter wrote that Paul's words were a little difficult to understand. Peter complimented Paul in his writings.

2Peter 3:14-18 Wherefore, beloved, seeing that ye look for such things, be diligent that ye may be found of him in peace, without spot, and blameless. (15) And account that the longsuffering of our Lord is salvation; even as our beloved brother Paul also according to the wisdom given unto him hath written unto you; (16) As also in all his epistles, speaking in them of these things; in which are some things hard to be understood, which they that are unlearned and unstable wrest, as they do also the other scriptures, unto their own destruction. (17) Ye therefore, beloved, seeing ye know these things before, beware lest ye also, being led away with the error of the wicked, fall from your own steadfastness. (18) But grow in grace, and in the knowledge of our Lord and Savior Jesus Christ. To him be glory both now and forever. Amen.

All of the books of the New Testament express different themes, but they all connect to the risen Christ and the plan of God for how mankind should behave and live life. Peter, James, Jude, and John finished the New Testament books. Paul refers to Peter, James, and John as pillars of the new church.

I have brought us up to the Revelation of Jesus Christ to the Apostle John. I will cover the complete book and how it relates to earlier prophecies and prophesies that are coming soon.

I will be drafting another book to cover the subject of prophecy and a coming Apocalypse. 100 A.D. TO PRESENT DAY

To keep the timeline moving, I will be brief as possible. I am about to cover 2,000 years of time since Jesus completed His first mission on earth.

I am only going to point out the high points of mankind's kingdoms of power and religious deceit which help create the confusion and obscure the purpose for which the bible reveals we are born.

Through the timeline of history, you will see the working of Satan, in a very subtle way, corrupting the truth just enough to confuse and keep mankind on a sure path of destruction in lieu of intended destiny.

INSET

Satan is very clever and deceitful. The following analogy will illustrate how Satan has manipulated the truth of God's plan to distract mankind from its intended purpose. When a pilot does the preflight check of his instruments, calibrate for sea level pressure, etc., he is placing confidence in the instruments he is checking during the flight to his destination. Now if he is off by as little as a half of a degree on the compass, guess what happens. By the time his flight of a thousand miles is completed, he will be hundreds of miles from his intended destination! He thinks he is on the right flight plan, but he is actually drifting farther away from the target destination with every mile he flies with that compass out of calibration a half a degree in direction. The source of his guidance is an indirect lie with every mile he flies.

Satan works the same way with the truth of the bible. Satan does not care how much truth you believe and obey as long as your belief system or guidance has a low percentage of untrue information. Enough false doctrine to get you off course and miss the intended mark, or in this case the intended purpose and education for your lifelong trip to destiny.

I am only sighting the high points of events and information makes changes in the world; especially the many concepts and opinions concerning religions of men as compared to what the bible reveals. The Bible is centered in God's interest in keeping His intentions for mankind through a new and better Redemption Plan as set forth by the sacrifice of Jesus Christ.

The education of mankind is continuing to accumulate with each passing century. Art, Literature, Science, are progressing throughout the world at a faster pace than ever. As I said before, the world ruling empires in Nebuchadnezzar's dream of the Great Image were the means of educational progress for all the nations under their domination. Rome is the lasting influence even to this present day.

What I see developing is a combination of religious authority and military enforcement of the whims and ideals of men in power. This began with the destruction of Jerusalem by the Romans and the murder of the apostles by the false accusations of the Jewish leadership.

Remembering the information covered to this point in time, we see the rejecting of belief in an Invisible God worldwide. The very nation of people God chose (Israel) to reveal His intentions for mankind is carnally corrupting themselves over and over. Up to this time, only the Old Testament prophets are still faithful to deliver the will of God for mankind.

After four hundred years of silence, Jesus was born and ministered to the chosen people of God, only to be rejected and killed. The impressive change I see in mankind is the willingness of these Christians to face death rather than compromise their faith in the principles Jesus taught them. This spiritual courage is still alive and well to present day (Kim Davis's moral integrity suffering her incarceration for uncompromising true values for living about the Kentucky same sex marriage issue for example)!

It is an invisible power in these people creating an unction from the Invisible God to live according to His will and not the ideals of men's religious hypocrisy, deceit, and compromising God's true values for life.

Carnal men are <u>assuming the chair of moral authority</u>, creating laws that contradict the divine principles of the Creator of Life. Many will suffer persecution and millions go to their death down through time for their belief in and commitment to Jesus. Their belief and commitment to the principles of Jesus makes their death a monument to the Redemption Plan. Their death is only a trumpet away from life eternal with God.

Hebrews 11:39-40 (39) And these all, having obtained a good report through faith, received not the promise: (40) God having supplied some better thing for us, that they without us should not be made perfect.

The coming of the Holy Spirit to indwell the minds of people makes a profound difference in the history of mankind. This Faith Once Delivered is a power available to the masses of people who choose to believe in the Invisible God and His son, Jesus Christ. These new believers are now facing two enemies, the Jews, and the Romans. The self-righteous and the un-righteous. The Jewish leadership handled initiating murder of the Apostles. The Holy Spirit replaced Jewish religious authority in the apostles, the Jews conspired against anyone who taught the Gospel of Jesus Christ.

They used the Roman government to enforce their false charges against these people. This persecution continued right up to the year 70 A.D. The Jews were upset, and angry Jesus did not overthrow the Roman government. They began their own insurrection against Rome. This action results in the very thing Jesus predicted would happen to Jerusalem and the Temple. The war waged against the Jews and Jerusalem was brutal and destructive.

What the Babylonians did to them in 604 B.C. and then Antiochus in 164 B.C. cannot hold a light to what Titus would later do to them in 70 A.D. (Read the actual account of the 70 A. D. destruction in Josephus's writings.) The persecution of the Jewish people began with Babylonian Empire. They were tolerated by the Persian Empire. The Greek Empire was a time of world conquest with leopard speed by Alexander the Great, only to be divided up by his 4 Generals. God used Greece to spread a higher understanding of ourselves intellectually. The great thinkers appear during these times. Out of these 4 notable ones, the Seleucids produced Antiochus Epiphanes. He was actually a forerunner of the ruthless military strength and hatred of the Jews. The military strength was obvious in the Iron Clad Roman Empire about 130 years after Antiochus. All of these are prophesied in the writings of Daniel.

In Daniel's writings he foresaw the downfall of the Greek Empire of Alexander the Great and the rising of the most dreadful and sustained Empire of influence upon the nations of mankind down through time to present day and beyond.

Daniel 8:8-12 Therefore the he goat waxed very great: and when he was strong, the great horn was broken; and for it came up four notable ones. Alexander died; the great horn was broken. The generals divided up the Empire before it came up four notable ones. These four Generals were the four notable ones: Seleucid, Cassander, Ptolemy, and Lysimachus. Out of these four notable ones came a little horn. Horn is a prophetic metaphor meaning Power of King.

Antiochus IV: This man is noted for plundering and desecrating Temples and sanctuaries. Never before even under domination of the Assyrians nor under the Babylonians did Israel receive such persecution as Antiochus IV prosecuted it. He hoped to destroy and crush the faith of Israel. He sent messengers with his laws for the Jews to keep. This man was like Satan himself, persecuting the people of God. The evil Satanic spirit influenced him. The statue of Olympian Zeus was set up in the Temple, which they had to worship. This was the abomination of desolation Jesus mentioned in His private teaching to His disciples.

- Traditional Patriarchal Sacrifices were abolished.
- There was to be no male child born to be circumcised. Disobedience of the above was punishable by death.
- He ordered The Old Testament Holy Scriptures destroyed. Antiochus IV Epiphanes the Manifest, the Illustrious, born 215, ruled the Seleucid Empire from 175 BC until his death in 164 BC.

He was a son of King Antiochus III the Great and the brother of Seleucus IV Philopator. His original name was Mithridates; he assumed the name Antiochus after he assumed the throne.

Notable events during the reign of Antiochus IV include his near-conquest of Egypt, which led to a confrontation that became an origin of the metaphorical phrase, line in the sand and the rebellion of the Jewish Maccabees (The Masada). To strengthen his hold over the region, Antiochus decided to Hellenize the Jews by ordering the worship of Zeus as the supreme god. This was anathema to the Jews, and when they refused Antiochus sent an army to enforce his decree with the tip of the Seleucid swords. According to the Books of the Maccabees, upon seizing Jerusalem his soldiers entered the Jewish Temple and slaughtered a pig, then forced Jewish men to eat the pig meat, impure by Jewish law. The men refused and the soldiers cut off the men's hands, feet, and tongues, then scalped the men and burned them alive on the altar of the Lord.

Antiochus's goal was to assimilate the Jewish people by Hellenizing their religion, which was extreme provocation against a people who until then had been content to live under Seleucid rule. Afterwards the Jews broke into a full-scale rebellion led by the Maccabees, who defeated the armies sent against them. This further undermined the Seleucid regime. It provided the Romans with opportunities to ally with the Jews.

Unwilling to give up control of Judea, Antiochus sent a commander named Lysias to deal with the Maccabees, while the King himself led the main Seleucid army against the Parthians. After first success in his eastern campaign, including the reoccupation of Armenia, Antiochus died suddenly of disease in 164 BC. I believe his death was providential, or he would have done what Iran wants to do to modern day Israel: wipe them off the face of the earth.

Daniel 8:11-12 Yea, he magnified himself even to the prince of the host, and by him the daily sacrifice was taken away, and the place of his sanctuary was cast down. (12) And a host was given him against the daily sacrifice by reason of transgression, and it cast down the truth to the ground; and it practiced and prospered.

Antiochus IV would have exterminated the Jews had he lived. We should be able to see a pattern of animosity and carnal hatred of the Jews in these following events of history. It is actually Satan's demon spirits influencing men to destroy what God once again is creating with the process of human beings living and learning about life. Before the invasion of the First Gentile Empire, the Assyrians killed as many Jews as possible and enslaved the Jewish people for the needs of the Assyrians.

In Luke 21:24, Jesus plainly says in the Olivet Discourse, the Jews and Jerusalem will be trodden down until the times of the Gentiles are fulfilled.

In the duration of the siege upon Jerusalem in 70 A.D. by Titus, was so bad women killed their own children for food. A powerful man rose and soon created a different religion to stop this persecution and discontent between the Christians and pagans. The irony is that it is called by the same name: Christian. He did this sort of in the same mantra as Zoroaster did after the Babylonian captivity back in the 500s B. C. Most of the deception this time was scripture tampering and changing the things Jesus taught just enough to pervert the true intent, purpose, and Faith in God. Flat out lies are not that hard to spot, but when truth is slightly altered, it is difficult to recognize deceit and compromise. It is like a faulty compass in an airplane out of calibration one decree. The farther the plane flies by that compass, the farther away from the flight plan it gets. This process is a great tool of Satan.

Satan has used people of power, pride, and prejudice countless times to promote a false Christ, to cloak the invisible God in false sense of truth. The result is a deceived innocent people following a carnal version of Christ that enslaves them to a different gospel than Jesus and the Apostles taught.

Satan is deceiving people about their true destiny and what God is actually creating through the process of human beings living and learning about life. The Jews were not persecuted because their religion was the only way of life intended; it was because they produced the Savior of mankind. The Jews added so much to their religion that it became like bondage. They rejected the New Covenant relationship Jesus set up.

Jesus paved the way for mankind to know the truth by the indwelling of the Holy Spirit which He promised to send, on the Feast of Weeks, which became known afterwards as the day of Pentecost. Satan hates mankind and attacked the remnant of the Jewish people through Rome. Then Satan used Roman influence to compromise the faith once delivered by Jesus and the apostles.

SCRIPTURE TAMPERING

I wish to explain what I have learned about the scriptures as legitimate writings ordained by God. I believe it is of paramount importance to base one's faith on true witnesses of the words Jesus spoke and the writings of the Apostles. Especially since the apostles themselves wrote warnings of people corrupting what they wrote.

Only two lines of Bibles have come down through history. They are the products of two religious systems with different agendas.

One system is dedicated to put the Inspired Word of God above everything else.

The other system is dedicated to putting something else above the Inspired Word of God. The other system allows human tradition to sit in a chair of equal authority with the Inspired Word of God. This is the work of carnal men seeking power and control of people. While the Apostles were still alive, the scriptures were pure, written by men inspired by the Holy Spirit from God to record and see through the scriptures, the Gospel of Jesus Christ, and God's intentions for mankind.

The murder of the Apostles opened the door to perversion for men to use for personal aggrandizement and power over the masses of people. The Encyclopedia is full of the history of manipulations and changes to the Bible. It is a subject to be pursued by the individual in a personal quest for the truth about Constantine's agenda to quell the fighting between Pagans and Jews. He did this to assure his domination of the masses for a world empire under his control, not to promote the ways of the Invisible God.

His conversion to the ways of Christ were convenient; a political move to set up control over people's lives. Here again we see the manipulation of mankind with personal or political agenda distorting the facts of truth.

They manipulate and pervert the writings of the actual witnesses to what Jesus Christ lives and teaches.

The Apostles were there. They lived with Jesus and saw His teaching and miracles for over 3.5 years. They had to be killed to cover up the truth of what they lived and documented as witnesses for the Son of God who pioneered the process for eternal life.

In the late fifties there were still books available that detailed the information about the foul play connected with the translation of Bible versions. Most all of these books are now out of print and nowhere to be found. I often wonder why this became the fate of these types of books. As I began a quest for truth about God and religions, it became noticeably clear why these books disappeared. The vanishing of information and death of true witnesses is common behavior for men of deceit.

There is a war going on just outside our physical vision between truth and error, good and evil. It is not unlike what Satan did to Adam and Eve in the Garden. He perverts the pure, childlike, belief of people and causes them to worship their creator in vain.

Mark7:7 How be it in vain do they worship me, teaching for doctrines the commandments of men.

The only bible God inspired was written in this world's two most perfect languages: Hebrew and Greek. I believe a person must research writings and dig deep into the original intent and language in which they were originally written.

I have found the older the book, the more truth in it. Faith, being the necessary element, makes the Christian believer strong because of the Words of God. It is important to be able to have confidence in the Bible we read, along with the revelation of the Holy Spirit to guide our thinking.

God never intended each person to manufacture their own bible.

Hebrews 4:12 The word of God is quick, and powerful, and sharper than any two-edged sword piercing even to the dividing asunder of soul and spirit, and of the joints and marrow, and is a discerner of the thoughts and intents of the heart.

Mankind assumed the responsibility of making his own Bible according to his own philosophy. This produced bibles which were not in agreement with each other because of the differences in men's carnal thinking. Most of these are called revised versions. There is a dramatic difference between a revised version and a translated version of the bible.

Even as early as 60 A.D., the Apostle Paul warned us about the sacred manuscripts of the Apostles being adulterated, corrupted, and used as articles of merchandise for selfish gain. 2Corinthians 2:17 We are not as many, which corrupt the word of God: but as of sincerity, but as of God, in the sight of God speak we in Christ. Peter also warned about men who use religion to make money for their own selfish agendas.

2Peter 2:1-3 There were false prophets also among the people, even as there shall be false teachers among you, who privately shall bring in damnable heresies, denying the Lord that bought them, and bring upon themselves swift destruction. (2) many shall follow their pernicious ways; by reason of whom the way of truth shall be evil spoken of. (3) And through covetousness shall they with feigned words make merchandise of you: whose judgment now of a long time lingers not, and their damnation slumbers not.

Now verse 2 of the scripture above is absolutely true of what I have run into with people when I encourage them to let the Bible say what it means. The information is automatically rejected because of pre-digested information from other longtime teachings about various aspects of death, the hereafter, and what mankind's intended potential is all about—some of which are not supported by the scriptures.

From the days of the Apostles and down through the ages, corrupters of Holy Scriptures have made progress in the art of deception. There are three God-Inspired Sentinels in the front, middle, and back of the Hebrew/Greek scriptures to guard over the combined book.

Deuteronomy 4:2 Ye shall not add unto the word which I command you, neither shall ye diminish ought from it, that ye may keep the commandments of the LORD your God which I command you.

Proverbs 30:6 Add thou not unto his words, lest he reprove thee, and thou be found a liar.

Revelation 22:19 And if any man shall take away from the words of the book of this prophecy, God shall take away his part out of the book of life, and out of the holy city, and from the things which are written in this book.

I do not wish to overwhelm with documentation of names and people who bring about this corruption of scripture. I will simply say that once again we are looking at what comes straight out of Babylon back in the days shortly after the flood: A carnal religion of men to replace or refute what God is intending for mankind started in ancient Babylon.

During my years of researching, I have found the King James 1611 is the most reliable translation from Hebrew and Geek to English; however, it has many errors in it because of Catholic influences. <u>The process that was used to translate the 1611 version of the bible is the reason it is trusted for its reliability of God's word to us.</u>

Beware of Revised versions of the Bible; they all come from a corrupted line of translators and men of religious and political agendas. The reason the 1611 King James is the most reliable translation from the Received Texts of Hebrew and Greek languages is because of the process used to translate the King James version of 1611.

This is a fact of history: In 1604 King James of England appointed Fifty-four Hebrew and Greek scholars to produce a Bible, which we have today as the King James authorized translation. These scholars were organized into Six groups that were commanded to meet separately: Two groups at Cambridge, Two at Oxford, and Two at Westminster. Each group was appointed a certain part of Scripture to translate into the English language.

Each individual scholar first made his own translation, then passed it on to be reviewed by each of the other members of his particular group. When each book of the Bible was completed it was sent to the other Five groups for their independent review and critiqued.

This process allowed each book to go through the hands and minds of the entire body of translators. To further ensure no collusion to deceive or that there were no errors, another committee was formed, selecting Two members from each of the Three institutional sites. The entire work came before this group to be completed. It took Seven years for the entire process to finish. There was no chance for collusion because these men were separated. These men felt a responsibility under the power of the Holy Spirit to create a means to show words not found in the Hebrew and Greek manuscripts but needed to be added to make the reading easier. They did this by printing <u>any words added by them in italics to name</u> <u>they were not of the original manuscripts.</u>

Besides this process, all learned men were invited to see and notify anyone concerned about the judgment process.

It is also a fact that the Received Text is of Apostolic Origin and dates to the 125 A.D. This is over 150 years before the famous Siniatic and Vatican manuscripts were written. They were created in 331 A.D., when Eusebius copied them for Constantine.

The Revised Standard Version was created in 1881 A. D. by a group of men sworn to absolute secrecy. They revised the Bible in <u>Secret meetings for 10 years</u> on each testament before dumping the completed work on the public for marketing. No public disclosure allowed, as was the King James version.

Not being aware of corruption of the bible texts is often the result of not looking up the original language of the words that are translated into English. The Greek and Hebrew languages have many specific words to stand for a thought or concept. The English words are not as specific and often do not express the original intent of the scripture.

God has allowed all these versions because it takes a belief and desire to know the truth coupled with work and effort to seek out the original intent. This is how God knows who really wants to know and who just follows the influences of men and religions.

CANONIZATION OF
THE SCRIPTURES

Canonization is taken from the Greek word KANON, meaning rule, or measuring rod. It is a process by which a collection of writings come to be valued as authoritative, definitive, and fixed by a particular authority. Because God inspired the sacred books of Israel. They were God Breathed. It is crucial that they are still separate from secular and pagan writings.

The books of the Bible were canonized to assure their position as the Inspired Words of God. This task, regardless of what the common opinion of historians say, was not the work of the so-called fathers of Judaism.

The canonization of the Old Testament is carried out under the Aaron/Levitical priesthood. The Bible is not a Jewish document; it is a Priestly Document. Hebrew Canon began to appear after the Babylonian exile. There was fear among the Levitical Priests that contamination of the writings will come out of the counterfeit form of Judaic worship coming from Samaria, north of Jerusalem, around 5 B.C. Samaria has long been occupied by Gentiles following Israel's exile (2 Kings 17).

After the Great Revival of Nehemiah 8, Ezra and the Great Assembly supervised and regulated the temple rites and sacrifices, priestly laws, synagogue rituals, and everything associated with the worship of God under the Old Covenant. Every act of worship of God within the Temple was approved by Ezra and the Great Assembly. Ezra's work was a major step in the preservation of the Hebrew Bible for Jews and the Old Testament for Christians.

There are five major works attributed to Ezra, the Priest of God:

1. The foundation of the Great Synagogue Assembly of elders

2. The canon of Scripture with three divisions of Law, Prophets, Psalms, and other writings

3. The substitution of square Chaldean characters for the Hebrew and Samaritan Script

4. The completion of the Chronicles and adding Nehemiah's story to His own book of Ezra

5. The establishment of synagogues throughout Persian Empire Chapters 29–31 of 2 Chronicles are a lengthy narration describing the restoration of the Priesthood to righteous service in the temple.

We learn from this brief amount of research that the Old Testament was overseen by God and completed by the Great High Priest of Revival, Ezra. He made the final edits, using the more developed language of his day to clarify many things in the writings of Moses, David, Solomon, and others up until his day.

This was finished around middle 400 B.C., after the restoring of the people and Jerusalem in the days of Darius the Emperor (speculation on my part).

By the time of the finished scriptures of the New Testament, we are looking at the only living witness to survive the persecutions of the Mystery of Iniquity, this being the Apostle John, writer of the final book of the New Testament, Revelation. There are eight writers who compose the completely New Testament. The coming change in priesthood by Jesus Christ is the determining factor for canonization of the New Testament Scriptures.

Hebrews 1:1-2 God, who at sundry times and in different manners spoke in time past unto the fathers by the prophets, (2) Hath in these last days spoken unto us by his Son, whom he hath appointed heir of all things, by whom also he made the worlds.

Under the new Covenant, Jesus Christ is the only High Priest and Mediator between God and mankind. Chapters 8-9 of Hebrews plainly say Jesus has replaced the Aaron/Levitical Priesthood.

Therefore, authority no longer rests on the temple priesthood to canonize scripture. It is now through the testimony of Jesus Christ men will write and canonize scripture. The New Testament writings plainly show us that God uses devout, righteous, converted men to pen the most important aspects of the witness and testimony of the saving power and faith in Jesus Christ. They document the Way of Life for the Christian Virtues that reflect the presence of Jesus Christ in people.

The facts are undeniable: Ezra the Priest of God set in order the Books of the Old Testament, and rightfully so, for he was the Faithful Priest of God who restored Israel back to the ways of the Lord after their captivity.

The New Testament was a work in progress during the life of Christ and for at least 70 years after the crucifixion. The Gospels were written and canonized by their authors. The Acts of the Apostles and Epistles or letters of Paul were set in order by Paul, Mark, and Luke. Last of all, John, Peter, and James finish the New Testament.

IGNORING THE SCRIPTURES

*T*here are two events I wish to relate from the scriptures about the foundational teaching for the church Jesus set up. What Jesus says was completely ignored in these two events. One of the events is an encounter with Peter. This scripture is later twisted from its intent by the Papacy to fabricate a premise for their authority.

Matthew 16:18 And I say also unto thee, that thou art Peter, and upon this rock I will build my church; and the gates of hell shall not prevail against it.

There is the Greek consideration upon the words, "thou art Peter [Greek, "petros" — literally 'a little rock],' and upon this rock [Greek, "Petra"] I will build my church." He does not promise to build His church upon Peter, but upon Himself, as Peter is careful to tell us. (1Peter 2:4-9).

Jesus built His church upon Himself, not Peter. The Church of Rome claims its church is built upon Peter as its first Apostle and founder. This is not what Jesus tells His disciples. On the night before His arrest, Jesus told His disciples how the government of His church would be set up. He also introduced the new Sacraments for sustaining church membership.

Matthew 26:26-28 And as they were eating, Jesus took bread, and blessed it, and brake it, and gave it to the disciples, and said, Take, eat; this is my body. (27) And he took the cup, and gave thanks, and gave it to them, saying, Drink ye all of it; (28) For this is my blood of the new testament, which is shed for many for the remission of sins.

Luke 22:24-26 And there was also a strife among them, which of them should be accounted the greatest. (25) And he said unto them, the kings of the Gentiles exercise lordship over them; and they that exercise authority upon them are called benefactors. (26) But ye shall not be so: but he that is greatest among you, let him be as the younger; and he that is chief, as he that doth serve.

These scriptures are the basic principles for recognizing the church Jesus was creating. But, as we shall see, this is not what men of carnal thinking; position and power are claimed for the church. If pollution can be found at the source of any stream, the whole will be permeated with contamination. Another way of saying this is things equal to the same thing are equal to each other.

Put poison anywhere in the bloodstream and the whole becomes poisoned. This is true of churches and carnal-minded people. Per Catholic doctrine, Jesus distinguishes Simon Peter to hold the first place of honor and authority. They promote the lie that Peter was first bishop of Rome.

Furthermore, they consider every bishop of Rome to be Peter's successor and the rightful superior of all other bishops. Although Peter never has the title of Pope or Vicar of Christ, in this sense the Catholic Church considers Peter the first Pope.

The church in Rome was already flourishing when Paul wrote his Epistle to the Romans about AD 57. He greeted some fifty people in Rome by name, but not Peter whom he knows. There is also no mention of Peter in Rome later during Paul's two-year stay there in Acts 28, about AD 60-62.

Church historians consistently consider Peter and Paul martyred under the reign of Nero, around AD 65 after the Great Fire of Rome.

My opinion is their Simon Peter was Simon Magus, known as Simon the Magician. I will take a moment to give my reasons: When you read the following scriptures about this Simon Magus, you will get the impression he could easily create the position of a Pope or Priest. He convinced the people he was a Great Man with the great power of God until Phillip and the apostles came to Samaria. He offered to buy the power of the Holy Spirit from them. He even wanted someone else to pray for him when he realizes he has made a mistake.

Confession booth, penance—sound familiar? Just a coincidence? He was a magician who bewitched the people with sorcery. I report, you decide. He was what I call your one day a week believer. He was baptized and believed in the name of Jesus.

But look what happened when the Apostle Peter and John showed up in Samaria. They found out that the Holy Spirit had not been received yet; they laid hands upon some for the receiving of the Holy Spirit. But when they came to Simon or Peter (Simon is Aramaic for Peter) he wanted to buy it. (Indulgences?) It is not that far of a stretch, is it?

Acts 8:8-24 (8) And there was boundless joy in that city. (9) But there was a certain man, called Simon, which before time in the same city used sorcery, and bewitched the people of Samaria, giving out that himself was some great one: (10) To whom they all gave heed, from the least to the greatest, saying, this man is the great power of God. (11) And to him they had regard because that of long time he had bewitched them with sorceries. (12) But when they believed Philip preaching the things concerning the kingdom of God, and the name of Jesus Christ, they were baptized, both men and women. (13) Then Simon himself believed also: and when he was baptized, he continued with Philip, and wondered, beholding the miracles and signs which were done. (14) Now when the apostles which were at Jerusalem heard that Samaria had received the word of God, they sent unto them Peter and John: (15) Who, when they were come down, prayed for them, that they might receive the Holy Ghost: (16) (For yet he was fallen upon none of them: only they were baptized in the name of the Lord Jesus.) (17) Then laid they their hands on them, and they received the Holy Spirit. (18) And when Simon saw that through laying on of the apostles' hands the Holy Spirit was given, he offered them money, (19) Saying, give me also this power, that on whomsoever I lay hands, he may receive the Holy Spirit. (20) But Peter said unto him, thy money perishes with thee, because thou hast thought that the gift of God may be bought with money. (21) Thou hast neither part nor lot in this matter: for thy heart is not right in the sight of God. (22) Repent therefore of this thy wickedness, and pray God, if the thought of thine heart may have forgiven thee. (23) For I perceive that thou art in the gall of bitterness, and in the bond of iniquity. (24) Then answered Simon, and said, pray ye to the Lord for me, that none of these things which ye have spoken come upon me.

The New Testament says nothing about Peter's connection to Rome, nor even that he founded a church anywhere, but Irenaeus of Lyons believed in the 2nd century that Peter and Paul founded the Church in Rome and appointed Linus as succeeding bishop.

The Catholic Church speaks of the Pope, the Bishop of Rome, as the successor of Saint Peter. This is often interpreted to imply that Peter was the first Bishop of Rome. However, it is also said that the institution of the papacy is not dependent on Peter being Bishop of Rome or on his ever having been in Rome. While accepting that Peter came to Rome and was martyred there, scholars find no historical evidence that he held episcopal office.

However, per Catholic belief, Jesus distinguished Simon Peter to hold the first place of honor and authority in the church. This is contradictory to what Jesus told His disciples. The Catholic Church's recognition of Peter as head of its church on Earth (with Christ being its heavenly head) is based on its own chair of authority interpretation of two passages, not what the actual Greek properly translated tells us.

I suppose it really does not matter to our salvation, but it is not how Jesus set up the administrative authority of His church.

CONSTANTINE

This is another turning point in the history of religious and academic history. Regardless of what institutions of higher learning teach, this man was just as responsible for corrupting the Words of God as those who misprinted and mistranslated the word.

We are still years ahead of mass printing of information. Information during this time of history was meticulously handwritten by men who dedicated their entire lives solely to being a scribe. Knowledge in any form is power.

During times of religious and political oppression, the deceivers use knowledge and writings as prized possessions to control the thinking of the masses of people. The information was not copied by these controlling people of power and spoon-fed to the common people. The people of those times had to rely solely upon the reading of scriptures from the Priests and Preachers, no different from what the ancient Babylonians did post flood.

Constantine was not a true follower of Jesus Christ. He was a Pagan, a murderer, and a politician. He was a carnal Pagan seeking a solution to the constant problems from the New Faith started by Jesus Christ. He solved the problem by professing Christianity and combining it with Paganism. Constantine was one of the first people of the Ecumenical Movement. Christianity was a political solution for Constantine. He could not conquer the New Faith, so he corrupted it.

Remember what I said earlier about history is full of "wolves in sheep's skin"? My understanding of the ecumenical movement comes from the Roman Catholic Church's attempts to reconcile with Christians who have become separated over theological issues.

This is still going on today. Compromise is not always the answer to differences in theological issues. Jesus said, You shall know the truth, and the truth will set you free. Compromising the truth to have a good relationship with someone does not solve the issues that separate people!

Jesus said if you believe and follow Him you will not always be able to have a good relationship with others who have their own interpretation and agenda for living life. A significant part of the Christian world of the 21st century is the reconciliation of the various denominations by overcoming the historical divisions within Christianity.

Even where there is broad agreement upon this goal, approaches to ecumenism vary. Generally, Protestants see the goal of ecumenism as agreements on teachings about central issues of faith, with mutual pastoral accountability between the diverse churches about the teachings of salvation. Just like the Jewish Priesthood, Constantine claimed a form of religious purity with no substance.

Later the Papacy did he same thing as they come to power in many phases of the changing power of nations they create and control. Both of these systems of religion were made by carnally driven by men seeking power and prestige rather than seeking God's will.

The revolt of the Jews against the Roman Empire resulted in complete destruction of the Jewish religious order, and the people were scattered over all the world. Their persecution of the followers of Jesus was diminished. Now the opposition to the Gospel of Christ is subtle under the flag of the ecumenical movement started by Constantine and continued into modern times.

The combining of Christianity and Paganism soon became the combining of Church and State. This is when the deceit and perversion began and grew into all types of persecutions against the true Gospel of Christ. Now we are entering the time of corruption of the teachings of Christ.

There are a couple of historic conferences that changed the influence of religion for masses of people. One was the <u>Council of Nicaea, 325 A.D. and the Council of Trent, 331 A.D.</u> These conferences were the result of several years of treachery and elevating the philosophies of men to a chair of authority over the scriptures for two reasons, one being to completely wipe out the Jewish faith; the other to show the Catholic Church as the sole authority speaking for Christ.

As we have discussed before, Jesus Christ was a created person who did not have eternal existence as God. Origen (185-254) taught this, and he was right on that one point. However, the later bishops of the Catholic Church did not seriously take him. Another historian of this time period was a man named Eusebius. He was a great admirer of Origen and a student of his philosophy. After Eusebius edited the Hexapla, Origen's bible, Constantine ordered Eusebius to prepare 50 copies for him.

Eusebius of Caesarea (260-340 A.D.) is called the first church historian. Constantine commissioned him to place the 50 copies in churches. This is where much of the changes began. Other perversions follow these times, even contradicting what the corrupted versions say.

By 325 A.D., Constantine, a wolf of paganism and sun worship, assumed openly the sheep's clothing of the Christian religion. He did this by merging Paganism with Christianity. From his self-appointed authority, Constantine began the long road of Gospel Perversions driven by pride, power, and prejudice over the poor masses of people in the world. He totally ignored the Holy Spirit Jesus sent to guide people into all of the truth taught by Him.

This is where I began to understand something clearly at last about wolves in sheep's skin. Just see how easy it is before the printing press, they were the sole authority for the things taught about life. This is not any different from what Nimrod and Semiramis did at the Tower of Babel. It is the same spirit of deceit. (Remember this about spirits, they never die.) Constantine, not the apostle Peter, was the true progenitor of the Roman Catholic Church. He created a church that resembles the church prophesied by the scriptures by using the statement Jesus said to Peter. It is the church pushing its influence on the peoples of the world and will do so until the second return of Jesus Christ. This will be a story revealing the long line of Dictators, Military Generals, Emperors, Bishops, and Priests who seek world dominance and assume the position of Jesus Christ as the head of the church.

A PROPHETIC HISTORY LESSON

Prophecy is a subject most people step away from. It is not a popular subject with most people, but it can be very instructive when understood in its context. God used prophets all through the times of the Old Testament. Sometimes it takes a period of time to pass before the prophecy makes sense. I think it is important to spend a little time explaining how prophecy is a large part of my understanding the purpose for mankind's future in light of God's intentions versus man's religious interpretations.

I am speaking plainly of a world of people who reject God, those who don't reject God, and those who are deceived about the whole process. There are so many contributors to prophetic interpretations causing confusion; I understand why people stay away from the subject. But that is a grave mistake. The bible interprets the bible when it is approached with an earnest desire to know what God's intentions are for the future of mankind.

PROPHECY REVEALS THE "DEEP THINGS" OF GOD

*C*onsider these words of testimony from the Apostle Peter: *2 Peter 1:16 For we have not followed cunningly devised fables, when we made known unto you the power and coming of our Lord Jesus Christ but were eyewitnesses of his majesty. 2 Peter 1:19-21 We have also a surer word of prophecy; whereunto you do well that ye take heed, as unto a light that shines in a dark place, until the day dawn, and the day star arise in your hearts: (20) Knowing this first, that no prophecy of the scripture is of any private interpretation. (21) For the prophecy came not in old time by the will of man: but holy men of God spoke as they were moved by the Holy Spirit.*

1. The Apostles are eyewitnesses to the presence of Jesus Christ and what He tells them about the past, present, and future.

2. No prophecy is of any private interpretation.

3. Prophecy comes not by the will of man.

4. These Biblical prophesies are on the men who speak to them by the Holy Spirit of GOD.

This does not mean, as God's children, we cannot explore these prophecies with the Holy Spirit guiding our minds to understand or at least guess on the meaning, warning, or significance of prophecies. We can certainly document from 2,000 years of history some prophecies that have been fulfilled or did not happen.

Jonah's prophecy to Nineveh is an example of Prophecy changing due to the conditions being met to prevent its fulfillment.

Amos 3:7 Surely the Lord GOD will do nothing, but he reveals his secret unto his servants the prophets.

God has pleaded with His people down through time to listen to the preachers He sent to warn them of the consequences that would come upon them for their disobedience to Him. With the information available to us in these end times, we have no excuse not to find out, within a small margin of speculation, what is going to happen to Christians in the last days before Christ returns.

As we study the Scriptures, it becomes clear there is a profound unity between the Old and New Testaments. This unity is proven by the fact that over one-third of the New Testament is made up of quotes from the Old Testament. In truth, many Old Testament passages simply cannot be understood without the New Testament.

Consider the many prophecies referring to Jesus Christ, such as those in Psalms 22 and Isaiah 53. Without the writings of the New Testament, we would never realize that Old Testament texts were Messianic in nature. Similarly, dozens of Old and New Testament prophecies about the end time cannot be understood without the book of Revelation. These examples show the unity of Scripture and are proof of God's inspiration of the entire Bible as the complete Word of God.

In the book of Isaiah God supplies us the standard by which to seek Him and understand His word, as well as discern those who speak the truth: Isaiah 8:20 "To the law and testimony! If they speak not according to this word, it is because there is no light in them." Revelation19:10 And I fell at his feet to worship him. And he said unto me, See thou do it not: I am thy fellow servant, and of thy brethren that have the testimony of Jesus: worship God: for the testimony of Jesus is the spirit of prophecy.

Hebrews 1:1-2 God, who at sundry times and in different manners spoke in time past unto the fathers by the prophets, (2) Has in these last days spoken unto us by his Son, whom he hath appointed heir of all things, by whom also he made the worlds.

The unlimited freedom which some preachers and teachers take with prophesies of the Holy Scriptures often cause, criticism, confusion, and controversy. The apostle Peter says, No prophecy is of any private interpretation.

From this I discern that the oracles of God, and especially the prophecies of Jesus Christ to His disciples and apostle John, are in no way dependent upon the solutions and opinions of carnal critics.

Anyone can study prophecy and make up a scenario that sounds plausible. The key to understanding prophecy has a lot to do with the history we just waded through about nations and God's intervention from time to time.

The matching of history to prophecy is essential. The knowledge of the origin of nations and where people have migrated helps. Knowing there is a great deception that is behind the scenes of governments of men, religions of men, and the orchestration of demonic spirits in the background makes it quite an adventure.

Although the past times are blending in with the present, the works of God in ages past are just beginning to develop, especially in these latter times or end of times of the 21st Century. Let the Spirit of Prophecy bear on us with what Jesus says about the future times, far beyond the kingdoms of men! God gives Daniel a peek at the overall events, just enough so those who are seeking the better way of life can have hope and confidence it will happen. There is truly little detail given in Daniel the 9th chapter, but the timeline covers over 2,000 years of living, including the birth of the Messiah, His death, resurrection and second coming!

Think about this: Jesus came, pioneered the way of salvation for us, and never wrote down one word of what He taught. It all comes to us through the witnesses that lived with Him, and even those who sought His death, sentenced Him to die, and convinced the Romans to carry out the execution via crucifixion. Christ left a lot of witnesses to testify of His coming and going and coming again. By their acts of treachery and violence, His enemies were witnesses to the life of the Son of God, Jesus the Christ.

THE SPIRT OF PROPHECY

So, it is with the Spirit of Prophecy. Its writings, spiritually discerned, produce both hope and confidence. While it is often, on the surface, speaking to individuals and nations, at the same time it is referencing doctrines and principles of a holy life as much as is possible while in this flesh. The reason prophecy is so important to the 21st century believer is its Spiritual authority in prophetic vision as set forth by the commands of God to regulate human life in preparation for ETERNAL LIFE!

We as Spiritually begotten Christians are privileged to understand these things by the power of the Holy Spirit given to believers as they accept Jesus Christ as Master and Savior of their lives.

INSET

<u>As you read through the next section of information, do not presume I am attacking the Catholic Church specifically.</u> I am reporting the historical facts of many different systems of religious order that have come out of the hearts of men. It is not my intent to prejudice anyone's thinking about who and what they choose to worship. I am just analyzing the choices that are part of history and prophecy with the Holy Bible as the guide.

Remember, life is a series of choices for us. The following information is what I discovered to base my understanding of the "Plan of God" for mankind's destiny.

The destinies are result of personal choice in lifestyle aligned with or apposed too God's intentions for mankind.

Remember I said Daniel was told to shut up; seal the book. John, on the contrary, was told (Rev.22:10) not to seal his visions. Daniel's prophecy refers to a distant time. Daniel 8:26 is implying the vision is not to be understood for the people in Daniel's time. What in Daniel's time was hidden is more fully explained in Revelation, and as the time draws nearer, it will be clearer still. But in Daniel 12:4, Daniel 12:9 (compare Daniel8:26), *the command is, Seal the book, for the vision shall be for many days.*

The fulfillment of Daniel's prophecy is distant; that of John's prophecy is near. This is why John does not to seal his visions (Revelation 22:10 "Seal not").

The New Testament explains the time of the end and fulfillment of the Plan of God for the end. The Church, for which John wrote his Revelation, needs more to be impressed with the shortness of the period, as it is inclined, showing its carnal origin, to conform to the world and forget the coming of the Lord.

The mainstream churches of today are caught up in high-tech programing and are looking more like the worldly than ever. The Revelation points, on the one hand, to Christ's coming as distant, for it shows the succession of the seven seals, trumpets, and vials. It proclaims, *Behold, I come quickly.*

So, Christ marks many events to intervene before His coming, and yet He also says *Behold, I come quickly,* because our right attitude is that of continual prayerful watching for His coming.

This attitude of watchfulness and personal preparation is diminished in the churches. Daniel is to shut up the words because it is not the time for the completion of God's Plan. There are several reasons for the command to Seal the Book.

The Jews were just coming out of captivity and given a chance to repent of their idolatry and sins.

- Salvation was to be taught and opened to all nations of mankind.
- The remaining kingdoms of mankind had not yet come to power on the earth as revealed by God in a dream to Nebuchadnezzar. The interpretation was given to Daniel for a position in the First world ruling kingdom of men.
- The Messiah had not yet been born to set up a NEW COVENANT. Can we see the working of God in the history of men's governments? God used them to spread His intentions for mankind.

If the Jews had not been taken to Babylon, how would the Babylonians have ever learned about the One True God, above all their idols? I think we sometimes do not see the overall wisdom of God working in His most precious creation, mankind. It is better to expose a lost person to the direction of Godliness than to just destroy them with punishment.

The punishment of death—is this not the lesson Jesus teaches as He walks among all of mankind? Jesus warns us about being judgmental with people who do not yet understand things He reveals to His disciples, and they pass on to us.

Remember, prophecy has a dual fulfillment. The key for us is the last part of the Scripture. Verses 21 and 22! Now we know from academic history that in 70 A.D. the Temple and city of Jerusalem is laid in ruins by Titus (First Fulfillment). It was a holocaust like the death camps of Nazi Germany in 1942-45.

The Great Tribulation in the future will be a time of trouble mankind has never experienced in all of the history of the world. Notice the context referring to the Great Tribulation:

Daniel 12:1 And at that time shall Michael stand up, the great prince which stands for the children of thy people: and there shall be a time of trouble, such as never was since there was a nation even to that same time: and at that time thy people shall be delivered, every one that shall be found written in the book.

Daniel 12:4 But thou, O Daniel, shut up the words, and seal the book, even to the time of the end: many shall run to and fro, and knowledge shall be increased.

There it is. The information has been sealed since Daniel's time, while knowledge has been increasing. Technology is growing extremely fast; it becomes obsolete months after it has been discovered. The times of the Gentiles will be over at the Second Coming of Jesus Christ.

Look at academic history. Jerusalem has been trodden down century after century until 1948. And even now they are attacked by rockets at least once or twice a month. This is when the information was sealed up until our time; the end time of man ruling man. And the last line of the 10th verse plainly says, The wise will understand. God wants us to know what is going to happen in the last days of man's governments in the world.

He has sent His message through His son, Jesus Christ, the only one who is worthy to open the seals binding up the information for the end time consummation:

To really understand the power of this Romani's system of church and state, I must go back into academic history and then overlay the bible information from Daniel and Revelation. This will produce understanding to the characterization Daniel expresses about the dreaded and terrible Fourth Kingdom. This turns out to be the worldwide influence of Roman Empire through the Catholic church. Daniel specifies this kingdom as a dreadful, diverse kingdom from the preceding three kingdoms and will dominate the world until Christ returns.

Daniel 7:7-8 After this I saw in the night visions, and behold a fourth beast, dreadful and terrible, and strong exceedingly; and it had great iron teeth: it devoured and brake in pieces and stamped the residue with the feet of it: and it was diverse from all the beasts that were before it; and it had ten horns. (8) I considered the horns, and behold, there came up among them another little horn, before whom there were three of the first horns plucked up by the roots: and behold, in this horn were eyes like the eyes of man, and a mouth speaking great things.

The information Daniel revealed is prophetic, and there is no way the people of the Roman Empire could follow his prophecy as a script to create the history we will cover. The Fourth Kingdom Daniel sees has 7 heads and 10 horns. Heads is metaphoric for kingdoms and Horns is metaphoric for power or Kings of Kingdoms.

This is the part of my story that most people get bored with, lose interest, and frankly do not have the patience to wade through the details of information needed to understand the language of the bible. The language of the bible makes more sense when I begin to compare these metaphors with academic history.

Again, this is what I believe is unique about knowledge when you combine the three things I choose to be the ingredients for this story. If you do not wish to understand and know the truth about the origin of Protestant Christianity and its roots set up on partial and perverted information, you need to stop now and read no further!

I wish there were a simple way to explain it, but there isn't. Think about this before you decide to stop reading.

Do you feel like we are living today in the end times of the governments of mankind?

Does it feel like the USA is falling behind the rest of the world and looking more like the third world countries?

Does it seem that crime, hate crimes, racial prejudice, terror, and moral depravity is on the increase?

Do you feel the effects of a government run by people with no common sense about the significant issues we face today as good hard-working people?

Do you feel less secure as a nation as countries in the Middle East fall to beheadings and all sorts of war and destruction?

Are you wondering why so many "natural disasters" are headlining the news these days?

Do you wonder why mainstream religious churches are dying on the vine and people are discontent with religion of all kinds? There is a reason for how you feel. I feel the same way and that is why I have been searching for the reason we get up, struggle through each day, and go to bed only to get up and do it again. I found my answer for why I was born, and I hope my writing it down for you will help you see your choices for destiny.

Ok, enough preaching, back to information that will eventually lead us to a conclusion for all this history and future events. The last part of the verse in Daniel 7:8 is the key to understanding the things Jesus tells his disciples in the Olivet Prophecy and what He reveals to John in the Revelation of Jesus Christ, the last book of the Bible. These Ten Horns will now be assigned to their place in secular History as far as time has passed. Most of the Horns are history, some are yet to appear in our time, the Latter Days.

Principle of interpretations for interpreting Bible prophecy are from the Bible either by direct explanation or are decided from the metaphoric language used by the author. This passage of scripture is a direct explanation. An angel explains: beasts stand for kingdoms. *"The four great beasts are four kingdoms that will rise from the earth."*

Daniel 7:17 These great beasts, which are four, are four kings, which shall arise out of the earth.

Animal horns stand for kings:

Daniel 7:20. And of the ten horns that were in his head, and of the other which came up, and before whom three fell; even of that horn that had eyes, and a mouth that spoke very great things, whose look was stouter than his fellows.

This description shows HORNS stands for Kings or Leaders of a Kingdom in power. This principle is derived from examples rather than by direct statement. The three examples are found by parallel paraphrase when the vision is set beside its interpretation. Daniel 7: (verse 7)"and it had ten horns", (verse 24) "the ten horns are ten kings" (verse 8)" there before me was another horn", (verse 24) "After them another king" (verse 8)" three of the first horns were uprooted before it", (verse 24) "he will subdue three kings". To place this scripture into world history I found the events of struggle for power during the demise of Roman Empire. "I considered the horns, and behold, there came up among them another little horn, before whom there were three of the first horns plucked up by the roots: and behold, in this horn were eyes like the eyes of man, and a mouth speaking great things."

Various Kings were warring for domination of the Empire. The little Horn is the one mentioned in Daniel the Seventh Chapter. It is the little Horn behind the Military power of specific nations that I will follow down through history and on into the future prior to the return of Jesus Christ. It reveals itself as the Papacy of Rome. This will be a detailed study of the multiple elements that make up the FOURTH BEAST from the book of Daniel. There will be a lot of history to research and compare with the scriptures to achieve understanding of who these HORNS or KINGS stand for.

I will expose the ROOTS of why the majority of the Christian believers are still in darkness about the things God expects from His Chosen people, Jew, or Gentile. It will be shocking and uncomfortable to read and digest. It will reveal false teachings concerning God's plan for mankind and life after death. It contradicts the true teachings of the Bible, and not the teaching men of carnal thinking have perpetuated from the 1st Century until present day. What I discover is not latest information. It has been available to us for no less than 500 Years. It is information that explains why the Jews are the most persecuted people on earth! It sorts out the reasons the term CHRISTIAN needs to be qualified in these end times!

It is a surprise to me and will be a shock to the majority of church people in the world, especially when the players rise to power once again for a final attempt to stamp out the teachings of Jesus Christ and the Apostles. It will show the Complete Gospel and revive the Faith Once Delivered by Jesus Christ and His apostles. It is our destiny. From this page on to the end of my story you will see the reason the fourth beast of Daniel's vision is so dreadful and influential upon the entire world. It is a beast with multiple lives down through the timeline of history, from history to the present, and on into the future.

Understanding the significance of this religious system backed with Military force has caused me to see the big picture of life and why I was even born. It is a manmade religious system that started after the flood of Noah and will continue until the second coming of Jesus Christ. Most people in the world could not care less about this information. I did not care either, until I began to search for answers concerning the continual wars, strife, and struggle all down through history for anyone who has ever lived. I only hope telling my story will help others to get a grasp on our ultimate purpose for being born.

IDENTIFYING THE RELIGIOUS SYSTEM

Because religion and faith are sources for many people to search for meaning and happiness in their lives, I feel it is the major study for me to dig out the reasons it is failing in the 21st century. It is a system of religion that teaches you not to think for yourself; the Priests and Preachers do it all for you. You will see the reason by the end of my research.

At the beginning of my story, I made a brief reference to the Babylon Mystery Religion. Cush started this, Semiramis, and Nimrod soon after the Flood. It is a carnal system of replacing the intentions of the Invisible God for mankind with a controlling carnal system of religion. It began as a system of dictatorial power over the masses. It flourishes on the mushroom concept of keeping people in the dark. You are taught that your potential is less than what God's word is telling you.

Anything that you question is sloughed off as being more than we are supposed to know about God. This is the system that Shem, Noah's son, fought most all his life after the flood and eventually brought to a halt for a brief time. Think about Shem's obedience to God; he had to eventually kill his own nephew, Nimrod, to put a stop to that system. It soon returned, identified as heathen paganism. It is a system of carnal promiscuity and perversions of the intended way of life for mankind. No sense of responsibility to a higher order of life ruling the universe.

Now we are at another time in the timeline of biblical and academic history when this carnal perversion is taking the chair of authority once again. The perversion becomes clear in the governments of powerful nations and a specific Empire. It begins with the subtle changes in the writings of the apostles and becomes intertwined with the military power of the Roman Empire. The prophet Jeremiah says it very plainly in the time of his inspired writing. It is a discourse that no doubt Martin Luther himself pondered over as he began the document that starts the Protestant Revolution in the 16th Century.

Jeremiah warned the people of God about this false religious system.

Jeremiah 51:6-7 Flee out of the midst of Babylon and deliver every man his soul: be not cut off in her iniquity; for this is the time of the LORD'S vengeance; he will make unto her a recompense. (7) Babylon hath been a golden cup in the LORD'S hand, which made all the earth drunken: the nations have drunken of her wine; therefore, the nations are <u>mad</u>.

The English word mad is properly translated in Hebrew as <u>not mad in the sense of anger</u>. But mad <u>in the sense of insane foolish ritualistic pride and vanity</u>, assuming a position of authority and glorification in the place of God.

Hâlal haw-lal' A primitive root; to be clear (originally of sound, but usually of color); to shine; hence to make a show; to boast; and thus, to be (clamorously) foolish; to rave.

causatively to celebrate; also, to stultify: - (make) boast (self), celebrate, commend, (deal, make), fool (-ish, -ly), glory, give [light], be (make, feign self) mad (against), give in marriage, [sing, be worthy of] praise, rage, renowned, shine.

Does this not describe the over-the-top rituals of the Church of Rome? Even in these modern times the Pope is surrounded by wealth and rituals carried on from centuries of its roots. The mad Jeremiah is referring to are the mysteries of the religious system.

It is common knowledge that the metaphoric word for church is woman in prophetic language. As early as 1825, Pope Leo XII struck a medallion with his picture on one side. The other side is a woman holding a Golden Cup in one hand and a Cross in the other. She is depicted as sitting on a huge orb standing for the world. The inscription around her says in Latin: "sedet super universum." *<u>The Whole World Is Her Seat</u>*. This is about as mad or bizarre as it can be plainly admitted.

This did not come into view during the decline of the Greek Empire after it was divided among Alexander's four Generals. However, the roots of this system began with one of the four Generals.

The Seleucids were early Roman people whose ancestors are the Etruscans of ancient times. Antiochus IV persecuted the Jews mercilessly in 164 B.C., about 130 years before Rome becomes the Roman Empire in 31 B.C.

As my timeline of academic history progresses I will insert the various heads of this beast down through time. We are now approaching the falling and demise of the 1st Head of the Roman Empire with the information covered about Constantine the Great of 300's A.D.

DANIEL'S PROPHECY OF THE FOURTH KINGDOM

This will be a quick lesson in the history of the Roman Empire and the Revived Roman Empire. It will include when the Catholic Church became the dominant influence over the Emperors and Empire and then the rest of the world.

The information is taken from my first 2009 book, "Researching the Faith Once Delivered." Visualize in your mind the Great Image of Nebuchadnezzar's Dream. See it as man figure standing for Four World Ruling Empires.

- A Head of Gold = Babylonian Empire beginning with Nebuchadnezzar as King.
- Arms and Breastplate of Silver = Persia beginning with Cyrus and Macedonia beginning with Darius. Both Kings of this Medo-Persian Empire continuing the ways of Babylon!
- Belly and Thighs of Brass = Greece beginning with Alexander the Great; then division between four Generals.
- Legs and feet of Iron with Toes of Iron and Clay = Roman Empire beginning with Augustus and Tiberius as Co-Ruling Emperors of the East and West Division of the Empire. Rome in the West; Constantinople in the East. Inside this Great Image is the Dragon. It is the heart and power behind these Kingdoms.

Once again, Satan is trying to deceive and destroy mankind! Now visualize a Great Stone hewn without hands crushing the feet of the Image and grinding it to powder. This is the OVERVIEW of the end of the TIMES OF THE GENTILES in prophecy.

The Stone is Christ returning to earth the Second Time with Power and Glory to end, for the last time, the attempts of men and the lies of Satan to destroy all of humanity.

Daniel 7:17-18 (17) These great beasts, which are four, are four kings, which shall arise out of the earth. (18) But the saints of the Most High shall take the kingdom, and have the kingdom forever, even for ever and ever.

The Fourth Beast is the most powerful and dreaded of the other Three. The fact is, the Fourth Beast carries more of Ancient Babylon in its religious character than its predecessors. Now let us begin to reveal this Fourth Beast and

its many sides from history, and its revival and prophesied participation in world events of the 21st Century.

The Roman Empire was set up in 31B.C. and was an estate run system with pagan religion dominating its culture. This Empire was the most vicious Empire with widespread dominance in all of its captured provinces. We are most familiar with its lust for entertainment and pleasure through the Caesars as depicted in movies with chariot races, gladiators, and staged wars in the huge arenas of its time. The mauling of Christians by wild beasts became popular for many years after Christ left the earth. The execution of the Apostles with influence of the Jewish leaders was carried out by the Roman government.

Persecution of the Christians was supported by Roman leadership in an attempt to bring about total peace within the provinces of Rome. The persecutions only emboldened the cause of Christianity and caused it to spread throughout the empire. A peaceful solution was achieved by the Roman Emperor, Constantine.

It was Constantine the Great who legalized Christianity and stopped the persecutions in 311 A.D. Christianity was brought into the government and tied to it so that it could be controlled. The following years he claimed to see a sign of the cross in the sky, and in 321 A.D. designated Sunday as a general holiday. By 330 A.D. he ceased issuing coins with the image of the Sun-god with whom he was named.

For the next 100 years or so, the paganism of Rome became the New Christianity. The power of the Emperor was dominated by an emerging

Papacy. Constantine selected Byzantium (later renamed Constantinople, modern day Istanbul) as its new capital in 324 A.D.

Like Rome, this city was built on 7 hills. This became the two legs of Iron on the Image in Daniel 2:33. Two capital cities, east and west! However, the Germanic tribes crossed the Danube into the Empire, led by the Visigoths. A few years later, Odovacar the Herulian deposed Romulus Augustus, the last Emperor in the west, Ravenna, 476 A.D. marking the traditional date for the end of the Roman Empire.

Little by little the empire collapsed; it was not a massive decline. It happened over a hundred-year period; a slow death.

The Fourth Beast is the Roman Empire. It is described by Daniel and John as having Seven Heads and Ten Horns. Before I can get the historical picture of the Fourth Beast sorted out, I have to first differentiate between the Fourth Beast before it is wounded to death and the Fourth Beast, resurrected with 7 heads and 10 horns.

Revelation 13:1-3 And I stood upon the sand of the sea, and saw a beast rise up out of the sea, having seven heads and ten horns, and upon his horns ten crowns, and upon his heads the name of blasphemy. (2) And the beast which I saw was like unto a leopard, and his feet were as the feet of a bear, and his mouth as the mouth of a lion: and the dragon gave him his power, and his seat, and great authority. (3) And I saw one of his heads as it were wounded to death; and his deadly wound was healed: and all the world wondered after the beast. [Just check out how much Roman influence has dominated the western civilizations for centuries!]

The Fourth Beast before it is wounded to death was The Roman Empire, 31 B.C. to 476 A.D. It was wounded to death by the Germanic tribes, and its resurrection came some years later in all parts of Europe.

Daniel 7:8 I considered the horns, and behold, there came up among them another little horn, (the emerging Papacy) before whom there were three of the first horns plucked up by the roots: and behold, in this horn were eyes like the eyes of man, and a mouth speaking great things.

It is beneficial to take the time to review a few points of history related to the 3 horns that are rooted up. This information will help confirm the fact it becomes the Papacy of Rome is behind the rooting up of the First Three Horns and is the power of influence behind the remaining 7 Horns and Heads of this Fourth Beast down through time.

As we read the historical information we can see the prejudice and animosity of Rome, influenced by the Bishops and Pope of the Fallen Empire. The treachery and murderous attitude of the Roman leadership infects the Fallen Empire as men war and murder to secure the Throne for themselves.

It should be noted that these 3 horns are all of German lineage. First is a list of the Three Horns rooted up and defeated by the Roman/Catholic Empire after 476 A.D.

* First Horn:

The Vandals In 400 or 401 A.D., possibly because of attacks by the Huns, the Vandals under king Godigisel, along with their allies (the Sarmatia Alans and Germanic Serbians), moved westwards into Roman territory. During the Emperor Valens's reign (364–78) the Vandals, much like the Goths earlier, accepted Arianism, a belief that was in opposition to that of Nicene orthodoxy of the Roman Empire.

In 429, political maneuvering in Rome was to change the landscape forever. The boy emperor Valentinian III ruled Rome (who rises to power at the age of 8), and his mother Gala Placida. However, the Roman General Flavius Aëtius, vying for power, convinced Gala Placida that her General Boniface was plotting to kill her and her son to claim the throne for himself.

When Boniface saw the letter from Rome and believed there was a plot to kill him, he enlisted the help of the Vandal King Geiseric. He promised the Vandals land in North Africa in exchange for their help.

Hilderic (523–530) was the Vandal king most tolerant toward the Catholic Church. He granted it religious freedom; so, Catholic synods were once more held in North Africa.

* Second Horn:

Heruli The Heruli (spelled variously in Latin and Greek) were a nomadic Germanic people who were subjugated by the Ostrogoth and Byzantines in the 3rd to 5th centuries. The name is related to earl (see erilaz) and is a honorific military title. One of the Heruli, Odoacer, deposed the last Western Roman emperor, Romulus Augustus. Odoacer (435–493), also known as Odovacar (from the Germanic Audawakrs, meaning watchful of wealth), was a Roman general and the first non-Roman ruler of Italy after 476. He deposed the last Western Roman Emperor, Romulus Augustus that year, but continued to rule as a client of the Emperor in Constantinople.

Odoacer is referred to as a king (Latin rex) in many documents, but the title is informal, though he himself uses it at least once and on another occasion it is used by the consul, Basalis.

In 476, Odoacer officially became the first Germanic King of Italy, and a new era began. Odoacer was an Arian Christian and is said to have been illiterate. The warriors and the families in Odoacer's federate received lands in Italy and became beneficiaries of a special tax policy. Odoacer kept the Roman administration, senate, law, and tax system of Italy. In return, he won a high level of support from the senate and people.

The Heruli lived here in peace only for a short time. The Ostrogoth king Germanrikis, the most powerful ruler of Europe, determined to annex the Herulian nation and their land to his own dominions.

About the year 370, the Ostrogoth army invaded the marshy maitis, and the Heruli were conquered. Those that survive were enslaved, and king Alkrikis was forced to become Germanrikis's vassal. The customs of the Heruli were just like those of the ancient Samogitians. According to the statements of Procopius (a historian A.D. 500-565),

the Heruli worshipped many gods; the prisoners of war were sacrificed to these gods. They used to get rid of their incurable invalids and the helpless aged people by killing them and burning their bodies. After her husband's death it was customary for a widow to burn herself on a pyre. They never tolerated slavery and they valued their liberty more than their lives. In war they were brave, enduring, and fearless of perils; on the battlefield they never wore armor.

Seldom did they even protect themselves with their shields. They were always dressed in fur coats, and while journeying, they folded and tied up the laps of their fur coats. If some Roman sneered at the "barbarian" fur coat, the Heruli said, "Warmth never cracks the bones!"

The Heruli were cordial to their neighbors, but if someone wronged them, they were extremely vengeful. In the year 405, Radagaisius, commanding a host of 200,000 men composed of Alans, Burgunds, Goths, Sueves, and Vandals, marched towards Rome. The whole of Italy is panic-stricken because Radagaisius made a public vow to burn the city of Rome and to sacrifice the Roman senators and all the Roman notables to his gods.

Why he wished to avenge himself upon the Romans, we have no definite information. As far as the city of Florence, Radagaisius met no resistance. But there a terrible battle took place. The Roman army gave no respite to Heruli, and being exhausted from a prolonged journey, the Heruli were defeated. The Herulian king Radagaisius was captured and beheaded.

*Third Horn:

The Ostrogoth The Ostrogoth (Latin: Ostrogothi or Austrogothi) were a branch of the Goths, an East Germanic tribe that played a major role in the political events of the late Roman Empire. The other branch is the Visigoths. The Ostrogoth set up a short-lived successor state of Rome in Italy and the Balkans, even briefly incorporating most of Hispania and southern Gaul.

They reached their zenith under their Romanized king, Theodoric the Great, who patronized such late Roman figures as Boethius and Cassiodorus in the first quarter of the sixth century. By mid-century, however, they were conquered by Rome in the Gothic War (535–554).

In 535, he commissioned Belisarius to attack the Ostrogoths. Belisarius quickly captured Sicily and then crossed into Italy, where he captured Naples and Rome in 536 and then marched north, taking Mediolanum (Milan) and the Ostrogoth capital of Ravenna in 540. At this point Justinian offered the Goths a generous settlement—too generous by far in Belisarius's eyes: the right to keep an independent kingdom in the Northwest of Italy and the demand that they merely give half of all their treasure to the empire. Belisarius conveyed the message to the Goths, although he himself withheld from endorsing it.

The Goths, on the other hand, felt there must be a snare somewhere. They did not trust Justinian, but because Belisarius has been so well-mannered in his conquest, they trusted him a little more and agreed to take the settlement only if Belisarius endorsed it. This condition made for something of an impasse. A faction of the Gothic nobility pointed out that their own king Witiges, who had just lost, was something of a weakling and they would need a new king. Eraric, the leader of the group, endorsed Belisarius, and the rest of the kingdom agreed. They offered him their crown. Belisarius was a soldier, not a statesman, and still loyal to Justinian. He made as if to accept the offer, rode to Ravenna to be crowned, and promptly arrested the leaders of the Goths and reclaimed their entire kingdom—no halfway settlements—for Byzantium.

October 552 or 553. Widin, the last attested member of the Gothic army, revolted in the late 550s, with minimal military help from the Franks. His uprising was fruitless; the revolt ended with Widin captured and brought to Constantinople for punishment in 561 or 562. With that final defeat, the remaining Ostrogoths went back north and (re)settled in south Austria. The Ostrogoth name died.

The nation practically evaporated with Theodoric's death. The leadership of western Europe therefore passed by default to the Franks. Consequently, Ostrogoth failure and Frankish success were crucial for the development of early medieval Europe.

The information supplied insight into the dreadful and terrible attributes of this Fourth Beast, the Roman Empire.

These Three Horns reflect the lust for Power and brutal tactics to achieve power by Roman Kings and Generals. Justinian did not even trust his own General Belisarius and became suspiciously jealous of him, as they all lusted for power.

<u>These Germanic Kingdoms brought down 500 years of Ancient Rome ruling the world, then fought among themselves for control and power over the remains of the Roman Empire.</u>

This is the Deadly Wound referred to in Revelation.

Revelation 13:3 And I saw one of his heads as it were wounded to death; and his deadly wound was healed: and all the world wondered after the beast.

The rooting out of these Germanic Kingdoms by Rome sets the stage for the healing of the Deadly Wound inflicted by the Germans causing the Fall of the Roman Empire (first 500 years of the Fourth Beast).

This will bring us to the evidence that the Deadly Wound was healed by the Papacy and began with the Emperor Justinian (the Fourth Horn, first of Seven Heads both Daniel and the Apostle John see in visions).

This Fourth Empire with many Heads has to be the Roman Empire and its many years of domination down through time. You will eventually realize that this religious system that hovered over Rome for centuries is still alive and well and will be a player in the End Times scenario just ahead of us in this 21ˢᵗ Century.

Daniel 7:7-8 After this I saw in the night visions, and behold a fourth beast, dreadful and terrible, and strong exceedingly; and it had great iron teeth: it devoured and brake in pieces and stamped the residue with the feet of it: and it was diverse from all the beasts that were before it; and it had ten horns. (8) I considered the horns, and behold, there came up among them another little horn, before whom there were three of the first horns plucked up by the roots: and behold, in this horn were eyes like the eyes of man, and a mouth speaking great things.

Two things in these verses: The Fourth Beast has Seven Heads and Ten Horns! Another little horn, but the Three Horns before it plucked up by the roots. This is prophetic language says the little horn takes power over the First Three Horns of power. Horns, meaning kings, are the kings of four nations within the crumbling Roman Empire fighting for dominance of the Kingdom.

This can be a little confusing at first, but as we develop the prophecy and relate it with world History, the description will become clear. Daniel's vision is the same Beast that John sees in his vision, 600 years later, as he describes it in his Revelation from Jesus Christ.

Revelation 13:1 And I stood upon the sand of the sea, and saw a beast rise up out of the sea, (sea = nations) having seven heads (heads = kingdoms) and ten horns, (horns = Kings) and upon his horns ten crowns, (crowns = religious authority) and upon his heads the name of blasphemy.

The Fourth Beast rising up among the peoples of the earth has Seven Heads and Ten Horns. The resurrected Fourth Empire. So, the Fourth Beast dies and is resurrected with Seven Heads and Ten Horns.

HISTORICAL BACKGROUND

*I*nformation leading up to the "Beast that was, is not, and yet is" I am going to insert events of academic history that are related to my personal education about the many aspects of religious changes and progressions down through time. The bulk of information is related to the roots of the Babylonian Mystery Religion corrupting the Gospel of Christ.

We are now looking at things around 500 A. D. The predicted scenario of the Fourth Beast of Daniel is a maze of information that I will try to keep as brief as possible. The Fourth Beast of Daniel's vision is all-inclusive of Rome up to 476 A.D., after the healing of the deadly wound, and on into the future till Christ returns.

During the last years of Rome's Glory Days, the slow decline begins with the Germanic Tribes rebelling against the establishment Roman Empire. This inflicted the deadly wound.

This will bring us to the evidence that the Deadly Wound which is healed by the Papacy and begins with the Emperor Justinian, (The Fourth Horn of the Ten and the first of Seven Heads). "FIVE ARE FALLEN, ONE IS, AND ONE IS YET TO COME"

Revelation 17:9-10 And here is the mind which hath wisdom. The seven heads are seven mountains, (kingdoms) on which the woman sits. (10) And there are seven kings: (horns) five are fallen, and one is, and the other is not yet come; and when he cometh, he must continue a short space.

Purely coincidence there are 7 actual hills in Rome. (Mountain = metaphor for kingdoms in prophetic language) The wisdom of this information in these verses is as follows: Seven Heads = Seven "Mountains." Interpretation = Seven Kingdoms The woman sits on these kingdoms. Interpretation = Babylon Religion Church.

What church today is based on this Babylon Mystery Religion? The Catholic Church. Seven Kings in the Seven Kingdoms Interpretation = Emperors of the Resurrected Fourth Beast. The next passages of scripture are expressed with brutal honesty about the religious order that empowers the Fourth Beast that was, is not, and is yet to appear on the world scene at the end time and bring with it Great Tribulation upon all who oppose its power.

I must wade through the details of these Seven Kings and Kingdoms because of what Jesus tells John to tell us about the end times. This prophecy deals with the near end of Jerusalem being trodden down by the Gentiles and the end of the Gentile Kingdoms of men.

Revelation 17:1-9 And there came one of the seven angels which had the seven vials, and talked with me, saying unto me, come hither; I will show unto thee the judgment of the great whore that sits upon many waters: (2) With whom the kings of the earth have committed fornication, and the inhabitants of the earth have been made drunk with the wine of her fornication. (3) So, he carried me away in the spirit into the wilderness: and I saw a woman sit upon a scarlet-colored beast, full of names of blasphemy, having seven heads and ten horns. (4) And the woman was arrayed in purple and scarlet color, and decked with gold and precious stones and pearls, having a golden cup in her hand full of abominations and filthiness of her fornication: (5) And upon her forehead was a name written, MYSTERY, BABYLON THE GREAT, THE MOTHER OF HARLOTS AND ABOMINATIONS OF THE EARTH. (6) And I saw the woman drunken with the blood of the saints, and with the blood of the martyrs of Jesus: and when I saw her, I wondered with great admiration. (7) And the angel said unto me, why didst thou marvel? I will tell thee the mystery of the woman, and of the beast that carries her, which hath the seven heads and ten horns. (8) The beast that thou saw was and is not; and shall ascend out of the bottomless pit and go into perdition: and they that dwell on the earth shall wonder, whose names were not written in the book of life from the foundation of the world, when they behold the beast that was, and is not, and yet is. (9) And here is the mind which hath wisdom.

These nine verses cover hundreds of years up to the present and on into the future. The language is found in other writings of the Apostle Paul and the Gospels. Daniel's 70-weeks prophecy is the overall outline with no details. The details must be sifted out as time moves forward. Much of the information has now become history. The rest of the information is yet ahead of us, sometime in this 21st century of the existence of mankind and the struggles for a one world government.

INSET

Please note from here on in this study <u>the frequency of German Domination and involvement in the affairs of the Church of Rome.</u> There is an ethnic proclivity in these people that has dominated their culture down through time. War is their specialty, along with a powerful sense of national pride. Present day Germany is more than 60 percent Roman Catholic.

Hitler was not a Catholic but certainly recognized and used their political power and influence. Germany's ancestors, the Assyrians, were used to punish Israel, and they show up in history in every attempt to set up a world ruling power down through time.

These 5 kingdoms that fall are all involved with the nations of Europe, especially Germany. Germany has a long history of remaining silent and then suddenly becoming active in world events. They have gone to great lengths to hide their true identity from the world. They are direct descendants of Assur, one of Shem's twin sons. The descendants of Assur are known throughout history as the ancient Assyrians.

In the bible narrative they were the very people God used to punish the nation of Israel many times. This is part of the manipulation of academic history of historians to appease the political agendas of men in power during the times of history.

THE FIVE KINGDOMS THAT FALL

evelation 17:9-10 And here is the mind which hath wisdom.

The seven heads are seven mountains, (kingdoms) on which the woman, (church) sits. (10) And there are seven kings: (horns) five are fallen, and one is, and the other is not yet come; and when he cometh, he must continue a short space.

There are no other events in world history during these time periods that can match these five kingdoms. These next five world-influencing kingdoms are the five heads that fall, and their spirit resurrects from the image of the Fourth Beast in world national politics.

*** Justinian, First Head, Fourth Horn:**

Known in English as Justinian I or Justinian the Great), 482/483 – 13 November/14 November 565, was Eastern Roman Emperor from 527 until his death and second member of the Justinian Dynasty after his uncle Justin I. One of the most important figures of Late Antiquity, Justinian's rule forms a distinct epoch in the history of the Byzantine Empire. The impact of his administration extends far beyond the boundaries of his time and empire. Justinian's reign is marked by the ambitious but failed renovatio imperii, or restoration of the empire. This ambition is expressed in the partial recovery of the territories of the Western Roman Empire, including the city of Rome itself.

The resurrection of the religious part of the Roman Beast becomes obvious under Justinian. The Recognition of the Roman See: The Holy See is the Episcopal authority of the Bishop of Rome, commonly known as the Pope, and is the preeminent See of the Catholic Church. It is also the sovereign entity headed by the Pope which governs the Vatican and stands for the Catholic Church in temporal affairs.

As the highest ecclesiastical authority stayed the cornerstone of his Western policy. Religious Relations with Rome: From the middle of the fifth century onward increasingly arduous tasks confronted the emperors of the East in ecclesiastical matters.

For one thing, the radicals on all sides felt themselves constantly repelled by the creed adopted by the Council of Chalcedon to defend the biblical doctrine of the nature of Christ and bridge the gap between the dogmatic parties. The letter of Pope Leo I to Flavian of Constantinople is widely considered in the East as the work of Satan so that nobody cares to hear of the Church of Rome.

The emperors, however, have a policy of preserving the unity between Constantinople and Rome. Justinian entered the arena of ecclesiastical statecraft shortly after his uncle's accession in 518 A. D. and put an end to the schisms between Rome and Byzantium since 483 A. D.

The Jews, too, suffered, for not only did the authorities restrict their civil rights and threaten their religious privileges, but the emperor interfered in the internal affairs of the synagogue and forbade the use of the Hebrew language in divine worship. The Jewish priests were threatened with corporal penalties, exile, and loss of property. The Jews at Borium, near to Syrtis Major, who resisted Belisarius in his Vandal campaign, were forced to embrace Christianity. Their synagogue was turned into a church. The emperor had much trouble with the Samaritans, finding them refractory to Christianity and repeatedly in insurrection. He opposed them with rigorous edicts but could not prevent hostilities towards Christians from taking place in Samaria toward the close of his reign.

The consistency of Justinian's policy meant that the Manicheans too suffered severe persecution, experiencing both exile and threat of capital punishment. At Constantinople on one occasion, not a few Manicheans after strict inquisition were executed in the emperor's very presence, some by burning, others by drowning.

This was the first step as a revived Empire. The Pope was recognized as authority in matters of state and church. This Credence given by Justinian was the First resurrection of the Old Holy Roman Empire (healing of the deadly wound)!

Justinian restored the empire from 554 to 586 A.D. This was the rebirth of the Roman Empire from the East and the first resurrection of the Empire. Eventually it withered away to a powerful Frankish Kingdom arising.

RISE OF ISLAM

*I*slam is an offshoot religion of Judaism that began in the 600s AD. However, its founding principles have degenerated to the terrorist Jihad infecting the world today! In Muslim tradition, Muhammad (570 –632 A. D.) is viewed as the seal of prophets. During the last 22 years of his life, beginning at age 40 in 610 A. D., Muhammad reported revelations that he believes to be from God conveyed to him through the archangel Gabriel.

The content of these revelations, known as the Qur'an, was memorized, and recorded by his companions. During this time, Muhammad in Mecca preached to the people, imploring them to abandon polytheism and to worship one God. Although some people converted to Islam, the leading Meccan authorities persecuted Muhammad and his followers. This resulted in the migration to Abyssinia of some Muslims (to the Aksumite Empire). Many early converts to Islam were the poor and former slaves.

The Meccan elite felt that Muhammad was destabilizing their social order by preaching about one God, racial equality, and in the process giving ideas to the poor and their slaves. By 629 Muhammad was victorious in the bloodless conquest of Mecca, and by the time of his death in 632 (at the age of 62) he united the tribes of Arabia into a single religious polity.

Islam struggled right along with the Jewish religion, and the Original Christians were forced underground because of persecution from the Romans. There are many changes in the other cultures of the world at this time. The Islamic Jihad is on a mission to set up a world domination of Islam. The bible shows this will never happen. This is another subject for another time.

<u>I am only concerned with the timeline of events created by the timeline of the bible</u> and the predicted attempts at world domination by the players appointed from the scriptures.

* Charlemagne, Second Head, Fifth Horn (800 A.D. - 924 A.D.):

This Frankish Kingdom was made up of Salian Franks (those who dwelt near the sea) and the Riparian Franks (those who dwelt near rivers). From these came many tribes and later the German tribe called Hesse. Charlemagne's crowning in 800 A.D. began the reign of the Carolingians. This is considered the _Second resurrection_ of the Roman Empire. This was regarded by most historians as the revival of the Empire. The Pope crowned Charlemagne while kneeling in prayer before the altar of St. Peter. His Empire included all the old Western Roman Empire plus large areas east of the Rhine never ruled by Rome. He even minted coins with the inscription: *"Empire Restored."* In German, Charlemagne reads Karl der grofie, and in Latin, Charlemagne reads Carolus Magnus, meaning Charles the Great!

* Otto the Great, Third Head, Sixth Horn (962 A.D.-1250 A.D.):

Over time from Charlemagne the German people dominated the peoples. These German Emperors of the Holy Roman Empire, Austro Hungarian were all crowned in the capital of Charlemagne's city.

INSET

<u>This is when the Reich philosophy of the Germans was born</u>. The first Reich was from 962-1806; the second Reich was from 1871-1918; and the third Reich was from 1934-1945. Make no mistake: German Emperors were the secular defenders of the Catholic Church.

Thus, we can see the <u>Beast/False Prophet</u> scenario as an alliance since the days of Constantine. Otto was crowned in Roman fashion. Pope John XII crowned Otto in February of 962.

This was the <u>Third resurrection of the Roman Empire</u>. Ten days later he and the emperor ratified the Diploma Ottonianum, which made the Pope the Guarantor of the independence of the Papal States.

Once again, fear and power struggles, and Pope John XII formed a league against Otto. Otto went to Rome and convinced a synod of Bishops to crown Leo VIII Pope, a layman of the church. Next, civil war broke out between supporters of John and Leo. Otto went back to Rome after John died and excommunicated Pope Benedict V.

He extracted a promise from the citizens of Rome not to choose a Pope without the Emperor's approval. The Crusades divided the Empire into East and West with the East mostly lands outside the Empire.

It is noteworthy to understand the east Frankish Kingdom, or Germany, led by Henry I and Otto I, <u>was the strongest power in Europe and a friend of the Roman Catholic Church</u>. Various German kings laid claim to the imperial title and were recognized by the Pope.

INSET

During these times of power changes in the Fourth Beast, there were minor rebellions against them. The Protestant Reformation was one of the largest events to break away from the influence of the Fourth Beast. World Wars One and Two were the largest put down of this desire to rule the world Fourth Beast. After these two world wars there is still a subtle attempt to revive the Holy Roman Empire when the League of Nations formed post WW2. This group became the United Nations.

THE REFORMATION OF THE PROTESTANTS

It was not until The Protestant Reformation, started by Martin Luther in 1517, that a swing back toward the intended church that Jesus started with the Apostles tried to happen. The reformation takes place between the 3rd and 4th revivals of the Holy Roman empires.

The only problem I see after more years of study and research is that the Reformation of 1517 did not leave all of the Roman Catholic Doctrines behind. But at least it was a spiritual awakening and a step away from carnal religion of men.

Martin Luther was a German priest and professor of theology who is a seminal figure in the Protestant Reformation.

Initially an Augustinian friar, Luther came to reject several teachings and practices of the Roman Catholic Church. He strongly disputed the claim that freedom from God's punishment for sin could be bought with money. He confronted indulgent salesman Johann Tetzel, a Dominican friar, with his Ninety-Five Theses in 1517. His refusal to retract all of his writings at the demand of Pope Leo X in 1520 and the Holy Roman Emperor Charles V at the Diet of Worms in 1521 resulted in his excommunication by the Pope and condemnation as an outlaw by the Emperor.

Luther taught that salvation is not earned by good deeds but is received only as a free gift of God's grace through faith in Jesus Christ as the redeemer from sin. His theology challenged the authority and office of the Pope by teaching that the Bible is the only source of divinely revealed knowledge from God and considers all baptized Christians to be a holy priesthood. (the bible supports the concept of a potential for Christians to become Priests in the coming Kingdom of God)

Those who identified with this and all of Luther's wider teachings are called Lutherans, even though Luther insisted Christian is the only acceptable name for individuals who profess Christ.

Today, Lutheranism constitutes a major branch of Protestantism and overall Christianity with some 80 million adherents. Luther's translation of the bible into the vernacular (instead of Latin) made it more accessible, which had a tremendous impact on the church and on German culture. It fostered the development of a standard version of the German language, added several principles to the art of translation, and influenced the writing of an English translation, the Tyndale Bible.

His hymns influenced the development of singing in churches. His marriage to Katharina von Bora set a model for the practice of clerical marriage, allowing Protestant priests to marry. In his later works, entitled On the Jews and Their Lies, Luther expressed antagonistic views toward Jews, writing that Jewish synagogues and homes should be destroyed, their money confiscated, and liberty curtailed.

These statements and their influence on anti-Semitism have contributed to his controversial status. Martin Luther died in 1546, still convinced of the correctness of his Reformation theology and with his decree of excommunication by Pope Leo X still effective.

Propaganda during the Reformation was enabled by the spread of the printing press throughout Europe, and within Germany.

J. Gutenberg. The printed literature caused new ideas, thoughts, and doctrines to be made available to the public in ways that had never been seen before the sixteenth century. The printing press was invented in approximately 1450 A.D. and quickly spread to other major cities around Europe. By the time,

the Reformation was underway in 1517, there were printing centers in over 200 of the major European cities.

These centers became the primary producers of Reformation work by the Protestants, and in some cases anti-Reformation works put forth by the Roman Catholics.

Protestant propaganda and church doctrine broke away from the traditional conventions of the Catholic Church. They called for a change in the way that the church ran and insisted the buying and selling of indulgences and religious positions be stopped, as well as the papal corruption that had been allowed to occur.

In addition to this, Reformers questioned the authority of the Church, in particular the Pope. Protestants believe that the main authority of their church should be the Gospel or Scripture (expounded by personal interpretation) and not by the Pope, who is the earthly head of the Catholic Church appointed by men.

Another dominant message is found in Protestant propaganda. It is the idea that every person should be granted access to the Bible to interpret it for themselves. This is the primary reason why Luther translated and published many copies of the New Testament during the Reformation years.

Protestants questioned the belief that the Pope had sole authority to interpret scripture. Luther's bibles were in the German language. This can be seen in Luther's publication, To the Christian Nobility of the German Nation, which criticizes the Catholic belief that the Pope is supreme and can interpret scripture however he sees fit.

To combat this, Luther put forth arguments from the Bible that show everyone can interpret scripture—not just the Pope. The Reformation messages were very controversial and often banned in several Catholic cities.

Despite the attempt by the Catholic Church to have and repress Protestant propaganda, the Protestant propagandists found effective ways of sending their messages to their believers. The use of pamphlets became the primary method of spreading Protestant ideas and doctrine. Pamphlets took little time to produce, and they could be printed and sold quickly, making them harder for the authorities to track them down, thus making them a highly effective method of spreading information. The sheer number of pamphlets produced during this time period showed that Protestant works during the Reformation were available on a consistent basis and on a large scale, making the controversial ideas accessible to the masses.

This is one reason the Protestants were successful in their propaganda campaign and the Reformation was a success. The dissension of the Reformers was not welcomed by Roman Catholics, who called this behavior and the works of the Protestant Propagandists heresy.

They disagreed with the Protestant Reformers and the messages that they presented to the public. Most Roman Catholics believed matters of the Church should not be discussed with laypeople but kept behind closed doors. This was the same way they translated their version of the bible.

The majority of the works published by Roman Catholics during the Reformation tried to dispel these ideas and restore the Roman Catholic faith. The Roman Catholic propagandists were very reactive with their works. On a number of occasions, they refuted Luther's and other Protestants' arguments after they were published.

An example of a reactive propaganda campaign publicized by Roman Catholics is with regards to the Peasants' War of 1525.

Charles V, Hapsburg Dynasty: Fourth Head, Seventh Horn (1273 AD - 1806 AD)

After the death of his paternal grandfather Maximilian in 1519, Charles V inherited the Habsburg lands in Austria. He was also the natural candidate of the electors to succeed his grandfather. With the help of the wealthy Fugger family, Charles defeated the candidacy of Francis I of France and was chosen on 28 June 1519. In 1530, he was crowned Holy Roman Emperor by Pope Clement VII in Bologna, the last Emperor to receive a papal coronation.

Charles was Holy Roman Emperor over the German states, but his real power was limited by the princes. Protestantism gained a strong foothold in Germany, and Charles was decided not to let this happen in the Netherlands. An inquisition was set up as early as 1522.

In 1550, the death penalty was introduced for all heresy. Political dissent was also firmly controlled, most notably in his place of birth, where Charles, aided by the Duke of Alba, personally suppressed the Revolt of Ghent in mid-February 1540. The Turks destroyed Constantinople in 1403 A.D. and <u>the Eastern Empire ended</u>. This was the end of the Fourth resurrection of the Roman Empire. Some aspects of the Eastern Empire transferred to Imperial Russia under the auspices of Ivan III, who was regarded as the first national sovereign of Russia.

Napoleon's Kingdom, The Fifth Head, Eighth Horn (1804 AD– 1814 A.D.):

Napoleon Bonaparte (15 August 1769 – 5 May 1821) was a French military and political leader who had a significant impact on the history of

Europe. He was a general during the French Revolution, the ruler of France as First Consul of the French Republic, and Emperor of the First French Empire. In January 1804, Bonaparte's police uncovered an assassination plot against him, sponsored by the former rulers of France, the Bourbons.

In retaliation, Bonaparte orders the arrest of the Duke of Enghien, in violation of Baden's sovereignty. After a secret trial, the Duke was executed in March. Bonaparte used the plot to justify the re-creation of a hereditary monarchy in France, with him as Emperor.

He believed a Bourbon restoration would be impossible once the Bonapartist succession was entrenched in the constitution. Napoleon crowned himself Emperor on 2 December 1804 at Notre Dame de Paris and then crowned Josephine Empress and forced Pope Pius VII to consecrate them. At Milan Cathedral on 26 May 1805, Napoleon was crowned King of Italy with the Iron Crown of Lombardy.

Napoleon annexed the Papal States because of the Church's refusal to support the Continental System. Pope Pius VII responded by excommunicating Napoleon and the Pope was then abducted by Napoleon's officers. Though Napoleon did not order the Pope's abduction, he did not order the Pope's release either.

The Pope was moved throughout Napoleon's territories, sometimes while ill, and Napoleon sent delegations to pressure him into issues including giving up power and a new concordat with France.

The Pope remained confined for 5 years and was not returned to <u>Rome until May 1814</u>. In 1810, the Austrian Archduchess Marie Louise married Napoleon following his divorce of Josephine. The marriage further strained his relations with the Church and thirteen cardinals were imprisoned for non-attendance at the ceremony.

After the French Revolution, Napoleon set out to re-create the Holy Roman Empire by an alliance with the Hapsburgs. <u>He convinced the German princes to quit the Holy Roman Empire and come together as the Confederation of the Rhine, including much of southern Germany.</u> Napoleon had to absorb most of the Western Roman Empire to survive. He ensured this by divorcing Josephine and marrying the Archduchess Marie Louise, the daughter of Emperor Francis II of Austria, Germany, in 1810 to give himself Roman legitimacy.

Their son became the King of Rome, and imperial eagles and banners adorned his cradle. Such is the history of men lusting for power and control of the masses of people and nations. Francis I, Louis XIV, and Napoleon—they saw themselves as the Holy Roman Empire's legitimate heirs. Not unlike the "rooting up of the first three horns" during the eventual demise of the first 500 years of the Fourth Beast, 1,400 years later Napoleon tried to recreate the Papacy for divine recognition of himself as Emperor of the Holy Roman Empire.

Napoleon was obsessed with power. In 1804 during the ceremony, he took the crown from the Pope and crowned himself, proclaiming himself to be the King of Italy.

This bears a striking resemblance to Hitler's rise to power later in this timeline. Later that year Napoleon annexed the Papal States, plundered the churches, and erected a Pagan edifice outside St. Peter's.

Many Catholics began to regard Napoleon as the Anti-Christ. What they meant by that statement was that Napoleon was the Anti-Pope. This was the struggle of the Papacy for the Deadly Wound Healed, influencing the Five Heads that eventually fell.

Revelation 17:10 And there are seven kings: five are fallen, and one is, and the other is not yet come; and when he cometh, he must continue a short space.

We have just finished naming these Five Fallen Kingdoms from history. The significance of knowing who these Kings and Heads are purely political and religious. The Holy Roman Empire was a political and religious power in Western Europe from 546 A.D. to 1806 A.D. It was identified as the Roman Empire in the 11 th Century and became the Holy Roman Empire in the 12 th Century. Though its borders shift many times throughout the 1260 years of these Five Heads, its principle area is always that of the German states.

From the 10th Century send its rulers had been chosen German kings who looked for but did not always receive imperial coronation by the Popes of Rome. The Holy Roman Empire was an attempt to revive the Western Roman Empire, whose legal and political structure deteriorated in the 5th and 6th centuries and was replaced by German nobles after the deposition of Augustus in 476 A.D.

The Popes in Rome keep alive the traditional concept of a temporal realm coextensive with the spiritual realm of the church. After finally severing its ties with the Eastern Empire because of its sovereignty, the Papacy continued to nourish dreams of a revived Western Empire like Ancient Rome of the 5th and 6th centuries. This concept was suppressed by Napoleon of the French Revolution.

This was the final phase of the Holy Roman Empire which is the origin of the concepts and philosophies of the 3rd Reich appearing in 1939. <u>On August 6, 1801, Francis II illegally abolished the Holy Roman Empire to prevent Napoleon from taking possession of it</u>. It actually became a secret Holy Roman Empire consisting of France and German Confederation of the Rhine in the West and the Austro-Hungarian Empire in the east.

It was known as the 2nd Reich 1871 A.D. – 1918 A.D. America and England destroy the 2nd Reich in 1918. Hitler tried it in 1939, calling it the 3rd Reich!

Sixth Head, WWI, Second Reich Kaiser Wilhelm, of Germany, once said to his troops, *"The German people are the chosen of God. On me, as German Emperor, the Spirit of God has descended. I am His weapon, His sword, and His Vice-regent."* (Sounds like the epiphany of Constantine when he saw the cross in the sky 1,600-years before Kaiser Wilhelm.)

SEVENTH HEAD, WWII, THIRD REICH

itler tried to carry out the beastly characteristics of the "Fourth Beast" in World War II. He patterned most of his philosophy after Napoleon. However, Hitlerism is a political burden that is eschewed by the upcoming modern advocates of the Reich concept.

Hitler once boasted his Reich would last a thousand years. Nazi parlance often refers to it as the "thousand-year Reich."

"The German form of life is definitely determined for the next thousand years." Hitler was founding an order for worldwide dominance.

Nazis stole monuments and wealth, of many nations of the world, to reform the culture of the world to their form of life. <u>If you destroy a nation's monuments, it is as if they never existed.</u>

Hitler's attempt at setting up a thousand-year Reich, was Satan's mockery of the Millennium when Jesus comes back to rule the world.

THE REICH CONCEPT

*R*eich is the German word for realm or empire. It is the idea of a master race of people destined to rule the world. This concept began in 1871 and continued until 1945 with the defeat of Adolf Hitler's Germany. The murder of over 6 million Jews in the prison camps of WWII are a grotesque reminder of claiming to be the superior race set on exterminating the lesser races of people. It embraces the belief in a mandate from divinity as a mission from God to rule the world and keep the purity of the Aryan races. Its philosophy goes against everything the Son of God came to educate mankind for the higher standard of life and human life's potential.

The German Reich concept promotes that the German race is the peace-giver of the world—that it is a joint Christian/Roman concept that needs to be in place for the regency of the Kingdom of God on earth.

Many of their writings state that the task of the Empire is to be God's protagonist on earth, to fulfill His will here while protecting the Christianity and church. Their goal is to preserve the righteousness of God and the divine order of the universe on earth. This Empire of physical men on earth is the transitory reflection of the eternal City of God (not unlike what Assur, Nimrod, and Semiramis tried to do with Nineveh and the Tower of Babel).

They claim God created the Holy Roman Empire for Christianity to expand over the entire earth. These German scholars and political elite still work in spirit. Frederick William IV of Germany dreamed of a revived Holy Roman Empire to replace the German Confederation. The Holy Roman Empire looks to recreate a united Christian Europe in similitude to the last years of the Roman Empire. <u>They secretly advocate a European Union.</u>

It is called holy because of the supremacy of the Pope in ecclesiastical affairs. The Pope as religious ruler and the German Emperors as the secular arm and defender of the Catholic Church.

Nazi scholars recognize the history of the European idea and try to convince independent nations to join with Germany in a U.S. of Europe, definitely dominated by the Germans. These concepts were around as early as 1943.

A common market with common legal rights and currency system. It is a reality at this present time. The European Common Market could become the 8th beast to enforce the resurrected Holy Roman Empire upon the earth for the last time! (The beast that is forming again is of the seventh!)

Revelation 17:6-13 (6) And I saw the woman drunken with the blood of the saints, (inquisitions and martyr of the saints down through history) *and with the blood of the martyrs of Jesus;* (the apostles and saints of the 1st century church) *and when I saw her, I wondered with great admiration. (7) And the angel said unto me, wherefore didst thou marvel? I will tell thee the mystery of the woman,* (Catholic Church) *and of the beast that carried her,* (military power of German Common Market) *which hath the seven heads and ten horns.(Seven Kingdoms and Ten Kings down through history) (8) The beast that thou saw was, and is not; and shall ascend out of the bottomless pit, and go into perdition: and they that dwell on the earth shall wonder, whose names were not written in the book of life from the foundation of the world,* (believers in the false prophet) *when they behold the beast that was, and is not, and yet is. (9) And here is the mind which hath wisdom. The seven heads are seven mountains (kingdoms), on which the woman (church) sits. (10) And there are seven kings: five are fallen, and one is, and the other is not yet come; and when he cometh, he must continue a short space.* (about 3. Years) *(11) And the beast that was, and is not, even he is the eighth, and is of the seven, and goes into perdition. (12) And the ten horns which thou saws are ten kings,* (ten kings over many nations of the common market) *which have received no kingdom yet; but receive power as kings one hour with the beast. (13) These have one mind and shall give their power and strength unto the beast.* (Germany is the facilitator of the military power to enforce the religion of the false prophet)

In one book, I read about a German historian and political figure, Prince Hubertus Loewenstein-Wertheim-Freudenberg (October 14, 1906 – November 28, 1984) an early opponent of Nazism. fled Germany and helped to promote Catholicism in the United States. He was a former Member of Parliament and is the author of over 40 books. He was the head of the Free German Authors Association and was decorated by Pope John XXIII for work toward reconciliation between the Roman Catholic and the Greek Orthodox Church.

"If only our voice could be joined with that of the Vatican, which today forms the one point of stability in the general madness… not Proletarians of all lands unite! But Catholics of all nations unite is the challenge that must precede the approaching revolution in the west. This Protestantism is the real forerunner of atheism and is guilty of having forced millions out of the Christian community."

This *man wanted to have a Catholic-dominated Europe. He continues:*

"There is no antithesis between the Reich and what true socialism affirms… what is needed is a collaboration between the idea of the Reich and the ideas of traditional European socialism… I call to mind the twelve men who wore the German-Roman Imperial crown and are my ancestors… A German Reich will arise to fulfill the history of all its centuries. A German Reich, in whose golden eagles is alive the idea of social, political, and spiritual liberty."

As my story develops, you will see this Reich concept is a carnal, humanistic interpretation of what God is doing and will do through the power of His Spirit and Jesus Christ when He comes again.

After World War II, for decades Europe was under the control of Russia in the East and by America in the West. This status changed a few years ago, and Germany is now reunited and holds gold wealth in reserves 2nd only to China.

BIRTH OF THE UNITED NATIONS

as anyone noticed how the Holy Roman Empire disappeared from view during the years of the rise of Britain and America? America, the icon of freedom and Democracy. These two nations smashed attempts at world conquest led by Germany and the axis powers in World Wars I and II. Even though the Holy Roman Empire disappeared, the Vatican is now an isolated empire of power.

Most people have forgotten the conferences held in San Francisco, California, in the late 1945 decline of World War II. Germany was soon be defeated, and the three main allies—the United States, Russia, and Great Britain—engaged in a quest to prevent another Worldwide War from happening again.

The League of Nations was the precursor to the forming of the United Nations in 1946. The San Francisco Conference is significant to this timeline because of its intended purposes and the warning from the leaders of the Catholic Church that without their oversight, the United Nations would eventually fail!

They were once again trying to revive that system of religion governing over the nations of the world. Radical Jihad today is trying to do the same thing by killing all the Christians. During the conference of 1945 there was a Solemn Pontifical Mass staged by the Roman Catholic Church. In an Auditorium that seated 10,000, every seat was filled. Most people aren't even aware of this event.

After much ritual and such, a sermon was given by Duane G. Hunt, radio spokesman for the church. (From 1927 to 1949, Hunt was the weekly speaker on NBC's Catholic Hour, a radio program on which he discussed Catholic doctrine.) Seated right in front of him were 300 delegates of the conference from Europe and South America.

The Catholic hierarchy was aware of the bickering and strife among the nations' delegates, even though the world leaders proclaimed otherwise.

The Catholic service offered the world leaders the world's last hope for peace. They characterized their offer as the Last Straw for the eventual drowning nations of the conference to grab, when they shall later see their world organization sinking into failure and oblivion.

Without divine help, the newly formed United Nations structure was doomed to collapse. The Roman Catholic Church offered divine help. Without the guidance and supervision of authority of the Church they were laboring in vain, is what was said. This sermon was a physiological seed destined to unite under Catholicism a Europe that would resurrect the Holy Roman Empire once again.

Their whole platform was built on men left to themselves, allowing their baser inclinations unrestrained, with selfishness given free reign. There could be no peace or order in the world. Hunt said that government derived its civil authority from God, and the Catholic Church was God's government over nations.

The Catholic interpretation is that God rules on earth through the Papacy and the Roman Catholic Church. Whatever the Pope binds on earth is bound in heaven. The Pope is the Vicar of Christ. He is supposed to be in authority over all kings and governments.

This conference was over 70 years ago, and the United Nations is still struggling to keep peace worldwide. The Catholic Church has remained satisfied with their converts all over the world. The various Popes are still influential in some nations of the world.

This concept of One World Government is still in the hearts and minds of the Europeans today. Every so often a step forward in show of religious influence and power comes out of the Papacy. (In 1989 the Catholic Pope had a 30-minute conversation with the Leader of Russia and the Berlin Wall came down. This divided city of Berlin in Germany had impeded Europe from restoring her vast Empire. The destruction of that wall reunited Germany once again.

However, over the past 20 years our politicians have overlooked the building of the United States of Europe. The politicians think this supporting of a U.S. of Europe or Common Market, is part of building a world superstructure for world peace.

Could this be the Beast Yet to Come? It is a fact we are dealing with another enemy—Radical Islam—but we must consider prophesy of the Bible God gives us concerning the Beast That Is Yet to Come.

It is not a Muslim Beast Power. Muslims have no history of conquest like the Germans. Muslims have no history of Roman Catholic Domination of the Kingdoms of Europe. Muslims have no Spiritual Leader with the influence and power of the Pope. Neither does Russia or China. The bible offers many clues as to how to recognize the coming Beast and False Prophet.

It will be looking something like the European Common Market of nations, led by a German Military power and influenced by the Catholic Church.

I will be authoring another book to make logical sense of who the players will be during the events prior to the Great Tribulation and the Apocalypse. It will be a book much different than any books on prophecy you can find today.

SUMMARY REFLECTION THUS FAR:

*A*ll of this information has brought us up to World War II and the demise of the 3rd Reich of the German peoples under Adolf Hitler. It sets the stage for the changing faces of evil in the world.

The Archangel Lucifer has wanted to take over the throne of God from the very beginning of rebellion in the spiritual realm. Because of lust for power this rebellion became the mission to remove the Invisible God from ruling the universe. Mankind was created and Lucifer, now called Satan, started on his mission to corrupt, and destroy God's most precious creation—human beings.

The behavior of mankind is easily influenced by Satan and his demons or the fallen angels. God fathered the process of what is to eventually become many Spirit Beings that begin as human beings. The firstborn son of this process is Jesus Christ.

This process of creating a Spiritual Family of God beings from the billions of created physical human beings that have lived and died down through time.

We have seen the Jews scattered all over the world. By the time of Adolf Hitler and the 3rd Reich there were over six million Jews murdered in death camps run by the Nazi SS soldiers of Germany. In the year 1945 A.D. the end of World War

II was a reality and the Allied Forces of the USA, England, and Russia divided up the territories.

<u>Germany lay in total destruction, a conquered nation.</u> <u>Berlin was cut in half by a huge wall.</u> Who would have believed that Germany could rise again to become a wealthy nation in gold reserves second only to China?

Japan lay in ruins after atomic bombs brought them to the peace table. Who would have believed they would be the thriving economic giant today? They come back to defeat America with transistors and technology, overwhelming our economy with better cars and products built cheaper and lasting longer.

In a little over 50 years America has lost its ability to stand up to the world. America is the nation who helps all nations in blind faith that the nations will be their allies and friends. We are sending billions of dollars to our enemies today. (Deals like Iran made with the USA) Mass murder in Syria and the Unite Nations writes threatening resolutions but no actions behind them. They did the same with Iran and Iraq.

However, about 68 years ago, one of the things the newly formed United Nations did act on is <u>allow Israel to become their own independent state</u>. This is a milestone for Israel. But it has been one conflict of war for the last 60 years to remain a sovereign state.

INSET

Though Israel is a small piece of land in the world, I have come to see why it is important to the future of mankind continuing to exist. Think about the fact that it is where the Invisible God begins to start a nation from Abraham. The expansion of the promise from God because of Abraham's faithfulness to God begins there with Jacob and then through Joseph in Egypt. By the time of Moses, the nation was chosen and marked among the other nations as the chosen people of God to carry the higher moral standard to the world. Even though they are the chosen, they fall into idolatry and bad behavior time after time down through their history.

God's message to us, from the Bible, is that God will allow the people to be punished for their apostasy but not forsaken. They are at present day a nation under attack. They are the center of the coming Apocalypse. Their existence and restoration is no accident.

Jesus will return to the city of Jerusalem someday in the 21st century. They are key in the plan of God for the steady process of progressive education for the potential development of mankind to reach our intended purpose in an eternal universe.

THE RESTORATION OF THE JEWISH STATE 1948

*A*ssyria and Babylon scattered Israel in 590-604 B.C. as prophesied by Jeremiah.

Jeremiah 30:10-11 Therefore fear thou not, O my servant Jacob, says the LORD; neither be dismayed, O Israel: for, lo, I will save thee from afar, and thy seed from the land of their captivity; and Jacob shall return, and shall be in rest, and be quiet, and none shall make him afraid. (11) For I am with thee, says the LORD, to save thee: though I make a full end of all nations whither I have scattered thee, yet will I not make a full end of thee: but I will correct thee in measure, and will not leave thee altogether unpunished.

Jeremiah 50:17 Israel is a scattered sheep; the lions have driven him away: first the king of Assyria hath devoured him; and last this Nebuchadnezzar king of Babylon hath broken his bones.

Ezekiel also prophesies:

Ezekiel 6:8 Yet will I leave a remnant, that ye may have some that shall escape the sword among the nations, when ye shall be scattered through the countries.

Ezekiel 11:16 Therefore say, thus says the Lord GOD; Although I have cast them far off among the heathen, and although I have scattered them among the countries, yet will I be to them as a little sanctuary in the countries where they shall come.

Ezekiel 11:17 Therefore say, thus says the Lord GOD; I will even gather you from the people and assemble you out of the countries where ye have been scattered, and I will give you the land of Israel.

The return of Jewish exiles scattered throughout the world actually began in 1948 A.D. Their return is sealed by becoming an Independent

Nation as outlined by the following document presented to and accepted by the United Nations. Following are some excerpts from the Declaration of Israel as an Independent sovereign state among the nations of the world.

On May 14, 1948, on the day in which the British Mandate over a Palestine expired, the Jewish People's Council gathered at the Tel Aviv Museum, and approved the following proclamation, declaring the establishment of the State of Israel. The new state was recognized that night by the United States and three days later by the USSR.

ERETZ-ISRAEL [(Hebrew) - the Land of Israel, Palestine was the birthplace of the Jewish people. Here their spiritual, religious, and political identity was shaped. Here they first reached to statehood, created cultural values of national and universal significance, and gave to the world the eternal Book of Books. After being forcibly exiled from their land, the people kept faith with it throughout their Dispersion and never ceased to pray and hope for their return to it and for the restoration in it of their political freedom. Impelled by this historic and traditional attachment, Jews strove in every successive generation to re-establish themselves in their ancient homeland. In recent decades they returned in their masses. Pioneers, ma'pilim [(Hebrew) - immigrants coming to Eretz-Israel in defiance of restrictive legislation] and defenders, they made deserts bloom, revived the Hebrew language, built villages and towns, and created a thriving community controlling its own economy and culture, loving peace but knowing how to defend itself, bringing the blessings of progress to all the country's inhabitants, and aspiring towards independent nationhood. The catastrophe which recently befell the Jewish people - the massacre of millions of Jews in Europe - was another clear demonstration of the urgency of solving the problem of its homelessness by establishing in Eretz-Israel the Jewish State, which would open the gates of the homeland wide to every Jew and confer upon the Jewish people the status of a fully privileged member of the comity of nations.

Survivors of the Nazi holocaust in Europe, as well as Jews from other parts of the world, continue to migrate to Eretz-Israel, undaunted by difficulties, restrictions, and dangers, and never cease to assert their right to a life of dignity, freedom, and honest toil in their national homeland.

In the Second World War, the Jewish community of this country contributed its full share to the struggle of the freedom- and peace-loving nations against the forces of Nazi wickedness and, by the blood of its soldiers and its war effort, gained the right to be reckoned among the peoples who founded the United Nations.

On the 29th of November 1947, the United Nations General Assembly passed a resolution calling for the establishment of a Jewish State in Eretz-Israel; the General Assembly required the inhabitants of Eretz-Israel to take such steps as were necessary on their part for the implementation of that resolution. This recognition by the United Nations of the right of the Jewish people to set up their State is irrevocable. This right is the natural right of the Jewish people to be masters of their own fate, like all other nations, in their own sovereign State.

ACCORDINGLY, WE, MEMBERS OF THE PEOPLE'S COUNCIL, REPRESENTATIVES OF THE JEWISH COMMUNITY OF ERETZ-ISRAEL AND OF THE ZIONIST MOVEMENT, ARE HERE ASSEMBLED ON THE DAY OF THE TERMINATION OF THE BRITISH MANDATE OVER ERETZ-ISRAEL AND, BY VIRTUE OF OUR NATURAL AND HISTORIC RIGHT AND ON THE STRENGTH OF THE RESOLUTION OF THE UNITED NATIONS GENERAL ASSEMBLY, HEREBY DECLARE THE ESTABLISHMENT OF A JEWISH STATE IN ERETZ-ISRAEL, TO BE KNOWN AS THE STATE OF ISRAEL. THE STATE OF ISRAEL will be open for Jewish immigration and for the Ingathering of the Exiles; it will foster the development of the country for the benefit of all its inhabitants; it will be based on freedom, justice and peace as envisaged by the prophets of Israel; it will ensure complete equality of social and political rights to all its inhabitants irrespective of religion, race or sex; it will guarantee freedom of religion, conscience, language, education and culture; it will safeguard the Holy Places of all religions; and it will be faithful to the principles of the Charter of the United Nations. PLACING OUR TRUST IN THE "ROCK OF ISRAEL," WE AFFIX OUR SIGNATURES TO THIS PROCLAMATION AT THIS SESSION OF THE PROVISIONAL COUNCIL OF STATE, ON THE SOIL OF THE HOMELAND, IN THE CITY OF TEL-AVIV, ON THIS SABBATH EVE, THE 5TH DAY OF IYAR, 5708 (14TH MAY,1948). END.

After 2,500 years since the siege on Jerusalem by Sennacherib and Nebuchadnezzar and as predicted by Jesus Christ (Matthew 24), the scattering of the Jews all over the world by the Romans, the Jews return to their original homeland. Yet it has been more than 60 years of continuous wars and fighting to stay the nation they want to be. History is violent. It is a series of men killing men for power and wealth. The confusion began when people of power and influence perverted the message from our Invisible Creator concerning how we relate to Him and our fellow human beings. This began a long line of deceit and religious activity created from human reasoning. The very people God chose to deliver His message were caught up in the delusional beliefs of carnal thinking and rejected God's first human created to live as an example and pioneer the process to eternal existence.

The books of Isaiah, Jeremiah, Ezekiel, Daniel, Matthew 24, Thessalonians, Jude, and Revelation are just a few of the books that must be combined in here a little, there a little reasoning to understand what the world is headed for in the 21st Century. There is a coming tribulation to the world at large that will make the destruction of Jerusalem in 70 A.D. and the Holocaust of the 1940s looks like child's play compared to what is coming upon Jerusalem and the world of nations in the near future.

All nations will be affected by the political power struggles of men in leadership. There is so much unrest in the world today that something has to happen to turn things around. American people are now raising their voices with discontent over how our government and leadership has run us into the ground financially and exposed us a weak in the eyes of our enemies. They are weary of political correctness and ready to get back to a commonsense approach to our problems.

Those who do not study history and prophecies of the Bible will not understand what is taking place during the coming tribulation. It is the darkness before the dawn of Jesus Christ returning to the earth to begin His saving plan for all people. We have been inadvertently deceived about our destiny for centuries.

The bible is very plain about mankind's agendas for world peace: they will never work. It will take Spiritual Power from outer space to correct the mess mankind has brought upon itself. God has a plan to eventually save as many people as wish to be saved from the destruction and wars orchestrated by Satan the Devil and his demons all down through history.

Therefore, Jesus came and then sent the Holy Spirit to help mankind change and be aware of the deceitful plans of Satan. Most of mankind is not interested or even aware of the invisible world just outside our vision. Though the language of Revelation may seem strange and unconnected, it is warning us of things to come.

Revelation 17:8 The beast that thou saw was, [Seven heads up through WW1 and WW2] *and is not;* [The Beast is asleep in the bottomless pit.] [Roughly a few decades of no world war, but close many times, a sort of uneasy peace with wars off and on in parts of the world.] *and shall ascend out of the bottomless pit and go into perdition: and they that dwell on the earth shall wonder, whose names were not written in the book of life from the foundation of the world, when they behold the beast that was, and is not, and yet is.*

This scripture is decisive as to why I was born into this world. I was born to get my name in the Book of Life. You were born to get your name into the Book of Life. The rest of my story is how I must come to grips with what the process is for me to remain in God's Book of Life for an eternal existence!

It is the real struggle we face against Good and Evil. I realized that I handle my behavior in this life, and I am free to choose how I am going to live it. This is when I began to dig deep into religious theologies and concepts that are part of our education to decide proper behavior and affect our destiny.

During this process, I discovered a long line of confusion, deceit, and power struggles surrounding the things of faith. I have sorted through the struggles and experiences in my life to arrive at the state of mind I presently own. It has been a long journey of searching for answers and truth about the things God expects compared to what men say God expects from us.

THIRD CENTURY DOCTRINE
VS FAITH ONCE DELIVERED

I was born four years after WWII ended. I am now 73 years of age and only recently am beginning to put the information I have accumulated for years into some form of order and perspective for me. All the information we have covered to this point in time comes from a world I had no influence upon. I was thrust into this world of ancient history and recent history because I was simply born into it.

But for me to confirm my existence, I had to understand the world I am in and discern from its successes and failures down through time. During the process of discovery, I found all of the deceit and confusion caused by an unseen force. As I explored the information I found that there is a purpose for the good and bad information. I must choose what information I will believe to create the responses and reactions in my life. I understand the concept of a purpose driven life, but it is of little meaning if I do not understand the destiny I was created to achieve.

It all begins when we are young and exposed to the world around us. Choices become clear through educational institutions, churches, and governments of men.

GROWING UP IN A
STRANGE CHURCH

I was 7 years old when my dad dropped out of the mainstream Protestant religions and joined a different type of Protestant religious order. He was not a churched person until he met my mom and got married. His friends were so rough and rowdy that the preacher who married them would not let any of them sign the license as witnesses. Dad became a member of the Baptist church and was baptized in 1956. After he became a deacon and Sunday school teacher, he asked the preacher a serious question one day. The preacher told him that what dad was saying about the information he had discovered in the bible was the truth. Then the preacher said, "But I cannot preach it that way and keep my job here." <u>An honest preacher.</u>

Dad left that church and joined a Christian church in south OKC. While attending there he came across a 50,000-watt station out of Mexico broadcasting a religious program that piqued his interest. It was a radio broadcast challenging people to get back to the bible and check things out for themselves. The radio church was exceedingly small in membership and did not have any local churches nearby. In fact, they only had two locations from which they were working: one in California and the other in Southeast Texas. They offered free literature and a bible correspondence course for personal bible study. Dad enrolled in the bible study course and began a long journey of personal bible studies.

In 1957, Dad took us to Texas to one of their yearly annual church festivals. Within three years they sent a pastor to OKC and started a local church there and in Tulsa. Within ten years there were about 700 hundred members in OKC. By then Dad was a deacon and had been through a leadership training class and a spokesman club designed after the Toastmasters International.

Long story short, he joined a religious order that quickly became a religious empire in a matter of a few years. Not unlike Jimmy Swaggart and Jim Bakker, and Copeland this organization's leadership fell to corrupt behavior, and unfortunately many people become disillusioned with religion when this happens in churches.

My point here is this: Do not put your trust in men. Men make mistakes.

Psalms 118:8 It is better to trust in the LORD than to put confidence in man.

Interesting this scripture is considered the literal center of the bible text.

SELF DISCLOSURE

At some time in the chaos, I left the organization myself and became an independent student of the bible and history. It would require another book to relate my 40 years of dealing with ministers of the Gospel, their charisma, and lack of discipline with the precious things of God in churches.

I have been a minister, board member, and servant of many different churches over the years. I spent 10 years proclaiming the gospel in music with a trio ministry to all churches. There is a scripture I want all who read this book to never forget when it comes to your relationship with God.

1Timothy 6:3-5 If any man teaches otherwise, and consent not to wholesome words, even the words of our Lord Jesus Christ, and to the doctrine which is according to godliness; (4) He is proud, knowing nothing, but doting about questions and strife of words, whereof cometh envy, strife, railings, evil surmising, (5) Perverse disputing of men of corrupt minds, and destitute of the truth, supposing that gain is godliness: from such withdraw thyself.

Please remember that your church cannot save you! Only Jesus can do that. Our responsibility is to believe in Jesus and check out who, what, and where we spend time together for life's values. I don't have to be a bible scholar or a rocket scientist to have a relationship with the Invisible God. Nothing can replace prayer and personal study of the bible. From this point on in my story I will compare what the Bible says about life, death, and the possibility of life after physical death. I will do this while comparing the information to what has been the main teaching of Christian churches and mainstream Protestant denominations.

Remember, I am reporting what I have discovered. <u>You decide if it is a choice for you.</u>

There is a better scenario than Heaven and Hell concepts. The better scenario is the Kingdom of God and the part we can have in it when our choices are honest with our Creator God. Based on just a little bit of the academic history you have just read through and inserting some biological scientific findings to help explain, I will let the bible tell us what I believe is God's plan for mankind.

It involves two destinies that are out there. Our choices will decide which destiny we will be ours. From the time, I was born until present day, the world has progressed with many innovations in industry, agriculture, and technology. Men have stood on the surface of the moon. That is an amazing feat. The trip to get to the moon and land safely is compared to shooting ½ of a BB from a BB gun and hitting a 1-inch square on the roof of a tall building 30 miles away!

All of these modern inventions and things that are products that make our life easier every day are wonderful. However, the one thing has not progressed in the long-standing beliefs of many Christian religions and churches. Concepts of heaven and hell related to what happens to good and bad people after they die have remained the same.

Churches are still promoting teachings of salvation from the 3rd century A.D. in a 21st century of increased and accumulated knowledge that could change our feeling of what is the purpose of our being.

Another area of little progress is people having a good relationship with people and nations with nations. Wars, murder, theft, and all kinds of crimes are committed every day all over the world. The United Nations is a failure at sustaining peace around the world.

Something is definitely missing in the overall quest for a world without strife, war, and poverty. Mankind without divine information and a personal willingness to handle its purpose is never going to bring peace to the earth. There are more churches than prisons in the world. The prisons are overcrowded, and the churches are in decline for attendance.

What is the reason for such a sad situation? I have to wonder what is missing in the churches causing so many to lose interest and drop out. I think part of the problem is the two-hour Christian. This is the fault of both individual and institutional religious behaviors that promote weak teaching and sugarcoat the consequences of sin and bad behavior in individuals. Ministers upholding whatever nets a large financial arrangement rather than principles of good behavior. Hypocritical behavior on the part of church leadership and service to the people. This spills over into our criminal justice system, giving the perpetrator of crimes more rights than the victims of crimes.

Human governments handle not enforcing the basic laws of the nation which were once founded on the laws God gave Moses. Now the laws are abandoned and rewritten by carnal-minded people who cave into the social whims and quirky beliefs and cultures of perverted behavior and thinking.

Another factor is the overcrowded courts and shortage of competent judges. Lady Justice is an icon of a woman holding the balance scales of measurement in one hand and a sword in the other while blind folded. A more realistic icon would be Lady Justice blindfolded with shackles binding her feet impeding progress, <u>a sword that is rusted from lack of use</u>, and lawyers, one on each side of her, trying to tip the balance scales while whispering opposing arguments in her ear! There is no such thing as swift judgment and punishment these days! Justice moves like the snail climbing uphill on ice. Even when a convicted criminal is sentenced to death for a horrendous crime, they live another 10 to 20 years. They are given three meals a day, a place to sleep, and shower and shave at the taxpayer's expense. They are also supplied educational and cable TV while filing appeal after appeal trying to change what Lady Justice has already decided.

We have just trudged through centuries of religious deceit and confusion in governments of nations and religious empires. There is a plain path of intentional abandonment of what Jesus sets up for His church.

Men have elevated carnal thinking to the chair of authority. Some have gone so far as to claim the position of standing for Christ on earth, changing what He says to do. Jesus warned us about this situation in the great Olivet Prophecy before His death and resurrection.

Matthew 24:4-5 And Jesus answered and said unto them, take heed that no man deceives you. (5) For many shall come in my name, saying I am Christ; and shall deceive many.

Jesus was not saying many will come proclaiming they are the Christ. He is saying many will come preaching <u>their version of Christ</u>. This is the process Jesus is showing where the deceit will originate. How are people being deceived? It is carried out through people of power claiming religious authority to speak for God.

It is sadly successful because most people do not study the bible personally for themselves. People do not compare what is being taught in their churches with what the Bible says about the subject; understanding that original Hebrew and Greek language must be applied to certain English words for true meaning. This is why there are hundreds of different Christian denominations and independent Christian churches in the world today.

It has been a project of mine for many years to make sense of all these religious differences in churches about the Oneness of God. I want to know what I am being deceived about and why there are so many plain contradictions in the writings of the bible. Preachers and teachers of Christ were deceiving me. The reason this happened to me was because I did not study and understand things in and about the bible personally. I spent too much time studying the information provided in religious literature provided by men who appeared to have wisdom and understanding about the bible.

It required an intentional desire to look for and search out the information of the bible personally. It required belief in what I was reading and an honest desire to know why I was even born. <u>The main thing I was missing was a daily supply of the Holy Spirit through God's word and honest prayer asking God to help me understand</u>. I didn't need a degree from a religious seminary to know God's will. I only needed a humble desire to know and believe what God had already provided through His word. His word taught me how to find God and communicate with Him. The power of His Holy Spirit is now available to help with all of us, thanks to Jesus Christ! Jesus says it very plainly:

John 8:31-32 Then said Jesus to those Jews which believed on him, If ye continue in my word, then are ye my disciples; indeed, (32) And ye shall know the truth, and the truth shall make you free.

Jesus says continue in His word. He doesn't say, "You shall continue in the word of those who say these things I say are His words." This gets back to choices and our personal responsibility for what we learn and understand. I lived many years in a church organization listening to the teachers, reading their literature instead of reading and studying God's word.

Other men's writings are to be treated like wheat and chaff going through a winnowing process of the word of God. The Bible will help me sift the wheat from the chaff. But even that is not enough if you really want to know the truth. It takes a belief in the power of the Holy Spirit of God impressing upon my mind what His will and ways are for me. It is a spiritual connection.

This is where I must talk about the human brain and how amazing it is in every person. I think it is important that we understand how our mind and body works relating to how we accumulate and process information. We are not born with instinctive knowledge like the animal kingdom. Human beings are designed to be taught and must learn everything we know. We only know what we have been taught. We are not creatures of instinct. How are we trained? We are taught from external sources and from internal sources. As babies and children, we are taught by our parents. For me, it helps me to better understand the various behaviors I am accepting or rejecting as I make choices for how I am living my life.

This will be a detailed study from the notes I made as I learn from Medical and Biological Science how my body and brain is designed to process information. All of this history and information affects how we understand why we were born.

SPIRIT, SOUL, AND BODY

he Apostle Paul wrote to the church about behaviors that would sustain us until the coming of the Lord.

1Thessalonians 5:14-22 Now we exhort you, brethren, warn them that are unruly, comfort the feebleminded, support the weak, be patient toward all men. (15) See that none give evil for evil unto any man; but ever follow that which is good, both among yourselves, and to all men. (16) Rejoice evermore. (17) Pray without ceasing. (18) In everything give thanks: for this is the will of God in Christ Jesus concerning you. (19) Quench not the Spirit. (20) Despise not prophecy. (21) Prove all things; hold fast that which is good. (22) Abstain from all appearance of evil.

These are the behaviors that will help you sustain and understand the real you. Next, he described the three components that makes you aware of who you are as a human being:

1Thessalonians 5:23 And the very God of peace sanctify you wholly; and I pray God your whole <u>spirit and soul and body</u> be preserved blameless unto the coming of our Lord Jesus Christ.

It is interesting to me that Medical Science names these three aspects exactly as the Greek words do for each of these English words.

Spirit: Greek word, pneuma is pronounced, pnyoo'-mah. A current of air, that is, breath (blast) or a breeze; by analogy or figuratively a spirit, which is (human), the rational invisible soul (by implication), vital principle, mental disposition, etc., or (superhuman) an angel, daemon, or (divine) God, Christ's spirit, the Holy spirit: - ghost, life, spirit (-ual, -ually), mind.

Soul: Greek word, psuchē, is pronounced psoo-khay'; breath, that is, (by implication) spirit, abstractly or concretely; which is the rational soul which is mere vitality, even of biological cells and plant life: these terms thus exactly correspond respectively to the Hebrew [H5315], [H7307] and [H2416]: - heart (+ -ily), life, mind, soul, + us, + you.

Body: Greek word, sōma, is pronounced so'-mah; The body (as a sound whole), used in a very wide application, literally or figuratively: - bodily, body, slave. Medical Science has found the different invisible frequency waves that are involved with the functions of the brain in relation to the body and spirit. This is where I find it interesting how Science and the Biblical narratives can be combined to enhance our understanding of the natural and supernatural. It becomes obvious there are some things invisible to our physical eyes.

Electricity is one example. A generator produces electrical current that cannot be seen until the coil on an electric stove or light bulb is energized to the point of glowing. The same thing happens with radio and television frequency waves. The waves are invisible to the eyes, but men have built physical machines that can send and receive these frequency waves enabling us to see and hear them from distances far beyond our physical eyes and ears.

This is similar to how the combination of our spirit, soul, and body works while we are alive. Science tells us that there are three specific frequency waves involved with a conscience awareness of ourselves: Alpha, Beta, and Theta frequency waves.

Our physical brain, consisting of a mass of connected biological cells, receives information by these three waves. These waves are our consciousness or mind often referred to as the "heart" of our thoughts, who we really are inside. Our brain, while our body is alive, generates, receives, and processes these frequency waves. The invisible activity is called the spirit in man in the bible, and the human spirit or consciousness by medical science.

So, as long as the body lives and breathes, our brain generates our spirit which is our conscious mind. These waves work in the physiological realm of our brain. They help images, thought, and how we process it as a living being. They give us our deductive reasoning, our personality, and the compositeness of our existence.

Our soul or active brain cells is <u>the bridge between the spirit realm and the physical realm</u>. In the physical body this is an electrochemical process. Medical science calls it a Process of Protein Synthesis. As active brain cells generate our thoughts repeatedly, protein synthesis occurs. Thoughts actually become permanently a part of our biological brain!

I see it as a software download into the hard drive of a computer. Now, there are two ways of loading software onto a computer. One way is from a CD inserted into the computer and electronically received by the hard drive. The other way is to electronically download the information from the Internet frequencies. This is how Theta and Beta waves of our brain are the two ways information is loaded into our brain during our learning process.

For example, as you are reading this story, or if you are listening to someone read this story, Beta brainwaves are entering your brain. They are allowing two of your five physical senses, sight, and hearing, or optical and audio, to pick up the images of sight and sound through the electrochemical process of protein synthesis in the brain cells. This is the physical eye and ear providing information to your brain, like a physical disc with information inserted into a drive and transferred electronically to the hard drive in a computer.

The other process of downloading information is spiritual. Scientists name these as the Theta brainwaves. It is the pathway of impressions, thoughts, and pictures allowing your brain, to be connected to your spirit in man. Your Theta brainwaves are your conscious thoughts speaking to your spirit. This is often spoken of in the terms like, "My heart tells me this is what I will do" or, "It's my gut feeling!"

The spiritual information comes from God or Satan. They are spiritual beings and can impress your thoughts with these Theta brainwaves. Your computer can receive updates downloaded into the hard drive from the internet connection, and you never see the information until it shows up on your computer. You can accept or reject updates the same as you can accept and reject the prompting of God's Spirit or Satan's Spirit.

But <u>you must make a conscience decision to accept or reject the information</u>. You must give the updates permission to load. The hypothalamus, (like an intel processor) in your brain is where this Theta activity is accepted or rejected before becoming a permanent part of your Alpha waves in the brain biology cells affecting your spirit. It is the biological part of the brain for the mind-body connection from the spirit world.

Because of the invisible spirit input, your feelings are not always you! At times you can become one with something that isn't you. For example, a spirit of fear can teach you to be so fearful through the spirit, soul (mind) and body connection it can cause your heart to race and you to physically shake from it.

Therefore, it is important to consider what we ingest into our minds through what we see, hear, and what our thoughts dwell on for any length of time. The protein synthesis process is causing the information to become part of our personality. The process is all a part of our education and experience for mental development in our lives.

This is where God wants us to make choices from information we become aware of as we live our life in this physical realm. The writer of Hebrews compares Mental Maturity to "meat." Babies cannot eat meat. Mature adults can. Spiritually speaking, this is making choices based on the knowledge and mature understanding what is good and evil.

Hebrews 5:14 But strong meat belongs to them that are of full age, even those who by reason of use have their senses exercised to discern both good and evil. (Once again, choices.)

Now, I said all of that to say this: It is our personal responsibility to check into things for ourselves whether they be true or some man's theory. What I have learned from the manipulation of history and the bible has led me to see that the many things the majority of the mainstream Christian religions teach are not what the bible is saying. Some of the errors relate to salvation and many of them do not.

However, there is error and false teaching in the churches today that Christ and the Apostles warn us about centuries ago. We have just waded through 2,000 years of men seeking power and

wealth by corrupting the Gospel of Christ. They are not teaching the complete Gospel Jesus gave us through the apostles.

Now the question is, "What has changed or been left out of the Gospel Jesus teaches?" Most people today couldn't care less about this information. They are part of a "herd instinct," following the media and majority of whatever their particular nation and culture promotes. People allow themselves to be spoon-fed by the preachers, teachers, and media culture, believing, buying, and clamoring for the latest technology and fads.

RESTORING THE FAITH ONCE DELIVERED

This is where the rubber meets the road as far as what the bible teaches and what mainstream Christian religion still believes—if you can have an open mind and for a while forget all you have ever heard about heaven, hell, and the judgment. Let the bible and a belief in the power of the Holy Spirit help you consider the rest of this story of why you and I were even born into this world.

The Faith Once Delivered is the phrase found in:

Jude 1:3 Beloved, when I gave all diligence to write unto you of the common salvation, it was needful for me to write unto you, and exhort you that ye should earnestly contend for the faith which was once delivered unto the saints. "That you should earnestly contend"—Compare.

Galations_2:5. The word here made "earnestly contend" is one of those words used by the sacred writers which have allusion to the Grecian games. Compare the notes in 1Corinthians 9:24, following. This word does not elsewhere occur in the New Testament. It means "to contend upon" (i. e., "for or about" anything) and would apply to the earnest effort put forth in those principles to obtain the prize. The reference here, of course, is only to contention by argument, by reasoning, by holding fast the principles of religion and keeping them against all opposition.

It would not justify "contention" by arms, by violence, or by persecution because:

(a) That is contrary to the spirit of true religion, and to the requirements of the gospel elsewhere revealed.

(b) It is not demanded by the proper meaning of the word, all that that fairly implies being the effort to keep truth by argument and by a steady life.

(c) It is not the most effectual way to keep up truth in the world to try to do it by force and arms.

"For the faith"—the system of religion revealed in the gospel. It is called faith, because that is the cardinal virtue in the system, and because all depends on belief. The rule here will require that we should contend in this manner for all truth.

"Once delivered unto the saints"—The word here used "once for all" in the sense that it was then complete and would not be repeated; or "formerly," to wit, by the author of the system. The more usual sense of the word would be, that it is done once in the sense that it is not to be changed or done again. Therefore, in the sense that it is then complete, and that nothing is to be added to it!

The "delivering" of this faith to the saints here referred to is made by revelation, or the system of truth which God has made known in his word. Everything which He has revealed, we are to defend as true. We are to surrender no part of it whatever, for every part of that system is of value to mankind.

By a careful study of the Bible, we are to learn what that system is, and then in all places, always, in all circumstances, and at every sacrifice, we are to keep its integrity.

As I have proven through history, the integrity of the Faith has been hijacked and manipulated by powerful, carnal minded men and institutions of learning to control people and appear to them as the only true administrators of Faith. Of course, this is Faith on their terms and interpretation. This is how they supported ignorance of what the Apostles taught until the Apostles were murdered.

When printing was invented they corrupted the text to meet their needs. The Faith began with John the Baptist as he came preaching repentance and baptism for sins committed. This was totally foreign to the Jewish community, for they were accustomed to sacrificial animals for sin. Something they must buy from the priests to then be sacrificed. They practiced physical salvation.

Matthew 3:1-3 In those days came John the Baptist, preaching in the wilderness of Judaea, (2) And saying, Repent ye: for the kingdom of heaven is at hand. (3) For this is he that was spoken of by the prophet Isiah, saying, The voice of one crying in the wilderness, Prepare ye the way of the Lord, make his paths straight.

The phrase John uses, kingdom of heaven, is raising salvation to a spiritual process. This phrase is just another way to express the Kingdom of God. The Kingdom of God in our hearts and minds and will eventually be physically set up on this earth by Jesus Christ at His second coming.

John keeps preaching of someone to come after him who would be the Messiah. He tells how Jesus will baptize them with water and the Holy Spirit and with fire. How Jesus will judge the world, save the righteous, and burn the wicked up with unquenchable fire.

Jesus shows up and is baptized by John. Upon His baptism the Holy Spirit descends upon Jesus and a voice from heaven declares this is the Son of God. Jesus is about thirty years of age at his baptism and goes into the wilderness to be tested by Satan. Afterward He returns and begins His ministry of the Faith in Him and God the Father. Part of His ministry is to reveal the character of the Father God to the people.

He refers to Himself as the image of the Father in obedience to His father's will. Jesus performs many miraculous events to assure the non-believers that He is sent from God. Jesus explains the new Faith many times in a one-on-one situation with various people and groups of the Jewish leadership.

An important aspect to Jesus ministry is His choosing of 12 men to become disciples of the Gospel He is presenting to the masses of people.

THE TWELVE DISCIPLES

atthew 10:1-4 And when he had called unto him his twelve disciples, he gave them power against unclean spirits, to cast them out, and to heal all manner of sickness and all manner of disease. (2) Now the names of the twelve apostles are these; The first, Simon, who is called Peter, and Andrew his brother; James the son of Zebedee, and John his brother; (3) Philip, and Bartholomew; Thomas, and Matthew the publican; James the son of Alpheus, and Lebbaeus, whose surname was Thaddaeus; (4) Simon the Canaanite, and Judas Iscariot, who also betrayed him.

It is interesting to note that this not a list of prominent people nor are any of them priests or students of the higher institutions of education in those days. They appear as more of a list of common people and blue-collar workers of their day, the only exception being Matthew, who was a tax collector of those days. He was an equivalent to the modern-day IRS agent, enforcing the collection of revenue commanded by the ruling government.

These men became the pillars of the church Jesus would begin with His departing commission to them at the Last Supper and the promise of the supernatural aid of the Holy Spirit after His death and resurrection.

Many of the principles Jesus applied to the Charter Leaders of His new church are ignored and murdered as presented earlier in the timeline of this story. Many of the principles the 12 disciples are to uphold and the problems they will meet are outlined in the book of John, Chapters 14 – 17. To set up the power of the changes Jesus introduced through the New Faith and Gospel; Jesus gave certain supernatural powers to the disciples.

Matthew 10:5-24 These twelve Jesus sent forth, and commanded them, saying, Go not into the way of the Gentiles, and into any city of the Samaritans enter ye not: (6) But go to the lost sheep of the house of Israel. (7) And as ye go, preach, saying, the kingdom of heaven is at hand. [Jesus is saying the Kingdom of God is embodied in Him and His example while upon this earth; a foretaste of the power and authority that will be set up when Christ comes the "Second Time"!

Daniel 2:44 is the coming Kingdom of God to earth. Jesus even mentions its coming in Matthew 6, the Lord's Prayer!]

(8) Heal the sick, cleanse the lepers, raise the dead, cast out devils: freely ye have received, freely give. (9) Provide neither gold, nor silver, nor brass in your purses, (10) script for your journey, neither two coats, neither shoes, nor yet staves: for the workman is worthy of his meat. (11) And into whatsoever city or town ye shall enter, enquire who in it is worthy; and there abide till ye go thence. (12) And when ye come into a house, salute it. (13) And if the house be worthy, let your peace come upon it: but if it be not worthy, let your peace return to you. (14) And whosoever shall not receive you, nor hear your words, when ye depart out of that house or city, shake off the dust of your feet. (15) Verily I say unto you, It shall be more tolerable for the land of Sodom and Gomorrah in the day of judgment, than for that city. (16) Behold, I send you forth as sheep in the midst of wolves be ye therefore wise as serpents, and harmless as doves. (17) But beware of men: for they will deliver you up to the councils, and they will scourge you in their synagogues; (18) And ye shall be brought before governors and kings for my sake, for a testimony against them and the Gentiles. (19) But when they deliver you up, take no thought how or what ye shall speak: for it shall be given you in that same hour what ye shall speak. (20) For it is not ye that speak, but the Spirit of your Father which speaks in you. (21) And the brother shall deliver up the brother to death, and the father the child: and the children shall rise up against their parents and cause them to be put to death. (22) And ye shall be hated of all men for my name's sake: but he that endures to the end shall be saved. (23) But when they persecute you in this city, flee ye into another: for verily I say unto you, Ye shall not have gone over the cities of Israel, till the Son of man be come. (24) The disciple is not above his master, nor the servant above his lord…

Jesus raised the laws and things of God to a spiritual level of understanding. His mission was clear, and He exercised caution so that His mission would not be preempted by the religious zealots who turned against Him because of the changes He brought to the Old Covenant system for salvation and worship.

A PERSONAL LESSON
FOR NICODEMUS

One of the first teachings Jesus introduced is presented in a private lesson to Nicodemus, a very well-known Jewish leader, who came to Jesus at night to avoid condemnation from his own people. The lesson with Nicodemus was an introduction to the literal process of salvation that would soon be pioneered by Jesus Himself through His crucifixion, death, and resurrection.

John 3:1-12 There was a man of the Pharisees, named Nicodemus, a ruler of the Jews: (2) The same came to Jesus by night, and said unto him, Rabbi, we know that you are a teacher come from God: for no man can do these miracles that you do, except God be with him. (3) Jesus answered and said unto him, Verily, verily, I say to you, except a man be born again, he cannot see the kingdom of God. (4) Nicodemus says unto him, how can a man be born when he is old? can he enter the second time into his mother's womb, and be born? (5) Jesus answered, Verily, verily, I say to you, except a man be born of water and of the Spirit, he cannot enter into the kingdom of God. (6) That which is born of the flesh is flesh; and that which is born of the Spirit is spirit. (7) Marvel not that I said to you, you must be born again. (8) The wind blows where it will, and you hear the sound thereof, but cannot tell where it comes from, and where it goes: so is every one that is born of the Spirit. (9) Nicodemus answered and said unto him, how can these things be? (10) Jesus answered and said unto him, are you a master of Israel, and know not these things? (11) Verily, verily, I say to you, we speak that we do know, and testify that we have seen; and you receive not our witness. (12) If I have told you earthly things, and you believe not, how shall you believe, if I tell you of heavenly things?

Nicodemus acknowledges that Jesus is a teacher come from God; his readiness and desire to receive instruction shows his belief in what Jesus says, so, Jesus begins with one of the fundamental truths of His advanced lessons.

It is no part of Christianity to conceal anything. Jesus declares to every man, high or low, rich, or poor, the most humbling truths of the gospel. Jesus tells Nicodemus that he must be born anew.

I know KJV says again, but that is a prejudice mistranslation from Catholic influence. The following response from Nicodemus is a clue that he doesn't get what Jesus is introducing. Nicodemus asks how can a man be born twice? Again, Jesus explains in simple terms, "Unless a person is born of water, (physical birth) and of the Spirit, (literal spiritual transformation), he cannot enter the kingdom of God." I think a better way of putting it in modern terms is to look at both phrases Jesus uses and consider the process in this way:

Unless a person is begotten of the Holy Spirit, (accepting and receiving Jesus Christ into your personal life as master), they cannot see the Kingdom of God.

The other phrase Jesus says is more specific, "Unless a person is born of water, (physical birth process from a woman) and of the Spirit, (Spiritual transformation from human to a

spirit being) they cannot enter the Kingdom of God."

Jesus clarifies the concept in verse: *(6) That which is born of the flesh is flesh; and that which is born of the Spirit is spirit.*

Later in scripture Paul says it too.

1Corinthians 15:50 Now this I say, brethren, that flesh and blood cannot inherit the kingdom of God; neither doth corruption inherit incorruption.

Jesus explains the spirit side of life in verses *(8) The wind blows where it will, and you hear the sound thereof, but cannot tell where it comes from, and where it goes: so is every one that is born of the Spirit.*

Paul again emphasizes the process.

1Corinthians 15:51-53 Behold, I shew you a mystery; We shall not all sleep, but we shall all be changed, (52) In a moment, in the twinkling of an eye, at the last trump: for the trumpet shall sound, and the dead shall be raised incorruptible, and we shall be changed. (53) For this corruptible must put on incorruption, and this mortal must put on immortality.

This is the lesson in a nutshell. This is the mission Jesus would fulfill at his crucifixion and resurrection later in 30 A. D. So, for the first time in history, God explained the after-death experience to people. This is only a broad sense of the matter. It is a mystery to the people because it had not been completed in all of earlier history; Jesus was the first to do it. Therefore, John writes in verse 13: "No man has ascended to heaven except He that came from heaven and was born of a woman."

John 3:13 And no man hath ascended up to heaven, but he that came down from heaven, even the Son of man which is in heaven. [Resurrected and gone to heaven.] Remember, John wrote this long after the event, this is why it reads like it does.

A LESSON FOR ALL PEOPLE AND THE SMARITAN WOMAN AT THE WELL

*A*nother new concept or teaching Jesus introduced appears when He met the Samaritan woman at Jacob's well.

John 4:5-26 Then cometh he to a city of Samaria, which is called Sychar, near to the parcel of ground that Jacob gave to his son Joseph. (6) Now Jacob's well was there. Jesus, therefore, being wearied with his journey, sat thus on the well: and it was about the sixth hour. (7) There is cometh a woman of Samaria to draw water: Jesus says unto her, give me to drink. (8) (For his disciples were gone away unto the city to buy meat.) (9) Then says the woman of Samaria unto him, how is it that thou, being a Jew, ask drink of me, which am a woman of Samaria? for the Jews have no dealings with the Samaritans. (10) Jesus answered and said unto her, if thou knew the gift of God, and who it is that says to you, Give me to drink; thou would have asked of Him, and He would have given you living water. (11) The woman says unto him, Sir, you hast nothing to draw with, and the well is deep: from where then have you that living water? (12) Are you greater than our father Jacob, which gave us the well, and drank thereof himself, and his children, and his cattle? (13) Jesus answered and said unto her, whosoever drinks of this water shall thirst again: (14) But whosoever drinks of the water that I shall give him shall never thirst; but the water that I shall give him shall be in him a well of water springing up into everlasting life. (15) The woman says unto him, Sir, give me this water, that I thirst not, neither come here to draw. (16) Jesus says unto her, Go, call thy husband, and come hither. (17) The woman answered and said, I have no husband. Jesus said unto her, thou hast well said, I have no husband: (18) For thou hast had five husbands; and he whom you now have is not thy husband: in that said thou truly. (19) The woman says unto him, Sir, I perceive that thou art a prophet. (20) Our fathers worshipped in this mountain; and you say, that in Jerusalem is the place where men ought to worship. (21) Jesus says unto her, Woman, believe me, the hour cometh, when ye shall neither in this mountain, nor yet at Jerusalem, worship the Father. (22) You worship you know not what: we know what we worship: for salvation is of the Jews. (23) But the hour comes, and now is, when the true worshippers shall worship the Father in spirit and in truth: for the Father seeks such to worship him. (24) God is a Spirit: and they that worship him must worship him in spirit and in truth. (25) The woman says unto him, I know that Messiah comes, which is called Christ: when He is come, He will tell us all things. (26) Jesus says unto her, I that speak unto thee is He.

This event is one that I did not understand until I realized that the concept was totally new to both Jews and all other religions of that day.

One reason the Jews ignored the Samaritans was their bias toward where they worshipped in the Mountains of Samaria instead of coming to the Temple in Jerusalem. Jesus revealed several things during this encounter.

(Verse 10) Everlasting life is a "Gift from God".

(Verse 10) He uses "Water" as a metaphor or icon for the Holy Word and Spirit of God.

(Verse 14) He tells her He is the only source of this "Water". He refers to an Everlasting Life that can happen from drinking in this "Water." (The Fountain of Youth myth comes from the pages of the Bible.)

(Verses 18, 19) He reveals Himself to her as a Prophet. (Verses 21, 22) He refers to a time when Worship toward God is not in the Mountains or Temple in Jerusalem.

(Verse 22) He says that Salvation of the Jews is about to be expanded to all peoples.

(Verses 23, 24) The time was coming and now it is here, God is referred to as a Spirit and Truth and is worshipped by this invisible power of Spirit and Truth by human beings!

(Verses 25, 26) The woman knows about a coming Messiah that will stand for and tell them about God, Jesus tells her plainly that He is this Messiah!

Thus far Jesus revealed the physical steps toward Salvation and the actual transformation process. Then He revealed that Salvation is a gift from God. It is started by believing in God's Holy word and Spirit. He also shows from this time forward, God can be worshipped anywhere, anytime!

God is not confined to a building or place on a mountain! (In other words, worshipping God is now a spiritual act not attendance and church ritual only) This is the first time Jesus openly professes He is the prophesied Messiah. With this exchange the Lord Jesus introduced the new concept of personal religion.

His knowledge of the heart and of the life set Him apart from physical ritualistic religion. He taught people to seize on all occasions; to lead sinners to the belief that Jesus is the Christ.

He begins to make use of parables, allegories, and all topics of conversation for examples to teach the nature of religion. People had not been exposed to a model of so much wisdom Jesus is speaking to them.

From the very beginning of His ministry, we see Jesus changing the very nature of religion. It does not consist merely in external forms. It is pure, spiritual, active, bubbling fountain of life sustaining knowledge and choices. It is the worship of a pure and holy God, where the heart is offered, and where the desires of a humble soul are breathed out, reaching for salvation. This is just a couple of the one-on-one teachings of the new Faith Jesus brings to earth. He also begins to teach publicly in the synagogues, introducing the fulfillment of many of the Old Testament prophets people have been taught by the priests. His first sermon is preached in Nazareth, His hometown.

JESUS PREACHES HIS FIRST SERMON

Luke 4:16-21 And He came to Nazareth, where He had been brought up: and, as His custom was, He went into the synagogue on the Sabbath day, and stood up for to read. (17) And there was delivered unto Him the book of the prophet Isaiah. And when He had opened the book, He found the place where it is written, (18) The Spirit of the Lord is upon me, because he hath anointed me to preach the gospel to the poor; he hath sent me to heal the brokenhearted, to preach deliverance to the captives, and recovering of sight to the blind, to set at liberty them that are bruised, (19) To preach the acceptable year of the Lord. (20) And He closed the book, and He gave it again to the minister, and sat down. And the eyes of all of them that were in the synagogue were fastened on Him. (21) And He began to say unto them, "This day is this scripture fulfilled in your ears."

I must tell you I had read this passage of scripture many times for many years and had never taken the time to compare it with the actual text from Isaiah from which Jesus was reading.

When I finally made the comparison I became suddenly aware of the last part of verse 2 and the remaining 9 verses of the prophecy that Jesus did not read that day in Nazareth.

Isaiah 61:1-2 The Spirit of the Lord GOD is upon me; because the LORD hath anointed me to preach good tidings unto the meek; he hath sent me to bind up the brokenhearted, to proclaim liberty to the captives, and the opening of the prison to them that are bound; (2) To proclaim the acceptable year of the LORD,(At this point in His reading that day, Jesus closed the book and sat down) *and the day of vengeance of our God;....*

Jesus stopped just short of the remaining part of the prophecy that will not be fulfilled until His second coming in our future. I know this sounds strange and , but as you continue in this story you will come to see it is a huge part of the Gospel that is connected to the Private Teaching to His disciples just a few days before His crucifixion and death. It is also found in the overall outlined plan of God prophesied in the ninth Chapter of Daniel.

When I began to read the remaining scriptures, Jesus was quoting in the very first sermon of His ministry, I became aware of why He stopped short, closed the book, and sat down. The remaining context of the prophecy is to be fulfilled upon His return to earth sometime before the end of the 21st Century. This is a lengthy prophecy. It is yet another step or phase of the overall Plan of God for mankind's rehabilitation from 6,000 years of slow progress in knowledge and understanding our purpose and the two possible Destinies.

Isaiah 61:2-11 To proclaim the acceptable year of the LORD, (At this point in His reading that day, Jesus closed the book and sat down) *and the day of vengeance of our God; to comfort all that mourn; (3) To appoint unto them that mourn in Zion, to give unto them beauty for ashes, the oil of joy for mourning, the garment of praise for the spirit of heaviness; that they might be called trees of righteousness, the planting of the LORD, that he might be glorified. (4) And they shall build the old wastes, they shall raise up the former desolations, and they shall repair the waste cities, the desolations of many generations. (5) And strangers shall stand and feed your flocks, and the sons of the alien shall be your plowmen and your vinedressers. (6) But ye shall be named the Priests of the LORD: men shall call you the Ministers of our God: ye shall eat the riches of the Gentiles, and in their glory shall ye boast yourselves. (7) For your shame ye shall have double; and for confusion they shall rejoice in their part: therefore, in their land they shall own the double: everlasting joy shall be unto them. (8) For I the LORD love judgment, I hate robbery for burnt offering; and I will direct their work in truth, and I will make an everlasting covenant with them. (9) And their seed shall be known among the Gentiles, and their offspring among the people: all that see them shall acknowledge them, that they are the seed which the LORD hath blessed. (10) I will rejoice in the LORD, my soul shall be joyful in my God; for he hath clothed me with the garments of salvation, he hath covered me with the robe of righteousness, as a bridegroom decks himself with ornaments, and as a bride adorns herself with her jewels. (11) For as the earth brings forth her bud, and as the garden causes the things that are sown in it to spring forth; so, the Lord GOD will cause righteousness and praise to spring forth before all the nations.*

When I say this is yet another phase of God's plan for mankind's salvation, I am referring to the Millennium or 1,000 years of Christ returning to rule on the earth. Understand, I am using rounded numbers for years and not specific time because this event is dependent upon Jesus responding to a direct order from His Father to return!

Matthew 24:36 But of that day and hour knows no man, no, not the angels of heaven, but my Father only.

Matthew 24:42 watch therefore: for ye know not what hour your Lord doth come. Matthew 24:44 Therefore be ye also ready: for in such an hour as ye think not the Son of man cometh.

Matthew 24:50 the lord of that servant shall come in a day when he looks not for him, and in an hour that he is not aware of,

Matthew 25:13 watch therefore, for ye know neither the day nor the hour wherein the Son of man cometh.

As I mentioned earlier, Jesus reserves this part of the prophecy concerning the activities that will begin after His second coming to earth for a private teaching with His disciples just before He is crucified. I will move on to more of the actual context of the "Faith Once Delivered" by Jesus and the Apostles at this timeline of my story.

JESUS PREACHES A NEW STANDARD OF PERSONAL RESPONSIBILITY

As His ministry expands, Jesus begins to preach the Gospel to the masses of people who gather to hear Him. He speaks to them plainly about the present religious practices of the Jews and elevates the laws of God to a higher standard of personal responsibility for everyone. Most of these principles are found in the famous Sermon on the Mount. This sermon can be found in the Book of Matthew, Chapters 5, 6, &7. It is full of concepts for personal interaction with fellowman and teaches a moral standard of personal responsibility. It is a great place to start young people who are interested in the bible. Its content includes many references to the coming Kingdom of God and raises awareness to hypocrisy in leadership of the existing priesthood of the Jewish religion.

As the ministry of Jesus progresses, His followers grow in numbers and begin to merit the attention of the Jewish leadership. They begin to view the Gospel of Jesus Christ as a threat to their authority and preeminence over the people.

JESUS IS PERSECUTED BY THE PAHARISEES

*A*s His ministry continues, Jesus is often followed by the sect of Pharisees and contested for His ignoring the many laws added to the Jewish faith by the Jewish Priests.

Mark 2:23-28 And it happened, that he went through the corn fields on the Sabbath day; and his disciples began, as they went, to pluck the ears of corn. (24) And the Pharisees said unto him, Behold, why do they on the Sabbath day that which is not lawful? (25) And he said unto them, Have ye never read what David did, when he had need, and was hungry, he, and they that were with him? (26) How he went into the house of God in the days of Abiathar the high priest, and did eat the showbread, which is not lawful to eat but for the priests, and gave also to them which were with him? (27) And he said unto them, The Sabbath was made for man, and not man for the Sabbath: (28) Therefore the Son of man is Lord also of the Sabbath.

Jesus plainly reminds the Pharisees that God created the Sabbath upon the 7 th day of the weekly cycle for mankind to

observe a physical rest from normal daily labors and activities. Jesus told the Jewish Priesthood the day He created, called Sabbath, is set apart for mankind. Mankind was not created to choose the purpose of the Sabbath and change its intended purpose for its own religious meaning.

INSET

This is also a now a tradition set up by the Catholic Church of the 3rd Century from the Emperor's chair of authority that has been changed to be seen upon the first Day of the weekly cycle. History is truly clear about changing the Sabbath from the day as God's Day of rest for mankind.

The Jews had already corrupted the intended meaning of the day and added worship and physical rituals to it that were not there in the beginning. The Catholic Church enforced the change to Sunday, under penalty of death, upon anyone who was found to be still being faithful to the seventh day observance.

As we have already covered in the early writing of this story, the Hijacking of the Faith Once Delivered by Jesus and the Apostles change many things. In the sense of disobedience, both the Jews and Romans were guilty of changing or adding to God's laws.

As I stated earlier, even the Protestant Reformation started by Martin Luther continues with many of the traditions of the Catholic Church even at present. The 21st Century protestant churches have tried to justify their day of worship through the scriptures when it is really not necessary nor possible to square with the bible.

Understand that there is no appointed or specified day of the weekly cycle appointed by God's Law for worship. The 7 th Day Sabbath is specifically as a day of rest from the 6 days preceding the Sabbath day. Any physical work or labor is to be only an emergency created by unforeseen circumstances. There is no problem with worshipping God on Sunday or any other day of the week. The Seventh Day was specifically set aside by God for man's physical and mental rest from the other six days of work and stress of life.

By the time, Jesus arrived, the Pharisees had made the Seventh Day of rest a yoke of bondage in what you can't do and made it their official worship day. They also made the temple the exclusive place of worship and forbade any other meetings of the minds in any other forum. In the creation of the Seventh day of rest you cannot find biblical authority making it a day of worship or a regular church service time; <u>although there is nothing in the bible that says you can't have a worship service on the Sabbath or any other day of the week.</u>

TEACHING WITH PARABLES

As the masses of people became greater and greater in numbers, Jesus began to use metaphors, allegories, and analogies in parable format to teach His lessons. By the end of His ministry, Jesus spoke no less than 40 parables. These were filled with simple context having latent, inherent deep meaning for moral living and future events to be fulfilled.

Jesus was asked by His own disciples why He spoke in parables to the masses. His answer was very direct and in no way sugar coated. It was certainly an answer that carried with it a formal accusation to anyone who took the Word of God with only a carnal sense of awareness and pride in their version of life.

There is a huge truth about the Plan of God for mankind in His statement behind the answer Jesus gives His disciples. *Matthew 13:10-16 And the disciples came, and said unto Him, why speak you unto them in parables? (11) He answered and said unto them, because it is given unto you to know the mysteries of the kingdom of heaven, but to them it is not given. (12) For whosoever hath, to him shall be given, and he shall have more abundance: but whosoever hath not, from him shall be taken away even that he hath. (13) Therefore, speak I to them in parables: because they are seeing see not; and hearing they hear not, neither do they understand. (14) And in them is fulfilled the prophecy of Isiah, which says, By hearing you shall hear, and shall not understand; and seeing you shall see, and shall not perceive: (15) For this people's heart is waxed gross, and their ears are dull of hearing, and their eyes they have closed; lest at any time they should see with their eyes, and hear with their ears, and should understand with their heart, and should be converted, and I should heal them. (16) But blessed are your eyes, for they see and your ears, for they hear.*

When I looked up the English words in their original context in Greek, I got a clear meaning of what Jesus was saying. Jesus was saying He spoke in parables because they really were so uneducated about the things He had come to raise to a spiritual level. It is best to just present the truth in parable format.

This is because His first mission upon earth was not to condemn the world for its ignorance in the higher ways of God. His mission was to live an exemplary life, raising the laws of God to a spiritual level, and then pioneering the process for an eternal existence. His Gospel is only perceived by an extremely limited number of people and totally rejected as a threat to the lifestyle of the Jewish Priesthood. Therefore, Jesus taught the masses in Parables and His Disciples with direct contextual doctrine in most cases.

INSERT

Many Christians today do not understand that personal salvation for mankind was only of a physical nature until Jesus fulfilled His mission to pioneer the way to spiritual salvation for an eternal existence. This is key understanding for what happened to those who lived before Jesus. His life was the "pivotal fulcrum" that opened the door to an eternal existence for anyone who will believe in Him, and the Father and principles Jesus teaches.

There is an ongoing Plan of God for the salvation of mankind that hopefully will become clear by the end of my book. Jesus taught in parables and ended most of what He taught with the phrase, "He that has an ear to hear, let him hear." This is saying, <u>If you understand what I am saying, the Father God is calling you, and now you are responsible to make a choice to accept or reject the information.</u>

JESUS EXPLAINS THE CALLING FROM GOD

John 6:44-45 No man can come to me, except the Father which hath sent me draw him: and I will raise him up at the last day. (45) It is written in the prophets, and they shall be all taught of God. Every man therefore that hath heard, and hath learned of the Father, cometh unto me.

This statement from Jesus was a response prompted by the objection by the Jewish leadership. Jesus told them His ministry is sanctioned by God the Father from heaven, elevating the laws of God given to Moses to a personal spiritual level of responsibility and making a complete change in the intercessory bridge between God and mankind.

They objected to His doctrine because He claims a greater position of authority than Moses. The Jewish priests saw Him to be a mere man, and that what He said was impossible. It is not to be expected that of themselves they would embrace the doctrine. His point is that when anyone believes in Jesus, it will be because they have been influenced by God the Father. When I think about the reasons why the Priests do not believe Jesus, they are for at least three reasons.

First of all, they have an improper regard for Moses, as if no one could be superior to him.

Next, they expressed an unwillingness to believe that Jesus, whom they know to be the reputed son of a carpenter and not of their priesthood, could ever be superior to Moses!

Finally, their rejection of Jesus was in the opposition of their will and that their love of their position and honor prevented their believing Him. The difficulty for their belief in Him is explained by Jesus.

John 5:38-44 And you have not His word abiding in you: for whom He hath sent, Him ye believe not. (39) Search the scriptures; for in them you think ye have eternal life: and they are they which testify of me. (40) And you will not come to me, that you might have life. (41) I receive not honor from men. (42) But I know you, that ye have not the love of God in you. (43) I am come in my Father's name, and you receive me not: if another shall come in his own name, him ye will receive. (44) How can you believe, which receive honor one of another, and seek not the honor that cometh from God only?

Jesus told them that their obsession with natural faculties or of power to do their duty generated mistaken opinions, pride, obstinacy, self-conceit, resulting in their deep-felt contempt for Jesus. (Verse 40) *"And ye will not come."* Jesus is telling the Jews the Old Testament bears evidence that He is the Messiah, though they professedly search it to learn the way to life, and though Jesus's works prove it, they refuse to accept Him and obtain life.

Life is to be obtained in Christ. He is the way, the truth, and the life, and only He can save us. Neither can Mohammad, Jewish Traditions, <u>or your church save you</u>. For us to begin the process of eternal salvation, we must come to Him—that is, must come in the way appointed, as lost sinners, and be willing to be saved by Jesus only.

This is why is because they are not willing to be saved. The only reason sinners die the second death (to be explained later) is because they will not come to Christ for life and happiness: it is not because they cannot, but because they will not.

It is our choice as free human beings. Sinners have an opposition to going to Jesus Christ for eternal life. They prefer any other way, and it is commonly not until all other means are tried that they are willing to give to Christ. This "humanistic, carnal, thinking" was the beginning of Cain's demise shortly after God created mankind. Seeking and worshiping God in his own way ignoring God's prescribed way.

John 12:32; "And I, if I be lifted up from the earth, will draw all men unto me."

In the conversion of the sinner, God enlightens the mind, inclines the will, and influences the soul by motives, by just views of God's law, by His love, His commands, by the Holy Spirit, which is applying truth to the mind, and urging a person to yield himself to the Savior. So that while God inclines that person and will have all the glory, man yields without compulsion; the obstacles are removed, and the person becomes a willing servant of God.

The following words of Christ sum this up for me. *John 6:65-69 And he said, therefore said I unto you, that no man can come unto me, except it was given unto him of my Father. (66) From that time many of his disciples went back and walked no more with him. (67) Then said Jesus unto the twelve, will ye also go away? (68) Then Simon Peter answered him, Lord, to whom shall we go? You are the words of eternal life. (69) And we believe and are sure that thou art that Christ, the Son of the living God!*

Modern mankind views Jesus as a human philosopher and not a Messiah from the Creator God.

IT'S OUR CHOICE TO ANSWER
THE CALL FROM GOD

*G*od will not force anyone to believe in Him or obey Him! He allows us to choose for ourselves whom, what, or how we will believe to answer the question of why we are born! Most people can quote the "Golden Rule," but do they not know what the rest of that passage of scripture says?

Matthew 7:12-15 (12) Therefore, all things whatsoever ye that men would do to you, do ye even so to them: for this is the law and the prophets. (13) Enter ye in at the strait gate: for wide is the gate, and broad is the way, which leads to destruction, and many there be which go in there at:

(14) Because strait is the gate, and narrow is the way, which leads unto life, and few there be that find it. (15) Beware of false prophets, which come to you in sheep's clothing, but inwardly they are ravening wolves.

Ask yourself why the clear majority of Christians believe 3rd century doctrine concerning Heaven, Hell, and Judgment.

Part of the Different Gospel espoused by the Catholic Church is rooted in the <u>Babylonian Mystery Religion</u> of the years before and after the Tower of Babel in Mesopotamia in 25th Century B.C. It is a manmade religion using the spiritual attributes from God to manipulate and rule people.

Not too many centuries after the Faith Delivered by Christ and the Apostles is massaged in with Paganism by the various Emperors, Bishops, and Religious Zealots of the 3rd through the 15th Centuries A.D., the truth from God becomes the corrupted Gospel through the Traditions of Men. Not only is it a different Gospel created by men of pagan inclinations; but also rejected by the chosen people of God, the Jews, as they refuse to accept the Faith Once Delivered by Christ and the Apostles.

I have showed to you earlier the only possible motive for the Murder of the Apostles and the persecution of the true believers all down through the history of mankind is to bury the true gospel. I do not condemn any church for trying to help people believe, see, and have faith in God and Jesus Christ. But <u>I cannot abide a perverted truth about the faith once delivered</u> by Jesus Christ and continued by the Apostles.

There is a plan for mankind that will help the eventual saving of all who choose to be saved. But it is not going to heaven if you are good enough or torture forever in a lake of fire if you are <u>not</u> good enough. The reward of the saved is an eternal existence with our Creator God. The reward of the wicked is eternal death with no chance for eternal life.

We don't have to fear the first physical death, but we do not want to be found in the spiritual second death. The truth of these destinies is what will hopefully change our lives personally. It is a personal choice. We cannot make it for anyone but ourselves. The choice to believe in an Invisible God is not popular; nearly six-thousand years of history has made that clear. Believing in an Invisible God is more important than believing some of the far-out concepts men and their religions offer. It is a spiritual matter. We must stay in touch with our spiritual conscience and educate it to understand why we are born. The truth about Heaven, Hell, and Judgment. These are the especially important tenants of Faith in our choices of belief for which destiny will be ours after physical death.

The deception associated with these subjects clouds the reason we are born into this world. The calling from God comes from the Heavenly Father. It is up to us to answer the call when it comes.

John6:44 No man can come to me, except the Father which hath sent me draw him: and I will raise him up at the last day.

John 6:65 And he said, therefore said I unto you, that no man can come unto me, except it was given unto him of my Father.

INSET

These truths, from the Bible, Science, and History, about these tenants of faith, are what changes my feeling of the meaning of life, why I was born, and which destiny I intend to end up with!

I have prayed to God that I can write this, my story, in a way that His Word and Holy Spirit will stir your will to Let it go; that is, of the third Century A. D. corrupted information about Heaven, Hell, and Judgment that is not in agreement with the prophesies, warnings, timelines, and teachings from our invisible God, the Patriarchs, Prophets, Jesus, and the Apostles of the scriptures.

We don't have to be experts in Greek and Hebrew to figure things out in the bible. James Strong made this easy when he produced one book that you must have when studying the bible: The Greek and Hebrew Concordance. The way the book is set up is simple. A number is assigned to every English word in the bible. Those numbers are tied to the Greek and Hebrew definitions. The process breaks through the malicious deceit written into the scriptures by translators with personal carnal agendas to change the context and intent of the scriptures.

Before I begin, ask yourself this question. Living in this 21st Century of an Apex of accumulated knowledge and information, why, am I still believing tenants of faith from the 3rd Century, adopted from an ancient mystery religion from 2,000 years prior to the 3rd century, when mankind doesn't even understand the Sun, Moon, and Stars are not God?

This is the question I asked myself not too long ago before this book was started. Once I understood the truth about Heaven, Hell, and Judgment, the book of Revelation became more understandable and made better sense. My next book will cover the information of Revelation as it relates to the 21st century and how we can be ready for the times ahead of the Great Troubles of Worldwide proportions.

WHAT THE BIBLE SAYS ABOUT HEAVEN, HELL, AND JUDGMENT

The truth of these three main subjects are crucial in understanding what my destiny can be. It is the difference between the reality of life and the fantasies of what mainstream religions teach. Understanding these three concepts points us to how to choose the intended destiny we were born to achieve.

Remember this; If you tell a lie long enough repeatedly, it eventually becomes accepted as truth. There is three types of Heaven, Hell, and Judgment. These scriptures inform us, from the Bible, the aspects of God's plan for humanity. What a loving God. God wishes that no person would perish forever from life with Him; yet, in God's great compassion, He has set forth a final punishment for those who do not wish to live the life God has set before us as His children. The punishment is everlasting death, not torment. There is no love in torture, it is the opposite of God's nature, it is an attribute of the devil to remind us of sin continually, and torture us with it.

Heaven, Hell, and Judgment <u>are real places and events in the plan of God for humanity</u>. How we are judged, and our destination is between the individual and God.

Heaven is expressed in terms of Paradise, or the hereafter and other pleasant uplifting ways. Many get the feeling it is a beautiful city with golden streets and mansions. There is such a city described by John in the book of Revelation. However, it is set in the context of a specific time of occupation by its tenants long after specific events take place in the timeline of God's master plan.

Isaiah 55:9 For as the heavens are higher than the earth, so are <u>my ways higher than your ways</u>, and my thoughts than your thoughts.

Isaiah sets the attitude for my thinking process while exploring the subject of Heaven! It is imperative that both you and I remember what is said earlier in this book about Traditions versus Scriptural Context as this subject is revealed from the Bible. The conceptual understanding of Heaven as one of two totally different destinies after the physical death of human beings is the most sensitive and important belief and faith of all peoples. I am trying to present the facts of truth from the bible, relying on the Holy Spirit of God to help me and you consider this information as a choice rarely presented in this format.

The ideology churches teach about Heaven is not what the Bible reveals. This will be difficult for me because it goes against what I have always heard about Heaven. However, it is an important subject to understand the Faith Once Delivered from Jesus to the Apostles.

The Faith the Apostles taught until they were martyred by the Roman Empire. Many of the things Jesus teaches were changed by the Roman Bishops a few years after Christ and the Apostles were gone.

The English word Heaven is found 583 times throughout the bible, 327 times in the Old Testament and 256 times in the New Testament. I find this an interesting comparison: 56 percent in the Old and 44 percent in the New. It means truly little as far a spiritual significance. It tells me that the knowledge of the meaning of heaven does not change in the progress of time if one only accepts the English meaning of the word.

A quick look at the original Hebrew and Greek definitions does reveal distinctive meanings. The Heavens or Heaven are words used to name the space in which the earth is suspended by its centrifugal rotation on its axis. This interpretation is derived from mankind's perspective as earthbound physical beings describing what can be seen from the earth. The view is expanded when the light from the sun is obscured by the rotation of the earth during what is defined as night.

There are three words, one from the Hebrew Language and two from the Greek language that describe Heaven. The actual English word shows up as the 7th word in the opening narrative of the Bible.

Genesis 1:1 In the beginning God created the <u>heaven</u> and the earth. *Genesis 1:7, 8 And God made the firmament, and divided the waters which were under the firmament from the waters which were above the firmament: and it was so. (8) And God called the firmament Heaven. And the evening and the morning were the second day.*

Hebrew sha^mayim and sha^meh pronounced shaw-mah'-yim, and shaw-meh' The second form being dual of an unused singular; from an unused root meaning to be lofty; the sky (as aloft; the dual alluding to the visible arch in which the clouds move, as well as to the higher ether where the celestial bodies revolve): - air, X astrologer, heaven (-s).

Greek G3771 ouranothen pronounced oo-ran-oth'-en from G3772 and the enclitic of source; from the sky: - from heaven. celestial, that is, <u>belonging to or coming from the sky</u>: - heavenly Greek G3772 ouranos pronounced oo-ran-os' From the same as G3735 (through the idea of elevation); <u>the sky; by extension heaven</u> (as the abode of God); by implication happiness, power, eternity; specifically, the Gospel (Christianity): - air, heaven ([-ly]), sky.

The difference between G3771 and G3772 is a matter of FAITH! The First Greek word is specific about proximity in relation to the earth and then expands the meaning to the proximity in relation to sky (atmosphere) and the celestial, (stars). The Second Greek word is similar to the first; adding the <u>descriptive of Faith and belief in the abode of God.</u> The concept of THREE heavens develops from the scripture because of what the Apostle Paul says in his letter to the Corinthians after being taught by visions from Jesus Christ. The Apostle Paul describes from his conversations with <u>an angel manifested as a man from the place where God dwells, calling it the Third Heaven.</u>

2 Corinthians 12:2 I knew a man in Christ above fourteen years ago, (whether in the body, I cannot tell; or whether out of the body, I cannot tell: God knows ;) such an one caught up to the third heaven.

Paul is referring to the appearance of a man, (an angel in the form of a man) coming from <u>the "THIRD" Heaven where Jesus and the Father dwell</u>. A detailed description of the Throne Room called a Third Heaven where God lives is described in the vision from Jesus to John in Revelation the 4th Chapter. When compared with the vision Ezekiel sees, (Ezekiel 1:) 700 years before vision John sees, (Revelation 4:) One significant attribute is clear! The heavenly throne of God is both a Stationary and Transportable (for lack of a better word to describe its ability to travel through the universe) Firmament appearing as a sea of translucent glass. The traditional teaching from centuries past in the churches of Christian Beliefs simply does not square up contextually with what the bible reveals.

I admit that traditional concepts of heaven are comforting to we who are still alive after someone dies, but I too must admit there are some illogical gaps that create uneasy feelings for families who think they are being watched by their loved ones from some place in heaven. The bible does not square with this concept either.

Simplified, there is only one type of audience watching you and I from somewhere we call heaven. God the Father, Jesus His Firstborn Son, innumerable created Spirit Beings called angels, Arch Angels, Cherubim, Seraphim, and Creatures. Only by the term 33.3% do we understand the different percentage of Fallen Angels, and only one Fallen Arch Angel of the 3 whose names are revealed from the scriptures. Lucifer, Michael, and Gabriel.

<u>Lucifer the one fallen whose name is changed to Satan</u> because of his conspiracy of rebellion against his own creator. This group of 1/3 plus one archangel is confined to the earthly realm as unseen prince and powers of the air surrounding earth.

I will list a few scriptures for consideration. First, consider the word Paradise used in the New Testament only 3 specific times. Once by Jesus, then Paul, and finally John when he was relating what Jesus tells him in the Revelation. So actually, twice by Jesus and once by Paul.

Luke 23:43 And Jesus said unto him, Verily I say unto thee today; shalt thou be with me in paradise.

Note:

Lest I add contradiction to the scriptures; I have expressed this scripture the way it must logically be done. As I explained earlier in this book about Scripture Translation and Punctuation, <u>there is no punctuation in the original Greek and Aramaic texts</u>. The comma was intentionally put in before the word translated, today, and it was then capitalized to conform with the Roman Catholic Influence of immediate transport of the dead to heaven in a conscious state of mind. This is a false teaching invented by Dante in his book called, The Divine Comedy.

Because the thief on the cross recognizes and takes responsibility for his crime and punishment, understanding Jesus has done nothing to deserve death, Jesus responds to him with this statement. Not that the thief would at once go to paradise; but because of his repentant attitude, it will be the man's ultimate destiny. Jesus, still performing His saving ministry even from the cross. *2Corinthians12:4 How that he was caught up into paradise, and heard unspeakable words, which it is not lawful for a man to utter.*

Revelation2:7 He that hath an ear, let him hear what the Spirit says unto the churches; To him that overcomes will I give to eat of the tree of life, which is in the midst of the paradise of God.

Actually, the churches have it correct about this word Paradise describing the place where God rules the Universe from His throne! However, they are not correctly informed of the major details of when, where, and how the process of human beings after death arrive and in what form and condition!

John plainly writes it after the resurrection of Jesus as He received it from Jesus before the resurrection; "*No man has ascended to heaven, only He, (meaning Jesus) who came from heaven*"! Paul plainly says, it is an angel in the form of a man who came from <u>paradise</u>, (3rd Heaven) to teach Paul some other information. Many preachers site the transfiguration narrative as proof of people already in heaven conscious with God.

Matthew 17:1-9 And after six days Jesus taketh Peter, James, and John his brother, and brings them up into a high mountain apart, (2) And <u>was transfigured before them</u>: and his face did shine as the sun, and his raiment was white as the light. (3) And behold, there appeared unto them Moses and Elias talking with him. (4) Then answered Peter, and said unto Jesus, Lord, it is good for us to be here: if thou wilt, let us make here three tabernacles; one for thee, and one for Moses, and one for Elias. (5) While he yet spoke, behold, a bright cloud overshadowed them: and behold a voice out of the cloud, which said, this is my beloved Son, in whom I am well pleased; hear ye him. (6) <u>And when the disciples heard it, they fell on their face, and were sore afraid.</u> (7) And Jesus came and touched them, and said, Arise, and be not afraid. (8) <u>And when they had lifted up their eyes, they saw no man, save Jesus only</u>. (9) And as they came down from the mountain, <u>Jesus charged them, saying, Tell the vision to no man</u>, until the Son of man be risen again from the dead.

Several points of interpretation plain here, that are always glossed over because of traditional Catholic teachings. They are on a physical mountain. Jesus only is transfigured before them. The patriarchs named have been dead for centuries; the text says these men appeared to be there. (In the context of an illusion sight or visionary mind's view not optical view.) There soon appears a cloud that overshadows them; <u>clouds are an earthly phenomenon</u>. An audible voice came from the cloud, relating a message from no visible being, just from the cloud.

The message was for their benefit. The disciples experienced actual fear. Jesus then touched them physically. They saw no one on that mountain except Jesus in the flesh! Jesus plainly said, Tell the VISION to no one, until His mission is complete via death and resurrection. Matthew does exactly what Jesus says. He writes about this mental visionary experience years later. This visionary event is not much different than what the Old Testament calls Dreaming.

Many prophets are contacted in this spirit brain phenomenon.

INSET

This is another example of comparing Medical Science with bible narratives for understanding the truth of what God is revealing! As I said earlier explaining the Spirit, Soul, Body, interaction with Alpha, Theta, Beta, invisible wave frequencies of communication, we also can dream via a Delta brain wave frequency.

Medical Doctors call it an Out of Body Experience. An out of body experience is termed, astral-projection of one thinking they have left their body. They didn't. <u>A spirit had access to their human spirit</u>. It was able to project pictures into the soul, so the person thought they had left, when in fact, they went nowhere physically. The spirit projects through theta wave activity in the physical brain, creating images that support the feeling of the experience.

The true information of what happens after death supports the medical evidence of this specific misleading phenomenon often used by evil spirits.

Psalms 146:4 His breath goes forth, he returns to his earth; in that very day, his thoughts perish.

HELL

Now, there is one more revelation in this insert that has been twisted for centuries. Many people have been convinced that during the time Jesus was in the tomb for 3 days and 3 nights, He somehow went to hell and visited people in hell for whatever reason. They cite the following scriptures to support this theory.

1Peter 3:18-20 For Christ also hath once suffered for sins, the just for the unjust, that he might bring us to God, being put to death in the flesh, but quickened by the Spirit: (19) By which also he went and preached unto the spirits in prison; (20) Which were disobedient, when once the longsuffering of God waited in the days of Noah, while the ark was a preparing, wherein few, that is, eight souls were saved by water.

2Peter 2:4-5 For if God spared not the angels that sinned, but cast them down to hell, and delivered them into chains of darkness, to be reserved unto judgment; (5) And spared not the old world, but saved Noah the eighth person, a preacher of righteousness, bringing in the flood upon the world of the ungodly.

The cases of those who had apostatized from the service of God. He appeals, therefore, to the case of the angels that had revolted. Neither their former rank, their dignity, nor their holiness saved them from being thrust down to hell.

The term "prison" is used in 1 Peter 3:18. The Greek word is phulakē, pronounced foo-lak-ay' From G5442; a guarding or (concretely guard), the act, the parson; figuratively the place, the condition, or (specifically) the time (as a division of day or night), literally or figuratively: - cage, hold, (im-) prison (-ment), ward, watch. In plain English it is a confinement to a specific place, not hell. Actually, they were confined to the earth after the rebellion.

Notice: *Luke_10:18 And he said unto them, I beheld Satan as lightning fall from heaven.*

Revelation 12:3-9 And there appeared another wonder in heaven; and behold a great red dragon, having seven heads and ten horns, and seven crowns upon his heads. (This is how Christ revealed the Devil to the Apostle John in vision) (4) And his tail drew the third part of the stars of heaven and did cast them to the earth: and the dragon stood before the woman, which was ready to be delivered, for to devour her child as soon as it was born. (5) And she brought forth a man child, who was to rule all nations with a rod of iron: and her child was caught up unto God, and to his throne. (Obvious reference to Jesus Christ) *(6) And the woman fled into the wilderness, where she hath a place prepared of God, that they should feed her there a thousand two hundred and threescore days. (7) And there was war in heaven: Michael and his angels fought against the dragon; and the dragon fought and his angels,* [This war was fought not too long before man is created] *(8) And prevailed not; neither was their place found any more in heaven. (9) And the great dragon was cast out, that old serpent, called the Devil, and Satan, which deceives the whole world: he was cast out into the earth, and his angels were cast out with him.*

Christ refers to this while on earth as human.

Luke 10:18 I saw Satan fall as lightening from heaven.

The problem with what has been traditionally taught about hell is the lack of scriptural comparison and seeing the overview of what the plan of God is about. We also need to consider that <u>there are 3 specific Greek words</u> that are different from the 1 English word Hell.

This is the key to the truth about the concept of HELL. The English word Hell to be the meaning for a place of constraint or finality for physical beings. The word is from an Indo-European word meaning to conceal, which is also the ancestor of English conceal, occult, eucalyptus, and apocalypse.

Following is a list of the different places or descriptions that the one English word is to stand for. Greek Word #86 Hades Pronounced: hades = - grave, hell. Considered by Protestant Religions to be a place for left souls to receive "everlasting Punishment." It is no more than a hole in the ground to bury dead bodies.

The bible says mankind's spirit returns to God. Ecclesiastes 12:7 Then shall the dust return to the earth as it was: and the spirit shall return unto God who gave it. The lake of fire hell is Geenna, pronounced; gheh'-en-nah Of Hebrew origin ([H1516] and 2011]); valley of (the son of) Hinnom; gehenna (or Ge Hinnom), a valley of Jerusalem, used (figuratively) as a name for the place (or state) of punishment: - hell. This word from the Hebrew origin and comparison with the valley of Hinnom, a valley in Jerusalem as representative of Hell Fire. This is because the valley of Hinnom in Old Testament times is a garbage dump where the refuse and trash of the city is burned up. A lake of fire in other words. Per the time-line of the bible, the Lake of Fire is not even lit yet.

Another fantasy of Dante Allegro the Italian poet. His book The Divine Comedy is the basis for what people believe about heaven and hell. G5020 tartaroo pronounced tar-tar-o'-o From <u>Tartaros-</u> (the deepest abyss of Hades); <u>to incarcerate in eternal torment</u>: - cast down to hell. This word hell (Tartaroo) is used only ONE TIME in the Bible about the English word HELL.

This particular HELL Peter is talking about is not the Lake of Fire. The Greek word tartaroō pronounced; tar-tar-o'o From Τάρταρος Tartaros- (the deepest abyss of Hades); to incarcerate in eternal torment: - cast down to hell. <u>This is a special hell prepared for the fallen angels and Satan. This will be their final destiny long after the Holy City comes from heaven.</u>

This is key information to understanding the specific type of punishment humanity will receive compared to what the Devil and his Demons will receive.

Jude 1:6 And the angels which kept not their first estate, but left their own habitation, he hath reserved in everlasting chains under darkness (Tartaroo) unto the judgment of the great day.

JUDGMENT

When God chooses a people to practice and perpetuate knowledge of His way of life for humanity, God commands obedience from His people. God's will be expressed by Commandments, Judgments, Statute, Ordinance, Precept, Covenant, and Testaments. These terms make up Law. Therefore, Judgment is based on the Laws of God for human behavior.

In the situation between Cain and Abel, Cain chose to worship God with his own human reasoning and suffered rejection from God. His worship was in vain because it did not follow the prescribed laws from God for worship.

I have done the same in these modern times. I see it as coming to God in our own way, which is not acceptable since Jesus has made worship plain and spiritual for us. Judgment is a complex issue. It is the heart of civil and moral choice, for consequences or reward are the result of its execution from a source of authority and power. This English word is used many times in the Bible to translate the intent of context from the Greek words used in scripture.

Here are three examples of the translations. G2917 krima Pronounce kree'-mah From G2919; a decision (the function or the effect, for or against ["crime"]): - avenge, condemned, condemnation, damnation, + go to law, judgment. G2920 krisis Pronounced kree'-sis (Subjectively or objectively, for or against); by extension, a tribunal; by implication justice (specifically divine law): - accusation, condemnation, damnation, judgment. G4232 praitōrion Pronounced prahee-to'-ree-on Of Latin origin; the praetorium or governor's court room (sometimes including the whole edifice and camp): - (common, judgment) hall (of judgment), palace, praetorium. Our judicial system is basic common knowledge to most everyone.

Judgment involves a decision based on the prescribed law as is applied to responsible or irresponsible actions. To fully understand the importance of these Judgments of God for humanity, you must study Exodus Chapters 21 through 24. God is speaking to Moses when He makes this statement. These are the Judgments of God, not Moses. Moses is the messenger!

Many of the laws in states and nations are based on these Judgments! H4941 mishpa^ṭ Pronounced mish-pawt' From H8199; properly a verdict (favorable or unfavorable) pronounced judicially, especially a sentence or formal decree (human or (particularly) divine law, individual or collectively), including the act, the place, the suit, the crime, and the penalty; abstractly justice, including a particular right, or privilege (statutory or customary), or even a style: - + adversary, ceremony, charge, X crime, custom, desert, determination, discretion, disposing, due, fashion, form, to be judged, judgment, just (-ice, -ly), (manner of) law (-ful), manner, measure, (due) order, ordinance, right, sentence, uses, X worthy, + wrong. This is the Hebrew word for the English Word Law.

We must not ignore the Judgments of God, for they are the redemptive force in preservation of life, liberty, and the pursuit of happiness. We as Christians, are concerned with Three aspects of Judgment.

1. The "Judgments of God" prescribed for the behavior of His people.
2. "Our Personal Judgment" in the affairs of this physical life in relationship to our brethren.
3. The GOD'S FINAL JUDGMENT. Judgment from God is set for an appointed time in our future.

OUR PERSONAL JUDGMENT

*O*ur Personal Judgment is the character development God is looking for in us as we live our lives as Christians in this world of injustice. God wants us as Christians to practice righteous judgment in the matters of this life.

Deuteronomy 16:18-19 Judges and officers shall thou make thee in all thy gates, which the LORD thy God gives thee, throughout thy tribes: and they shall judge the people with just judgment. (19) Thou shall not wrest judgment; thou shall not respect persons, neither take a gift: for a gift doth blind the eyes of the wise, and pervert the words of the righteous.

Proverbs 18:5 It is not good to accept the person of the wicked, to overthrow the righteous in judgment.

John 7:24 Judge not according to the appearance but judge righteous judgment.

This is a part of our learning experience in this life. It will prepare us for leadership in the coming Kingdom of God to this earth.

1 Corinthians 6:2-3 Do ye not know that the saints shall judge the world? and if the world shall be judged by you, are ye unworthy to judge the smallest matters? (3) Know ye not that we shall judge angels? how much more things that pertain to this life?

We are to judge with the upright and moral principles after we have exhausted all information and evidence. We are warned about making judgment based on the outward appearance of a situation.

1 Corinthians 4:1-5 Let a man so account of us, as of the ministers of Christ, and stewards of the mysteries of God. (2) Moreover, it is needed in stewards, that a man be found faithful. (3) But with me it is a small thing that I should be judged of you, or of man's judgment: yea, I judge not mine own self. (4) For I know nothing by myself; yet am I not hereby justified: but he that judges me is the Lord. (5) Therefore, judge nothing before the time, until the Lord come, who both will bring to light the hidden things of darkness and will make manifest the counsels of the hearts: and then shall every man have praise of God.

There are some circumstances in which we must wait before we can start our judgment. Do not be premature in judgment. Can we now see the importance of the Judgments of God set forth to the children of Israel, God's chosen people to lead the world? These disciplines or judgments are evidence of our character as we try to be Christ-like in our responsibilities and conduct before men and the world. Now is our time to prove ourselves worthy of the judgment bestowed upon us by the grace of Jesus Christ.

1 Peter 4:17-18 For the time is come that judgment must begin at the house of God: and if it first begin at us, what shall the end be of them that obey not the gospel of God? (18) And if the righteous scarcely be saved, where shall the ungodly and the sinner appear?

GOD'S FINAL JUDGMENT

*T*his Final Judgment begins with our relationship with Jesus Christ. The Heavenly Father has given all judgment over to Jesus.

Matthew 12:18 Behold my servant, whom I have chosen; my beloved, in whom my soul is well pleased: I will put my spirit upon him, and he shall show judgment to the Gentiles.

John 5:21-22 For as the Father raises up the dead and quickens them; even so the Son quickens whom he will. (22) For the Father judges no man, but hath committed all judgment unto the Son:

John 5:27 And hath given him authority to execute judgment also, because he is the Son of man.

Please take the time to read these next verses. It is incomprehensible that some human beings will take this attitude against the one who created them in His own likeness.

Romans 1:21-32 Because that, when they knew God, they glorified him not as God, neither were thankful; but became vain in their imaginations, and their foolish heart was darkened. (22) Professing themselves to be wise, they became fools, (23) And changed the glory of the incorruptible God into an image made like to corruptible man, and to birds, and four-footed beasts, and creeping things. (24) Wherefore God also gave them up to uncleanness through the lusts of their own hearts, to dishonor their own bodies between themselves: (25) Who changed the truth of God into a lie, and worshipped and served the creature more than the Creator, who is blessed forever. Amen. (26) For this cause God gave them up unto vile affections: for even their women did change the natural use into that which is against nature: (27) And likewise also the men, leaving the natural use of the woman, burned in their lust one toward another; men with men working that which is unseemly, and receiving in themselves that recompense of their error which was meet. (28) And even as they did not like to retain God in their knowledge, God gave them over to a reprobate mind, to do those things which are not convenient; (29) Being filled with all unrighteousness, fornication, wickedness, covetousness, maliciousness; full of envy, murder, debate, deceit, malignity; whisperers, (30) Backbiters, haters of God, despiteful, proud, boasters, inventors of evil things, disobedient to parents, (31) Without understanding, covenant breakers, without natural affection, implacable, unmerciful: (32) Who knowing the judgment of God, that they which commit such things are worthy of death, not only do the same, but have pleasure in them that do them.

Romans 2:1-11 Therefore thou art inexcusable, O man, whosoever thou art that judges: for wherein thou judges another, thou condemns thyself; for thou that judges does the same.

There is an appointed time for final Judgment from God upon the incorrigible wicked. One of our main goals as Christians is to remain obedient and faithful to the ways of our Lord that we may be able to stand righteous before on Judgment Day.

2 Corinthians 5:9-10 Wherefore we labor, that, whether present or absent, we may be accepted of him. (10) For we must all appear before the judgment seat of Christ; that everyone may receive the things done in his body, according to that he hath done, whether it be good or bad.

Whether good or bad, we will ALL be brought before the Judgment Seat of Jesus Christ to receive reward or punishment for our deeds!

Hebrews 9:27 And as it is appointed unto men once to die, but after this the judgment:

It is important to understand that when we die, <u>judgment is not immediate. There is an appointed time for judgment just as there is an appointed time for resurrection</u>.

2 Peter 2:9 The Lord knows how to deliver the godly out of temptations, and to reserve the unjust unto the day of judgment to be punished:

2 Peter 3:7-9 But the heavens and the earth, which are now, by the same word are kept in store, reserved unto fire against the day of judgment and perdition of ungodly men. (8) But, beloved, be not ignorant of this one thing, that one day is with the Lord as a thousand years, and a thousand years as one day. (9) The Lord is not slack concerning his promise, as some men count slackness; but is longsuffering to us-ward, not willing that any should perish, but that all should come to repentance.

God wants us to be saved and live for eternity with Him. He has a plan that gives opportunity for the billions who have lived, to believe, understand, and repent of sin and come to the saving sacrifice of Jesus Christ!

Some do not realize we as the "First Fruits" of the First Resurrection will have a part with Jesus Christ in executing righteous Judgment on the world. This will be during the Kingdom of God when we will be priests of the High God to rehabilitate the wicked of the world.

Jude 1:14-15 And Enoch also, the seventh from Adam, prophesied of these, saying, Behold, <u>the Lord cometh with ten thousands of his saints</u>, (15) <u>To execute judgment upon all</u>, and to convince all that are ungodly among them of all their ungodly deeds which they have ungodly committed, and of all their hard speeches which ungodly sinners have spoken against Him. Revelation 20:4-5 And I saw thrones, and they sat upon them, and judgment was given unto them: and I saw the souls of them that were beheaded for the witness of Jesus, and for the word of God, and which had not worshipped the beast, neither his image, neither had received his mark upon their foreheads, or in their hands; and they lived and reigned with Christ a thousand years. (5) But the rest of the dead lived not again until the thousand years were finished.

This is the first resurrection. There will be more than one resurrection according to the bible. Jesus even eluded to more than one. God, repent of their sins, and begin a personal effort to conform their daily living to the behavior.

John 5:28-29 Marvel not at this: for the hour is coming, in the which all that are in the graves shall hear his voice, (29) And shall come forth; they that have done good, unto the resurrection of life; and they that have done evil, unto the resurrection of damnation.

Revelation 20:11-13 And I saw a great white throne, and him that sat on it, from whose face the earth and the heaven fled away; and there was found no place for them. (12) And I saw the dead, small and great, stand before God; and the books were opened: and another book was opened, which is the book of life: and the dead were judged out of those things which were written in the books, according to their works. (13) And the sea gave up the dead which were in it; and death and hell delivered up the dead which were in them: and they were judged every man according to their works.

This is the appointed time, the Great White Throne Judgment of God upon the people of the earth, both good and bad. This is the FINAL JUDGMENT for mankind. It is when you will receive one of TWO DESTINIES. Judgement must be tied in with the Book of Life and the Book of Works.

THE "BOOKS" OF RECORDS

God keeps our "Spirit!"

*T*he spirit in man is how God keeps record of His created physical beings.

Psalms 139:7 Whither shall I go from thy spirit? or whither shall I flee from thy presence?

Psalms 139:13-16 For thou hast possessed my reins: thou hast covered me in my mother's womb. (14) I will praise thee; for I am fearfully and wonderfully made marvelous are thy works; and that my soul knows right well. (15) My substance was not hidden from thee, when I was made in secret, and curiously wrought in the lowest parts of the earth. (16) Your eyes did see my substance, yet not being perfect; and in thy book all my members were written, which in continuance were fashioned, when as yet there was none of them.

Psalms 56:8 Thou know my wanderings: you put my tears into thy bottle: are they not in thy book?

Is there a spiritual Book in heaven, with God, where He keeps information about our character and our existence on a continual basis, until we die? <u>Yes, there is</u>. Does God, by some means, preserve our spirit when we die; and keep it until the resurrection and judgment? <u>Yes, He does</u>. It is not that far of a stretch for us to understand this process.

Records are kept in books during ancient times. Books, or papyrus scrolls, are the means of preserving and remembering information accumulated over time. The term books is a metaphor for describing the preservation of spiritual information in heaven.

Today we have audio and video recording abilities to preserve what we hear and see. Computer science allows us to store billions of bits of information in tiny electronic chips. Information can be preserved in drives of Zeros and Ones converted to language, images, and such at the click of a mouse. Disks of plastic can be inscribed with information and put in other computers or machines for making the information appear to us. When we see what man can invent to store information, how can we doubt God has a means of storing spiritual information of our character and existence?

God keeps information about all of His creation including the number of hairs on your head.

Matthew 10:29-31 Are not two sparrows sold for a farthing? and one of them shall not fall on the ground without your Father. (30) But the very hairs of your head are all numbered. (31) Fear ye not therefore, ye are of more value than many sparrows.

Luke 12:6-7 Are not five sparrows sold for two farthings, and not one of them is forgotten before God? (7) But even the very hairs of your head are all numbered. Fear not therefore: ye are of more value than many sparrows.

Some Bible scholars say the following scripture references are referring to the books of the Bible. Bible means books. There are all kinds of different books. This passage is <u>referring to specific books that God keeps</u>. The Book of Works and the Book of Life; God's Books.

Here is an example of one of the Books of God that holds information that only Jesus can open and explain.

Revelation 5:1-4 And I saw in the right hand of him that sat on the throne a book written within and on the backside, sealed with seven seals. (2) And I saw a strong angel proclaiming with a loud voice, who is worthy to open the book, and to open the seals thereof? (3) And no man in heaven, nor in earth, neither under the earth, was able to open the book, neither to look thereon. (4) And I wept much, because no man was found worthy to open and to read the book, neither to look thereon.

Revelation 20:12-13 And I saw the dead, small and great, stand before God; and the books were opened: <u>and another book was opened, which is the book of life</u>: and the dead were judged out of <u>those things which were written in the books, according to their works</u>. (13) And the sea gave up the dead which were in it; and death and hell delivered up the dead which were in them: and they were judged every man according to their works.

Notice the word Book is plural. Notice there are Two subject matters or conditions of human activity. These books are opened after man's activities on earth have ended in death of the physical body. Humankind is then resurrected to live with conscious awareness of themselves and are then judged out of Two different books.

Revelation 20:15 And whosoever was not found written in the book of life was cast into the lake of fire.

Revelation 20:12 the dead were judged out of those things which were written in the books, according to their works.

To understand this completely in this spiritual context we must remember what we learned about the difference between sons of men and sons of God. Remember what sets the Two phrases apart? The Holy Spirit indwelling us is the difference.

Romans 8:12-14 Therefore, brethren, we are debtors, not to the flesh, to live after the flesh. (13) For if ye live after the flesh, ye shall die but if ye through the Spirit do mortify the deeds of the body, ye shall live. (14) For as many as are led by the Spirit of God, they are the sons of God.

As sons of men, we must accept and obey Jesus Christ, receive the Holy Spirit, and then we become sons of God. I'm convinced therefore, why I was born.

I was born to become a literal spirit being child of God; it's my intended destiny.

It is the intended destiny for all human beings. But it is a choice only you alone can make.

Revelation 20:15 which says "whosoever was not found written in the Book of Life was cast into the lake of fire!

Revelation 20:12 says everyone is judged out of the Book of Works. It is plain there are two books holding personal information on each of us. Now apply what we know about the Spirit in man sustained by physical life and elements of our physical environment with these books. We are all born into this world as sons of men. The Book of Works holds the lives of all humans who draw the breath of life and eventually die! The Book of Life holds the names only the lives of those who accept, obey, receive the Holy Spirit, and follow Jesus Christ! (Sons of God) Remember this moment between Jesus and the apostles?

Luke 10:19-21 Behold, I give unto you power to tread on serpents and scorpions, and over all the power of the enemy: and nothing shall by any means hurt you. (20) Notwithstanding in this rejoice not, that the spirits are subject *unto you; but rather rejoice, because <u>your names are written in heaven</u>. (21) In that hour Jesus rejoiced in spirit, and said, I thank thee, O Father, Lord of heaven and earth, that thou hast hid these things from the wise and prudent, and hast revealed them unto babes: even so, Father; for so it seemed good in thy sight.* Yes, it requires childlike faith to believe the things we have just explored. Such information is not understood or received by everyone.

1 Corinthians 2:7-14 But we speak the wisdom of God in a mystery, even the hidden wisdom, which God ordained before the world unto our glory: (8) Which none of the princes of this world knew: for had they known it, they would not have crucified the Lord of glory. (9) But as it is written, Eye hath not seen, nor ear heard, neither have entered into the heart of man, the things which God hath prepared for them that love him. (10) But God hath revealed them unto us by his Spirit: for the Spirit searches all things, yea, the deep things of God. (11) For what man knows the things of a man, save the spirit of man which is in him? even so the things of God know no man, but the Spirit of God. (12) Now we have received, not the spirit of the world, but the spirit which is of God; that we might know the things that are freely given to us of God. (13) Which things also we speak, not in the words which man's wisdom teaches, but which the Holy Spirit teaches, comparing spiritual things with spiritual. (14) But the natural man receives not the things of the Spirit of God: for they are foolishness unto him: neither can he know them, because they are spiritually discerned.

2 Corinthians 5:10 For we must all appear before the judgment seat of Christ; that everyone may receive the things done in his body, according to that he hath done, whether it be good or bad.

This scripture from 2 Corinthians shows <u>the Book of Works affects the judgment of God</u>. This concept of Books as a metaphor to describe how God stores the records of all of humanity's actions or works when a person dies; and also, a record of when person chooses to perform actions or works to follow Christ, makes logical sense.

It helps us know we are special when we give ourselves to God and behave accordingly. Not being found in the Book of Life is chilling information about the consequences of not living God's way of Life on this earth.

SCRIPTURE REFUTES DOCTRINES OF MEN

Revelation 3:5 He that overcomes, the same shall be clothed in white raiment; and I will not blot out his name out of the book of life, but I will confess his name before my Father, and before his angels.

Revelation 20:15 And whosoever was not found written in the book of life was cast into the lake of fire.

<u>Jesus is saying our name can be erased from the Book of Life</u>. This is not "once saved, always saved" as some religions teach. As long as we are in this flesh, we have choices to make. We need a daily supply of God's Spirit.

We can quench the Spirit of God in us and lose salvation! This is how free moral agency allows us to make choices for our eternal existence.

1 Thessalonians 5:19-23 Quench not the Spirit. (20) Despise not Prophesies. (21) Prove all things; hold fast that which is good. (22) Abstain from all appearance of evil. (23) And the very God of peace sanctify you wholly; and I pray God your whole spirit and soul and body be preserved blameless unto the coming of our Lord Jesus Christ.

The books were opened suggests these are spiritual books where the Spiritual records of our lives are kept when we die. This is not taught in mainstream religion.

This information contradicts the notion we go to heaven as a conscious spirit being at once when we die. The Bible teaches that consciousness as a literal born into Spirit child of God, will be at an appointed time in our future.

Teaching our spirit is conscious when it goes back to God when we die, does not concur with the scriptures.

Hebrews 11:39-40 And these all, having obtained a good report through faith, received not the promise: (40) God having supplied some better thing for us, that they without us should not be made perfect.

1 Corinthians 15:50-52 Now this I say, brethren, that flesh and blood cannot inherit the kingdom of God; neither doth corruption inherit incorruption. (51) Behold, I show you a mystery; we shall not all sleep, but we shall all be changed, (52) In a moment, in the twinkling of an eye, at the last trump: for the trumpet shall sound, and the dead shall be raised incorruptible, and we shall be changed.

1 Thessalonians 4:13-17 But I would not have you to be ignorant, brethren, concerning them which are asleep, that ye sorrow not, even as others which have no hope. (14) For if we believe that Jesus died and rose again, even so them also which sleep in Jesus will God bring with him. (15) For this we say unto you by the word of the Lord, that we which are alive and remain unto the coming of the Lord shall not prevent them which are asleep. (16) For the Lord himself shall descend from heaven with a shout, with the voice of the archangel, and with the trump of God: and the dead in Christ shall rise first: (17) Then we which are alive and remain shall be caught up together with them in the clouds, to meet the Lord in the air: and so, shall we ever be with the Lord.

When you consider what God says in Psalms 53:1-3 and read the consequences of the sons of men in Genesis 6:5,6; it is obvious we cannot live any great length of time with carnal thinking and behavior as our only guide. We need spiritual intervention to sustain our existence or time and chance will eventually end our lives forever.

The doctrine of men teaching consciousness when going to heaven when we die must be qualified with what the Bible teaches.

It is our Spirit in man that goes to heaven when we die. <u>The spirit in man is placed in the book of works</u>; it is the record of our physical life while on the earth. Anything more than this is just not in the Bible. This is where these things become the speculation of men with good intentions but no spiritual understanding of the scriptures or why God made us physical human beings instead of Spiritual Beings.

Notice the word Book is plural. Notice there are Two subject matters or conditions of human activity. These books are opened after man's activities on earth have ended in death of the physical body. Humankind is then resurrected to live with conscious awareness of themselves and are then judged out of two different books.

Revelation 20:15 And whosoever was not found written in the book of life was cast into the lake of fire.

Revelation 20:12 the dead were judged out of those things which were written in the books, according to their works.

To understand this completely in this spiritual context we must remember what we learned about the difference between sons of men and sons of God. Remember what sets the two phrases apart? The Holy Spirit dwelling in us is the difference.

Romans 8:12-14 Therefore, brethren, we are debtors, not to the flesh, to live after the flesh. (13) For if ye live after the flesh, ye shall die but if ye through the Spirit do mortify the deeds of the body, ye shall live. (14) For as many as are led by the Spirit of God, they are the sons of God.

As sons of men, we must accept and obey Jesus Christ, receive the Holy Spirit, and then we become sons of God.

Revelation 20:15 which says whosoever was not found written in the Book of Life was cast into the lake of fire!

Revelation 20:12 says everyone is judged out of the Book of Works. It is clear there are two books holding personal information on each of us.

Now apply what we know about the Spirit in man sustained by physical life and elements of our physical environment with these books. We are all born into this world as sons of men. The Book of Works holds the lives of all humans who draw the breath of life and eventually die.

The Book of Life holds the names only the lives of those who accept, obey, receive the Holy Spirit, and follow Jesus Christ. (Sons of God)

Yes, it requires childlike faith to believe the things we have just explored. Such information is not understood or received by everyone. This scripture from 2 Corinthians shows the Book of Works affects the judgment of God. This concept of Books as a metaphor to describe how God stores the records of all of humanity's actions or works when a person dies; and also, a record of when person chooses to perform actions or works to follow Christ, makes logical sense. It helps us know we are special when we give ourselves to God and behave accordingly. Not being found in the Book of Life is chilling information about the consequences of not living God's way of Life on this earth.

We should prioritize our time with the things that keep us on the intended path for our destiny. The bible encourages us to consider our options when there are serious choices to be made.

Ephesians 5:16 Redeeming the time, because the days are evil.

Colossians 4:5 Walk in wisdom toward them that are without, redeeming the time. Choose your path and seek God's approval.

SUMMARY

We have waded through pages of information to give a background of understanding for what all this business of power, government, and religion has become down through time. We have seen some of the manipulation of historical and biblical information down through time.

I have also touched on some scientific information that the bible supports.

I have only exposed the tip of the iceberg of information and understanding available to us in these modern times of the information highway.

I have uncovered a plan for mankind that the majority of churches do not teach. There are more details and information about the Plan of God for mankind than I have covered in this book.

I have shown how the process of becoming a literal born of the Spirit, has been pioneered by Jesus Christ and how through the process Christ has supplied a way for us to experience salvation and this process through believing in Him and accepting Him as our personal savior.

We have seen how men have tried to make the salvation process something they control through rituals and teachings that do not square up with what Jesus and the apostles taught. We are living in the last days before many catastrophic events will soon occur.

We live in an extremely dangerous and complex world of information and choices for living our lives. The things of this world are all connected to our destiny and potential to become a part of the final Kingdom that will rule this world, the coming Kingdom of God. This is not preached or taught in most churches and religions of the world today. They spiritualize our potential away into a fantasy created by men of carnal minded agendas.

It is time to lay aside 3rd century understanding and move into the 21st century of understanding. The reason I was born is the same reason you were born; <u>to become a literal born of the spirit child of God with a spiritual body and eternal existence with the Invisible Creator God</u> who designed this process for us to reach our intended destiny.

The world says we must keep church and state separated. <u>The bible does not separate the two, men do.</u> This nation was founded on most of the very principles and laws God bestowed upon His chosen nation of Israel.

But this nation is far removed from what God intended for the behavior of people and nations. America as allowed political agendas of men and false religions to lead us toward the end time prophesies.

There is a day of reckoning coming for all the nations and especially everyone of all nations. I have shared what I have learned and remembered over the years from available books on many subjects.

By combining them with the bible timeline a reason is revealed for mankind's very existence. I have found the reason I was born. <u>I was born to become a Spiritual child of God and live forever with the Creator of all mankind can see and find in this Universe.</u> There is no other place like our spaceship, Earth. There is much more to learn and figure out before mankind destroys itself with its own forms of government and philosophies about the purpose of being born into this world. All the information in this story happens long before I am born into this world. But the information is necessary for me to understand how to cope with the world I am born into and what my intended reason for being born is all about.

I did not choose to be born. I am here because of life that preceded me. Life comes from life. Man can clone life, but man cannot create life or live forever by his own devices.

I can surround myself with the best doctors, policeman, scientists, and smartest people alive; it will not stop me from what everyone must face, death!

Hebrews 9:27 (27) And as it is appointed unto men once to die, but after this the judgment:

The judgement after our physical death decides which one of two destinies we will receive. What we believe shapes our destiny.

Every person is born into this world with the potential and possibility of finding out why they came into existence without choosing to be born.

Choices for how we live our life is the only freedom we have to decide our destiny.

I choose to follow Jesus and do the best I can to promote the goodness to my fellow man as He did. What will your choice be? What will it say next to your name in the book of works in the spiritual files of the Invisible Creator God?

Will it say, Please refer to the <u>Book of Life</u>, this person has received Jesus Christ as their Lord and master. Only you and I can make the choice for your name to be found in the Book of Life.

Born into this world as sons of men, we must accept and obey Jesus Christ, receive the Holy Spirit, and then we become sons of God; first in our hearts and actions while in this flesh and at the appointed time born as a spiritual person into the Kingdom of God when Jesus comes back.

I'm convinced why I was born! <u>I was born to someday, at the appointed time and along with many others, become a literal spirit being child of God; it's my intended destiny!</u>